Contents

P
91.3
.R83
1996

Contents

Foreword

Communication Research: Strategies and Sources is designed to acquaint students of communication with research and the vast array of information sources available in the discipline. It describes the strategies involved in selecting, refining, and researching communication topics. It is a guide to the literature, explaining the content and utility of significant and representative communication research sources. It is also a communication research manual, providing an opportunity for students to use and become familiar with communication research materials. Throughout the book, we stress the overall strategy of searching the literature for information on a particular topic.

This book provides a comprehensive overview of the necessary steps to begin communication research and describes published sources that are available in or accessible through most medium-sized college and university libraries. The works that are described are used when conducting documentary, archival, or library research. This type of research is necessary before any other research methodology is attempted.

Communication is a broad discipline in which researchers are interested in many different subject areas. Thus, we explain the structure of the communication field, the types of research done by students of communication, and focus on the basics of documentary and library research. These basics include developing and refining research questions, writing and organizing, beginning investigation of a topic, and acquiring the tools that make the research process more efficient. We also describe each type of communication research source that is available for accomplishing a research goal.

This text is beneficial for both undergraduate and graduate students who need to become acquainted with the variety of available communication research resources and procedures. We introduce students to sources in interpersonal, group, organizational, public, and mass communication and to common research strategies.

Because the book is designed as a supplemental text, there is a fair amount of flexibility in its use—from one or two students working independently, to a module within a course, to an entire class focused on communication research. Any undergraduate or graduate communication course that requires students to use the literature of the field is an appropriate vehicle for offering instruction in researching topics.

For example, this text is a helpful introduction to research procedures and the communication literature in Introduction to Graduate Studies classes as well as in undergraduate and graduate Communication Theory and Research classes. It is appropriate for a variety of introductory-level undergraduate classes in which it is desirable to acquaint students with the literature and research procedures of the field. In addition, instructors may select from among the many sources cited those that are pertinent to their specific courses, such as Freedom of Speech, Media Law, Organizational Communication, Investigative Reporting, Interpersonal Communication, and Media Research. This book is also a useful manual to aid research-paper writing and development by students working on independent studies. It is most helpful for graduate student preparation of thesis and dissertation proposals and for the literature reviews required in many graduate and undergraduate courses.

Students unfamiliar with the library will need some general orientation instruction. The library staff will be able to clarify such matters as the use of the library catalog, location of periodicals, and any special location symbols used in the library.

Some chapters include exercises that require students to use several annotated sources. Generally, these questions hypothetically place students in a specific course and present a need to acquire information for a specific project. For example, "You are preparing to lead a discussion on the effects of cartoon violence on children in your Group Communication class. . . ." These assignments lead students to important communication research sources and provide perspective on how the sources are useful in a variety of courses and situations. Questions reiterate points made in the text of the chapter and show how the sources can be used to build a comprehensive bibliography on a chosen communication topic. Answers to the Exercise questions for Part Two are available to instructors from the authors. Chapters in other sections of the book include exercises for classroom discussion.

Users of previous editions will notice a new chapter about searching the Internet, a worldwide information superhighway. We have also updated all sources, adding new ones and eliminating some older materials, and have changed several Exercise questions. There have been some changes in APA style since the last edition. We explain these changes and the new reference style in Appendix A.

We are grateful for the comments and suggestions of several people who helped us refine our ideas throughout our four editions: Alan Albarran, Southern Methodist University; Alison Alexander, University of Georgia; Steven Beebe, Southwest Texas University; Roger Desmond, University of Hartford; William Donahue, Michigan State University; James Fletcher, University of Georgia; Karen Foss, University of New Mexico; Claudia Hale, Ohio University; Peter Hamilton, Pittsburg State University; Eva McMahan, University of Alabama; Dale Hample, Western Illinois University; Fred Hilpert, California State College–Stanislaus; Ken Ksobiech, Marquette University; Marilyn Mathias-Root, Boston University; Andrew Rancer, University of Akron; Lawrence Rosenfeld, University of North Carolina; Edward Springer, Villanova University; James Witterbols, Niagara University; Janet Yerby, Central Michigan University; and Stephanie Zimmerman, San Jose State University.

R.B.R.
A.M.R.
L.J.P.

Introduction

We believe that university students actively seek to master the available tools when learning about the field of communication. The library contains many of these communication research tools. Our aim is to introduce these tools to you and to explain how they can be used to help increase your knowledge of communication. How much effort you give to this learning process will determine how much you personally gain.

Introduction

This book is divided into three main parts. In Part One, we explain why and how communication research is done. After surveying the field of communication, we look at the research process, selecting and narrowing research topics and questions, searching the literature, and using computers to search databases and access information on computer networks.

In Part Two, we explore the available types of communication research sources or reference materials. We consider general communication research sources such as subject handbooks, textbooks, encyclopedias, and annual reviews. These materials are helpful in defining subjects or topics you may wish to investigate. We also examine finding tools such as bibliographies, guides to the literature, indexes, and abstracts. These tools are needed to locate sources and materials. In the next two chapters we discuss more specific communication research sources, namely communication periodicals (scholarly journals and professional magazines) and information compilations (collections, statistical compendia, government publications, yearbooks, directories, dictionaries, and manuals). These periodicals and compilations are important for finding primary and factual data and for developing research projects.

In Part Three, we explain how to design and conduct research investigations and how to complete literature reviews and other projects. The final chapter ties together the ideas presented throughout the book.

Because we try to highlight a representative sample of references in each chapter, not all works important to the study of communication can be discussed at length. Numerous sources, though, are listed at the ends of the chapters and are indexed at the end of the book. The sources we have selected do not constitute an exhaustive list. We chose them because they represent the many diverse areas of communication research, they are written in or translated into the English language, and they are available at many college and university libraries. We also identify some specific sources, such as archival and legal references, which are available via specialized libraries, because they are accessible and of particular utility to communication researchers.

As with any book, materials become dated, and new or revised sources become available between the time a book is written and is available for use. You will undoubtedly uncover other important bibliographic tools in your literature searches. As you do, just add them in the chapters and to the source index for quick reference in the future.

We mentioned earlier that a major goal is to introduce and explain bibliographic tools that are available for investigating communication topics. In so doing, we hope we will accomplish a secondary goal of reducing the anxiety many students feel when researching a communication topic for the first time or when confronted with so much information that they don't know where to start. We anticipate that this book will be a useful starting point and a reference guide and that it will assist you in learning about communication.

Helpful Hints

Students who have used earlier versions of this book have offered some helpful hints. These tips make a lot of sense.

First, get to know the physical layout of the library you will be using. Find the reference section, the reserve desk, and the library catalogs or computer stations. Discover how books and periodicals are arranged in your library. This information is usually available in printed form when you enter the library. Ask about the availability of CD-ROM databases, on-line search services, and accessibility of the Internet. Consult a reference librarian or staff member at an information desk if you have a question, *any* question.

Second, complete the Exercises at the ends of the chapters. Be sure to read thoroughly each chapter before trying to answer the questions. In fact, we constructed the Exercises so that reading the chapter first will be an enormous aid to completing the questions. Students who were looking for shortcuts in the past became frustrated. Your amount of effort will actually be reduced by reading the chapters before trying to answer the questions.

There are no trick questions in the Exercises. Each reference source you are asked to use is explained in the chapter text. Read the *annotations* carefully. The sources that are annotated or described in detail in the text sometimes provide clues for answering the questions. When you locate reference sources that are new to you, examine them carefully. Explore the table of contents, examine the preface and introduction, and look for an index. In so doing, the sources themselves may provide you with a more efficient method of use. If you find yourself spending more than 15 minutes on any one question, your approach to the problem may not be the best. Ask a reference librarian for advice. Also, ask for help when you cannot find a source you need. It may be shelved in a different location in the library.

Third, if you are working on a research paper, literature review, or research prospectus as you read this book, keep in mind the sources you examine as you develop a research topic or question. You might find it advantageous to return to the materials discussed in earlier chapters for a more thorough examination. For instance, the Exercises in Part Two will sometimes ask you to look at only one volume of a multivolume work. Once you have solidified your own research topic, you might want to go back to the other volumes to see if they can help lead you to additional references. Because you already will be familiar with how these sources are used, it will require little effort to check them for pertinent information.

In a similar vein, if you have a clear-cut topic in mind as you progress through the chapters, do not hesitate to examine each source thoroughly as you use the guide. This will save you time in the future. You can easily compile a thorough bibliography as you proceed through the chapters of this book.

Fourth, update the references in this book whenever possible. Students in the past have found that they misplace additional or updated references if they do not add them when they are first located. The space provided at the ends of the chapters and in the index can be used to update and to add references. You may also want to augment the annotations and citations with your own notes on using the materials. In this way, the book will become an even more useful and comprehensive collection of communication research materials.

PART ONE

Communication Research Strategies

The essence of strategy is careful planning. Accordingly, communication research requires a comprehensive plan of action. Part One focuses on conventional search procedures used to investigate communications topics.

In Chapter 1, we discuss the types of research projects students typically undertake and then describe the general structure of the communication discipline. Next, in Chapter 2, we outline search procedures and provide an orientation to library research. In Chapter 3, we explain the strategies used to search computerized bibliographic databases. And in Chapter 4, we explain how to use the Internet to search other bibliographic databases.

Part One of the book, then, is an orientation to the process of communication research. We include end-of-chapter exercises to help you formulate a strategy—a plan of action—for completing research projects. If you are using this text in a college course, you will find it worthwhile to ask your instructor for feedback about how well you understand the research strategies by discussing your answers to the exercises.

Chapter 1

Studying Communication

Why should we study communication? Those who do will tell you that their work is driven by a need to know more about human interaction and the communication process. To discover how communication works, we need to develop skills for acquiring and using information throughout our professional lives.

Research is often defined as systematic inquiry into a subject. The key word in this definition, *systematic*, points to the need to examine topics methodically rather than to plunge haphazardly into sources. Two major goals in this book are to acquaint you with this step-by-step procedure of inquiry and to provide guidance for following these generally accepted principles and practices of research.

In this chapter, we explain how communication students and professionals become involved in the research process. First, we look at the types of projects that require systematic inquiry in the communication discipline. Then we explore the profession and how the discipline is organized. This will give you an idea of the interdisciplinary nature of communication and a sense of what interests communication researchers.

Communication Research Projects

Throughout a college career, a communication student faces a wide variety of assignments requiring the use of research tools and skills:

Compiling bibliographies

Completing take-home exams

Conducting audience or consumer surveys

Conducting original research investigations

Giving speeches or oral readings

Investigating and writing news stories

Leading seminars

Preparing advertising or public relations campaigns

Preparing debate cases or group discussions

Writing abstracts, research reports, theses, or dissertations

Writing television, radio, or film scripts, or critiques

Writing term papers, seminar papers, or literature reviews

To complete these assignments effectively, we need to know the methods and materials of communication research—the tools within and outside the library that provide the needed information. We also need to know how to use these tools.

Class assignments require locating and documenting facts and finding pertinent supporting materials. Sometimes instructors suggest that you read a specific study (for example, McCroskey and McCain's 1974 article on interpersonal attraction, Hart and Burks' 1972 essay on rhetorical sensitivity, or Horton and Wohl's 1956 discussion of parasocial interaction). How would you go about finding these with such limited information? One way would be to consult an index (see Chapter 6) to find complete bibliographic citations for journal articles.

Sometimes you will just want to explore the scholarly journal literature for research on a particular idea or topic of interest. At other times, you may need specific facts—the current number of employees in the television or newspaper industry or the most recent decision of the Federal Trade Commission about advertising, for example. You may need to choose a method of running a meeting in a particular organization. You may need information on media markets and advertising rates to design a public relations campaign. Or you may need specific census information for a debate case you are preparing or a research paper or feature article you are writing. How would you find these facts?

Academic Pursuits

Preparing a term paper, literature review, research study, or thesis or dissertation prospectus requires extended use of the communication literature and the library. Also, students often conduct their own research investigations, where research questions are asked, a study is designed, and data are collected and analyzed. These projects require you to examine and understand past research in the area so that you can determine what important communication problems still need to be addressed. This process will also help you determine whether your research question has already been satisfactorily answered. It gives you a solid foundation on which to build the investigation or to generate hypotheses about how the communication concepts or ideas are related to one another.

For example, suppose you decide to conduct a research investigation and you conclude, after browsing through the literature, that you want to study the variable "eye contact" (which may vary from a great deal of eye contact to very little—thus the term **variable**). After reading some more of the literature, you decide to examine the effect of eye contact on a second variable, the "length of conversation" during an interpersonal interaction (which may vary from a few seconds to many minutes). You will need to give a reason for proposing this study (why it is important) and a question or prediction about how the variables (eye contact and length of conversation) might be related. The first section of a research proposal summarizes and analyzes the findings of research studies that have previously examined these variables, and the **hypotheses**, educated or informed guesses about the relationships between the variables, are the end product of this exhaustive literature search.

Sometimes there is not enough research to allow an educated guess, so a research question is posed that will guide the study. Or, perhaps, your method is first to gather multiple observations about people's eye contact with others while interacting, and then to arrive at an explanation about the role of eye contact in interpersonal interaction. This latter method is more *inductive* than *deductive* in nature, that is, we reason from specific observations to a general principle. We will discuss the different approaches to conducting a research study in Chapter 9.

Professional Pursuits

The need to seek information and the importance of knowing what information is available are certainly not limited to the academic world. Communication professionals use and refer to many of these materials on a daily basis. For example:

Film critics search past film reviews for references to particular directors.

Public relations specialists consult directories for names and addresses of organizations.

Television producers check current statistical sources to ascertain that a documentary is current.

Communication consultants use abstracts and indexes to learn about new teaching or training methods.

Advertising or media researchers search scholarly studies for relevant communication research.

Political speech writers examine collections of speeches and editorials for themes and issues.

Journalists check grammatical usage or news style by consulting a wire service handbook.

Professors keep abreast of the field by reading professional and scholarly periodicals.

Being able to answer questions systematically and knowing what materials are available and how to find and use them are essential in any career. These materials are the tools of the trade.

The projects and assignments given in your classes help you understand how communication researchers satisfy their need to know more about communication. Such assignments teach you the systematic methods of searching for knowledge. In effect, your link to the communication discipline is through your participation in scholarship.

The Communication Discipline

Communication is how people arrive at shared meanings through the interchange of messages. Although *communication* has been defined in a variety of ways, when we define it as the process through which meaning and social reality are created, many things become communication events. Political scientists, educators, business executives, linguists, poets, philosophers, scientists, historians, psychologists, sociologists, and anthropologists, to name but a few, are concerned with communication within their specific areas of inquiry. It is little wonder that no other discipline of knowledge is quite as broad as communication.

Communication researchers examine the processes by which meanings are managed—in other words, how people structure and interpret messages and use language and other symbol systems in a variety of contexts: interpersonal, group, organizational, public, and mass. Thus, the focus of communication inquiry is broad, and the contexts in which the communication process is examined are diverse and interrelated.

Communication is a time-honored and yet modern field of inquiry. The Greek philosopher Aristotle (384–322 B.C.) devoted much thought to examining the constituent elements of *rhetoric*, or the available means of persuasion. From 1600 through the early 1900s, speech theorists focused on effective delivery of the spoken word. Early students of mass communication were intrigued by the effects of media-delivered messages. Contemporary communication researchers have also expanded their interests to interpersonal, group, and organizational communication contexts and to the processes that occur during communication. In examining the flow of information and the interchange of messages between individuals in a variety of contexts, researchers today are also probing the uses and effects of modern communication technologies in a world where societies and people are linked by instantaneous transmissions via satellites and computers.

Communication has a rich history. For more information on the history of the communication discipline, consult the following sources:

Benson, T. W. (Ed.). (1985). *Speech communication in the 20th century.* Carbondale: Southern Illinois University Press.

Cohen, H. (1994). *The history of speech communication: The emergence of a discipline, 1914–1945.* Annandale, VA: Speech Communication Association.

Crowley, D., & Heyer, P. (Eds.). (1991). *Communication in history: Technology, culture, society* (2nd ed.). New York: Longman.

Delia, J. G. (1987). Communication research: A history. In C. R. Berger & S. H. Chaffee (Eds.), *Handbook of communication science* (pp. 20–98). Newbury Park, CA: Sage.

Rogers, E. M. (1994). *A history of communication study: A biographical approach.* New York: Free Press.

Schramm, W. (1980). The beginnings of communication study in the United States. *Communication Yearbook, 4,* 73–82.

Schramm, W. L. (1988). *The story of human communication: Cave painting to microchip.* New York: Harper & Row.

Because communication is studied in several allied disciplines, you may sometimes find it difficult to focus on one particular research topic and to find all the available literature about that topic. And, because communication is of interest to those other disciplines, many research sources exist in the social and behavioral sciences, the arts, and the humanities. With so much information available, determining which sources are most pertinent becomes difficult.

For example, if you were interested in organizational communication, you would find pertinent reference materials in health, education, business management, sociology, psychology, personnel, and other communication-related sources. However, the differences in the language and vocabulary used within each of these disciplines might make understanding the works in those disciplines somewhat difficult for someone not in those fields. As a communication scholar, you are thus faced with learning about the communication process within one of several traditionally defined communication contexts, while also trying to integrate knowledge about the process generated in other disciplines.

Structure of the Field

As a result of this breadth and diversity, the communication literature includes a variety of subjects that define the field. Knowledge of these subjects will help you discover the most appropriate sources for your research. We have grouped these subjects into six major content categories: interpersonal communication, small-group communication, language and symbolic codes, organizational communication, public communication, and mass communication. The study of communicators and their messages is common to all areas of communication. What differentiates one subject area from another is the focus on different settings or dominant modes of interaction.

1. *Interpersonal communication* involves the study of people and their interactions or relationships. Researchers in this area study the use of verbal and nonverbal messages in developing and maintaining relationships between people. Some topics

they find interesting are interpersonal competence, impression formation, spousal conflict, interpersonal attraction, communication apprehension, and relational communication.

2. *Small-group communication* covers communication in groups of three or more persons. Researchers often study how groups emerge, accomplish their goals, and solve programs and how group leaders function. Topics in small-group communication include small-group effectiveness, cohesion, conflict, group roles, consensus, productivity, group culture, and family communication.

3. *Language and symbolic codes* is concerned with verbal and nonverbal codes of communication. When examining these codes, researchers focus on how language and nonverbal symbols are transmitted, received, and come to have meaning for people of the same or different cultures. Topics cover issues such as text or discourse, language intensity, proxemics, language development in children, conversational flow, listening, nonverbal immediacy, and relational power.

4. *Organizational communication* is concerned with the processing and use of messages between and within organizations. It focuses on the complexities of communication in formal structures where many interpersonal and group relationships already exist. Researchers look at organizational networks, systems, conflict, negotiation, superior/subordinate relationships, and other aspects of organizational life.

5. *Public communication* covers communication in nonmediated public settings and focuses mainly on one-to-many communication. Primary topics include rhetoric, public address, analysis and delivery of speeches, persuasion, argumentation, and debate. Research focuses on speaker credibility, ethics, interpreting literature, propaganda, political campaigns, and communication education.

6. *Mass communication* focuses on communication from a source or organization to many people via mediated channels such as television or newspapers under conditions of limited feedback. Those who study mass communication are concerned with how such mediated messages are formulated and received and how they affect individuals and society, as well as the control of power in society. They are often interested in media effects, history, ethics, formation of public opinion, policy and regulation, international broadcasting, and critical or textual analysis of messages.

These six subject areas are listed, along with several terms that describe subareas of study relevant to each of the larger topics. These subareas may be useful when deciding on a research topic or locating materials in a library. Naturally, many of the subareas could be placed under two or more of the broader headings because of the interdisciplinary and fluid nature of communication inquiry.

Interpersonal Communication

Dyadic communication
Gender and communication
Instructional communication
Interpersonal influence
Interpersonal perception
Intrapersonal communication
Relational communication

Small-Group Communication

Decision making
Family communication
Group dynamics
Intergenerational communication
Leadership
Problem solving

Language and Symbolic Codes

Developmental communication
Intercultural communication
Linguistics
Nonverbal communication
Semantics
Semiotics

Organizational Communication

Business and professional speaking
Health communication
Human communication technology
Negotiation and mediation
Organizational behavior
Socialization and assimilation
Training and development

Public Communication

Argumentation
Communication education
Debate
Environmental communication
Freedom of speech
Legal communication
Performance studies
Persuasion and attitude change
Political communication
Public address
Rhetorical criticism and theory
Voice and diction

Mass Communication

Advertising
Broadcasting and telecommunications
Comparative media systems
Criticism and culture
Economics of media industries
Film and cinema
Journalism
Media effects
Media ethics
New technologies
Policy and regulation
Popular culture
Public relations

These topics help us see how diversified the communication discipline is. Students have many avenues of scholarship available to them. Scholars often need to know about more than just one topic, so they conduct research on many, often overlapping topics during their careers. This interest in multiple areas influences scholars' memberships in professional communication organizations. Many members of the communication discipline belong to several organizations or to several divisions within one or more organizations. Professional communication associations, then, reflect the many interests of their members.

Structure of Professional Communication Organizations

Because of the diversity of their members' interests, major professional communication organizations have developed classifications for interest groups in the field. For example, the Speech Communication Association (SCA) has several divisions: argumentation and forensics, feminist and women studies, health communication, instructional development, international and intercultural communication, interpersonal and small group interaction, language and social interaction, mass communication, organizational communication, performance studies, political communication, public address, public relations, rhetorical and communication theory, and theatre.

The International Communication Association (ICA) has similar divisions: communication and technology, health communication, information systems, instructional/developmental communication, intercultural/development communication, interpersonal communication, mass communication, organizational communication, philosophy of communication, and political communication. The subject-area divisions of the ICA are reflected in earlier volumes of the *Communication Yearbook*, first published in 1977. This source, along with *Communication Abstracts*, first published in 1978, provides important access to and integration of communication knowledge. Both publications are constantly updated and are valuable sources for those who study communication, as is the more recent addition of *ComIndex*, a computerized database. These sources are described in more detail in Chapters 3, 5, and 6.

Thus, the **discipline** of communication can be partitioned into more specific topical areas, even though the work of researchers in the various divisions is often relevant to researchers in other areas. For example, health communication researchers may find information on interpersonal, organizational, and mass communication pertinent to their own studies.

Mass-communication organizations also have specialized divisions that reflect several concerns and content areas. The Association for Education in Journalism and Mass Communication (AEJMC) has the following divisions: advertising, communication technology and policy, communication theory and methodology, history, international communications, law, magazine, mass communications and society, media management and economics, minorities and communication, newspaper, public relations, qualitative studies, radio/television, secondary education, and visual communication. The Broadcast Education Association (BEA) also contains several divisions: broadcast news, communication technology, courses and curricula, gender issues, history, international, law and policy, management and sales, multicultural studies, production, research, student media advisers, two-year colleges and small colleges, and writing.

Activities

Among other activities, professional communication associations publish journals and hold yearly conventions around the country. The papers presented at these conventions represent the most current concerns of communication researchers and may be helpful in your research projects. Some of these papers are submitted to the Educational Resources Information Center (ERIC) for inclusion in the Resources in Education (RIE) system (see Chapter 6). This system places the papers on microfiche, and many libraries receive the entire collection. Some of these papers are collected in proceedings, which are published by the association.

Other authors may choose to submit their papers for publication in a scholarly journal. Unfortunately, there could be a 2- to 3-year delay (or longer!) between the time the paper is first submitted and the time it is published. It is often possible, though, to receive a copy of a paper by attending the convention, by writing to the author (see the discussion of professional association directories, pages 183–186), or by having paper copies made from the microfiche (for a small fee).

Publications

Professional organizations also publish many materials of interest to communication scholars. The SCA, for example, publishes a number of monographs, tapes, books, reports, and bibliographies. The SCA newsletter, *Spectra* (published monthly, except in July), is sent to members to inform them of: new developments in the field; fellow members' promotions, grants, and new appointments; and job openings in communication. Issues also contain reports on publications and conventions that are of interest to members. Both the ICA and the AEJMC publish general newsletters with news of issues, events, people in the field, and job listings. The BEA publishes *Feedback*, its official communicator of association news (in addition to essays and articles). The BEA also sends monthly packets of materials (including news; grant, paper, and scholarship announcements; and job openings) to members. Several divisions of these four organizations also have their own newsletters, which are sent to members of those divisions. All organizations publish directories. These may be helpful if you wish to contact researchers directly about their work.

For more information about these professional organizations, contact them directly:

- Association for Education in Journalism and Mass Communication, 1621 College Street, Columbia, SC 29208
- Broadcast Education Association, 1771 N Street NW, Washington, DC 20036
- International Communication Association, P.O. Box 9589, 8140 Burnet Road, Austin, TX 78766
- Speech Communication Association, 5105 Backlick Road, Suite E, Annandale, VA 22003

Types of Associations

The associations in the preceding list are national scholarly associations. Graduate and undergraduate students are encouraged to join these organizations, although most members are academic faculty and professional communicators. The organizations offer special student memberships. Meetings of regional and state communication associations also provide valuable opportunities for students to attend and to present their research. Four regional associations that are affiliated with the SCA are:

- Eastern Communication Association (ECA), Department of Communication and Marketing, University of New Haven, West Haven, CT 06516
- Central States Communication Association (CSCA), Box A-6, East Central University, Ada, OK 74820-6899

- Southern States Communication Association (SSCA), Box 5131, University of Southern Mississippi, Hattiesburg, MS 39406-5131

- Western States Communication Association (WSCA), Communication Department, University of Utah, Salt Lake City, UT 84112

An organization that affiliates with some of the preceding organizations is the World Communication Association (WCA). It publishes one journal and meets regularly in countries around the world. For information, write to:

- World Communication Association, Golden West College, 15744 Golden West St., Huntington Beach, CA 92647-0592

Some professional organizations focus on the practical activities of their members' careers. Such organizations also distribute newsletters, hold annual conventions, and compile directories of members. They differ from the more scholarly organizations in their emphasis on information and techniques for dealing with practical problems and situations arising in practitioners' lives. Many have student chapters. Contact the following organizations for more information:

- American Association of Advertising Agencies, 666 Third Avenue, New York, NY 10017-4056

- American Forensic Association, Speech Communication and Theatre Arts Department, Box 256, University of Wisconsin, River Falls, WI 54022

- American Marketing Association, 250 S. Wacker Dr., Suite 200, Chicago, IL 60606

- International Association of Business Communicators, One Hallidie Plaza, Suite 600, San Francisco, CA 94102

- International Listening Association, 4105 Squire Court, Muncie, IN 47304

- Lambda Pi Eta (Communication Honor Society for Undergraduate Students), 5105 Backlick Rd., Suite E, Annandale, VA 22003

- National Association of Broadcasters, 1771 N Street NW, Washington, DC 20036

- National Forensic Association, Speech Communication Department, Otterbein College, Westerville, OH 43081

- Pi Kappa Delta (National Honorary Forensic Organization), Box 5075 University Station, North Dakota State University, Fargo, ND 58105
- Public Relations Society of America, 33 Irving Place, New York, NY 10003-2376
- Radio–Television News Directors Association, 1000 Connecticut Avenue NW, Suite 615, Washington, DC 20036
- Society of Professional Journalists, P.O. Box 77, Greencastle, IN 46135-0077
- Women in Communications, Inc., 3717 Columbia Pike, Suite 310, Arlington, VA 22204-4255

Summary

Communication research, like all research, must be systematic to be effective. Communication researchers study the processes through which meaning and social reality are created. Researchers examine the flow of information and the interchange of messages between individuals in several contexts. Although the study of communication is broad-based and interdisciplinary, the field can be divided into several major areas of focus. Professional communication associations publish scholarly journals, organize conventions and conferences, and produce materials and newsletters to keep their members informed.

References

Hart, R. P., & Burks, D. M. (1972). Rhetorical sensitivity and social interaction. *Communication Monographs*, 39, 75–91.

Horton, D., & Wohl, R. R. (1956). Mass communication and para-social interaction: Observations on intimacy at a distance. *Psychiatry*, 19, 215–229.

McCroskey, J. C., & McCain, T. A. (1974). The measurement of interpersonal attraction. *Communication Monographs*, 41, 261–266.

_____

_____

_____

_____

Exercises

1. Describe two situations in your anticipated career that would require you to have a knowledge of communication research. To help, speak to a professional in the area and ask about communication research in that profession.

2. Identify three key terms or headings in the communication subject areas listed in this chapter that now interest you. Explain how these key terms can be applied to projects you plan to complete in the near future, such as a literature review, speech, news story, group discussion, or term paper.

3. Indicate the main subject area described in this chapter with which you most closely identify at this point in your education. Find a national scholarly communication organization that has a division in that area. Contact the organization for information about the division.

4. Examine some newsletters from the professional associations identified in this chapter. What issues are currently of concern to members? What functions do these newsletters serve for members?

Chapter 2

Searching the Communication Literature

The process of searching the communication literature is fairly standard, no matter what sort of project you are attempting. Literature reviews, research reports, thesis or dissertation prospectuses, debates, speeches, news editorials, and feature articles all begin in the same way. Specifics on many of these projects are explained in Chapter 11. Most important is starting early so that there is enough time to complete a systematic and thorough search of the literature. The first milestone is identifying and developing a narrowed, focused topic.

The Topic

Selecting, Narrowing, and Adjusting a Topic

1. Select a Topic
Often the most difficult part of the research process is selecting a topic and then defining the research area. To gain a comprehensive

picture of the communication field, you will need to find some general sources that will acquaint you with the various facets of communication. Some of the sources described in Chapter 5 of this book—handbooks, textbooks, encyclopedias, and annual reviews—can serve this purpose.

You may get ideas for possible research topics by examining the textbooks used in your courses. Handbooks and encyclopedias in communication and related disciplines may also help you find a topic that interests you. Specific topic areas may also be found in annual reviews, in indexes (which list articles published in scholarly and professional journals), and in abstracts (which generally give paragraph-long summaries of research studies). These sources are helpful in narrowing a general topic to a specific research area because they identify subtopics or research problems that are particular to the research topic and list the current studies in these subtopics. Bibliographies and guides to the literature can also be used when defining and refining a problem area for investigation. These communication research sources are discussed in Chapters 5 and 6.

2. Narrow the Topic

Once you have chosen a general topic or research problem, the next step is to narrow it so that you can formulate a specific *research question*. By constructing a specific research question, you narrow the focus of your research, and you can channel all your energies into a productive purpose. The research question also provides a theme for your research that helps you unify disparate elements and eliminate or reduce nonproductive efforts. A specific research question sets a goal for your efforts and helps you save time. We often develop specific research questions by thinking about a topic, talking to and brainstorming with others, and most of all, reading about the topic or research problem in the literature of the field.

For example, let's imagine you are interested in both mass communication and organizational communication and that you want to investigate the interface of these two general areas. At this point, your broad topic might be "The Use of Media in Organizations." By examining some textbooks and bibliographies, you find such subtopics as advertising, in-house publications, public relations, organizational training programs, institutional media, corporate television, and so on. This may start you thinking, conversing with others, seeking out past research, and reading about the experiences of those people in organizations who must communicate with the public by working with journalists.

Your initial research may cause you to ask whether these organizational professionals receive any training in dealing with the press or reporters. At this point, you have identified a more specific research problem and can formulate a preliminary question to examine, such as "What types of training programs in media relations and public interviews do organizations provide for their management personnel?" This is a viable question that is sufficiently narrow in focus to study and discuss in a research paper. Another possible research question would be "Which type of media training program is the most effective for management personnel?"

3. Adjust the Topic

Once you have decided on a specific preliminary research question, the next step is to conduct a more extensive review of the available literature related to that preliminary question. In other words, what is the status of published research and information about your topic? If the subject area is still too broad, you'll find yourself doing extraneous work and feeling uncertain about what to include. If you find it difficult to choose pertinent sources, reexamine your research question and try to limit it further. In the preceding example, for instance, you may decide to exclude government and other nonprofit organizations from consideration and to focus on commercial organizations. Naturally, you don't want to go to the other extreme and make the research question too narrow, or you will have very little information to examine.

How will you know whether your question is sufficiently narrow in focus? Your examination of the literature should tell you. If the topic area is too broad, your treatment of it may be too superficial, and there may be too many sources with which to deal. But if the topic is too narrow, the answer to the question may be obvious or insignificant.

Adjusting a question to a manageable size also depends on the scope of the assignment or your personal goal for the project. If you are working on a literature review or on a thesis or dissertation proposal, the amount of literature you will consult will be greater than if you are completing a 10-page research report.

This notion of adjusting a research question as a search of the literature progresses is difficult for a beginning researcher. Discussions with instructors, advisers, and librarians can prove helpful in this process. Some suggestions follow.

The Search

Preparing for the Literature Search

4. Choose a Search Strategy

With some assignments, a general-to-specific **search strategy** is most beneficial. When little is known about the topic or when the assignment involves a comprehensive overview of the literature, it is best to begin with general sources such as encyclopedias, annual reviews, and handbooks, then move to bibliographies, guides, indexes, and abstracts (and their computerized equivalents), and finally complete the **literature search** by examining the original journal articles, books, or media. With this search strategy, you limit the topic as you continue through the search, rather like the strategy used in searching computerized databases (see Chapter 3).

Key terms are combined to enlarge the search (for example, adding "radio" to "television" to find out more about the broadcast media). Key terms are separated to limit the number of sources you will find (for example, removing "radio" from the descriptors examined).

In other situations, you may find it advantageous to use a specific-to-general search strategy. For example, if you have found a key **reference** or article, you will want to enlarge the search beyond that one reference. Again, indexes, abstracts, and bibliographies provide additional information. Citation indexes are particularly helpful in locating related studies. (These are all discussed in Chapter 6.)

One handy way of planning this search is to list the main sources necessary for the search and to update these as the search progresses. We've found it useful to complete a search strategy sheet (Figure 1). Here you can identify the main reference sources you think will be useful for your topic. As you read through Chapters 5 and 6 of this text, you'll notice sources that are very much related to your topic and others that are not related. List the related ones on the search strategy sheet and use the sheet when you visit the library. It will also help you keep track of sources you have consulted and those that remain.

5. Become Familiar with the Library

In later chapters, you will be introduced to many reference works, periodicals, and finding tools useful to communication researchers. To locate them, you will need to acquaint yourself with

---

SEARCH STRATEGY SHEET

Name:

Research Question: *What do researchers know about . . .?*

Relevant Subject Terms and Headings:

SOURCES TO CHECK

Handbooks:

Textbooks:

Encyclopedias:

Guides to the Literature:

Annual Reviews and Series:

Bibliographies:

Indexes:

Abstracts:

Figure 1. Search strategy sheet.

the organization and services of the library you are using and with the special catalogs and lists maintained by that library.

Many libraries conduct orientation sessions or offer self-guided tours and handouts for new users. Be sure to take advantage of these if they are offered because the basic information and tips you will learn will save you much confusion and frustration. Lacking such an orientation, the best approach when using a library new to you is simply to ask a **reference librarian** to explain: (a) the workings of the library's catalog and what it includes; (b) the location of periodical indexes, abstracts, and other reference books and how that location is indicated in the catalog; (c) how to determine which periodicals the library owns and where they are located; and (d) where government documents are found and what lists or catalogs are available to identify and locate them. Of course, as you go about using the library for your research and completing the exercises in this book, you will inevitably come up with many additional questions. Never hesitate to ask reference librarians to help you. They realize that libraries are somewhat complicated to use and that students will have many questions.

The library **catalog**, whether in card or computer format, is the most obvious and well-known part of a library. Most students are familiar with the use of such catalogs before they enter college.

(College library catalogs are often more complicated or arranged differently from high school catalogs, but the general principles of use are the same.) In fact, many students turn to the library catalog first when they begin a research project. There are problems, however, with relying on the library catalog. Most catalogs provide detailed subject access only to books, and only to those books owned by the library. Books provide only one type of information, and the information is often dated (the lag between the time a work is written and the time it is published is often considerable). When writing a research paper, you should support material from books with more recent information from **journal** articles. Indexes and abstracts will help you locate pertinent journal articles, as we discuss in Chapter 6.

Furthermore, libraries have to be selective about what books they purchase. No college library can own every book that has been published. So library catalogs do not truly represent all the materials available to a researcher. By limiting yourself to the holdings of one particular library, you will miss some important sources and perhaps use sources that are not entirely relevant to the topic.

Finally, the catalog does not help you judge the relative authority or relevance of books on your topic. For this reason, a selective bibliography, such as those found in encyclopedias, handbooks, and textbooks, is often a more efficient starting place for research projects. Once you have found a bibliography on your research topic, you may wish to consult the subject catalog to see what sources have been published since the date of the bibliography. Other tips on using the library catalog are found in the section "Develop Subject Headings," discussed shortly.

Among the information sources often *not* found in the library catalog but of interest to the researcher are research reports, statistical information, media accounts, and government publications. Libraries often have separate catalogs of government publications. In addition, to determine which periodicals a library owns and where they are located, you sometimes must use a separate listing (often in computerized printout form) located in the reference area.

Computerized searching procedures are available in most libraries. In fact, most libraries have converted their card catalogs to computerized catalogs. Procedures for using computerized catalogs vary widely, but instructions for using them should be readily available near the catalog terminal or through on-line help screens. The principles of searching computerized databases described in Chapter 3 can be applied to using on-line library catalogs, as well.

In addition, many libraries now provide their users with access to a computerized union catalog for finding out what books (as well as films, records, and other nonprint media) are available in hundreds of libraries throughout the United States. The largest and most widely available union catalog of this type, *WorldCat*, is produced by OCLC (the Online Computer Library Center). *WorldCat* is made available through OCLC's FirstSearch on-line database search service. Information on how to access *WorldCat* can be found in libraries where the service is available. *WorldCat* will tell you whether your library owns a particular book, and, if not, the system can be asked to display a list of libraries that do own the work. RLIN (Research Libraries Information Network) is a similar system used by 20 to 30 of the largest research libraries in the country.

The **interlibrary loan system** is a useful service libraries provide. Because libraries are selective about the books they buy, a national interlibrary loan system has been created so people can borrow a book from another library for a period of time (typically 2 weeks). Requests for such loans are usually filled out at the reference desk, the circulation desk, or the interlibrary loan department.

It is also possible to request copies of specific articles published in periodicals (such as scholarly journals) through an interlibrary loan. Interlibrary loan also helps overcome one complication that may arise when the journal you want is "at the bindery." If you know what journal article you want (as opposed to just wanting to browse through an issue), it may be possible to request a paper copy through interlibrary loan.

Borrowing materials through an interlibrary loan usually takes 2 or more weeks. This is one reason you need to begin research projects early in the semester. If there is no time for an interlibrary loan, a library in your area or region may own the work that you wish to read. OCLC's *WorldCat* can specify which libraries own the materials, but unfortunately, it cannot tell you if the materials have been checked out or are kept in the noncirculating reserve collection of those libraries. However, if your college or university has a campus computer network that is connected to the national Internet network, you will probably be able to access the catalogs of other libraries in your region or state. These catalogs will usually be able to tell you if items are available. Ask at the reference desk about the availability of these services.

Library procedures differ, library-by-library. You need to be aware of the different protocols followed in the libraries you use. If a book has been checked out, some libraries may allow you to put a "hold" on it when it is returned or to recall the book from the borrower. Because libraries' protocols differ, it is best to inquire about specific procedures at the main information desk of the library visited.

For basic guidelines on using research libraries, see:

> Beasley, D. R. (1988). *How to use a research library*. New York: Oxford University Press.

Using Effective Search Procedures

As we have said, documentary or library research is much easier to conduct if it is done systematically. Disorganized researchers find that they waste much time searching for and consulting sources that were previously located but forgotten. You can simplify the organization of effort in any research project if you construct bibliography cards, prepare a subject-headings list, and keep a search record.

6. Keep Bibliography Cards

A **bibliography card** or record holds complete information for each source examined. It lists a complete and accurate citation, as well as where the source is found. You should also include a capsulized summary of the pertinent contents of the source.

Bibliography cards or records serve three major purposes:

1. They furnish a complete current record of sources for later use in compiling a bibliography or citing references.

2. They eliminate the practice of repeating or retracing steps by allowing recently located sources to be checked against what was previously examined.

3. They provide a record of needed sources that have yet to be found in the research process.

Cards are suggested here, instead of notebook paper, because they are handy, sturdy, and easy to organize and alphabetize. Note-taking programs are now available for home and portable computers, and students with these resources will find them useful to prepare bibliography records. Figure 2 shows an example of a bibliography card.

People have found a variety of note-taking styles useful for summarizing what has been read. You should use the system that works best for you. We suggest you use a citation format similar to the one shown in Figure 2. This is a modification of the style used by the American Psychological Association (APA), which is explained later in this book. This modified style for the bibliography card begins with full information on the author(s), the year (and month) of publication, and the title of the article. Then the publication name, volume number (both underlined), and inclusive page numbers follow. This modification is necessary because,

---

Rubin, Alan M. (Winter 1983). Television uses and gratifications: The interactions of viewing patterns and motivations. Journal of Broadcasting, 27, 37–51.

TV uses and gratifications study. Qs: (1) What are the interactions among TV motives, behaviors, & attitudes? (2) What TV motive pattern can explain viewing attitudes & behaviors? Survey sample—464 adults, ages 18 to 89; secondary analysis. Findings: TV motives—pass time/habit, information/learning, entertainment, companionship, escape. Motives interrelated.

[Card 1 of 2]

Rubin ('83). JOB. #2

Canonical roots: (1) entertainment & pass time motives with TV affinity, viewing levels, & realism: (2) information & nonescape with news, talk, game shows & viewing levels. Predictors: entertainment, pass time, companionship, & information motives predict viewing levels and affinity; information & entertainment motives predict realism. Discussion: TV dependence emphasizes the medium, not content; "...heavy users of television are not necessarily motivated by a desire to escape from reality." (p. 49)

[Card 2 of 2]

Figure 2. Bibiography card.

although the APA style does not require authors' first names or the journal issue (if each issue does not begin with page 1), some other bibliographic styles do. By including this information here you may save much time in the future should you use the information in a project requiring a different style or if you need to use a masculine or feminine pronoun to refer to his or her work.

The *Publication Manual of the American Psychological Association* (pp. 189–222) gives the details of bibliography form and provides a quick reference guide for writing style, editorial style, typing and submitting manuscripts, and proofreading. Communication researchers often use it when they prepare final versions of papers. You should, however, use one style during the entire research process. It is unnecessarily time-consuming to convert references written on bibliography cards or records in one format to another format for the paper. Learning a style early can save time in the future.

We use the APA format throughout this book because it is used in most major communication journals. Use our citations as guides for your own bibliographic citations. However, be aware that typed references will have a slightly different format from those printed in this book. When typing, you indent the first line, like a normal paragraph. When it is typeset, it takes the form of an indented overhang, where the first line is flush with the left margin and all other lines are indented three spaces.

Students often find photocopying an article preferable to sitting in the library and taking notes on bibliography cards. Keep in mind, though, that this practice can be very costly and more time-consuming than it may first appear. Often you scan a newly discovered article first to see if it is relevant to your topic and make some initial judgment about the article's worth. This means you are preparing yourself to take notes on a bibliography card, but stop short. Later, you'll have to reread the article and repeat this preparatory process. Also, by stopping at this point and filing the photocopy of the article for later use, you are not making full use of the article's reference list for other places to search. Finally, by photocopying everything, you tend to put off reading the articles to just before writing, so writing is delayed and hurried. By reading articles and taking notes immediately on bibliography cards or bibliography records in a notebook computer, you're ready to organize and write once all sources have been found. So, you may be tempted to photocopy everything, but doing so can add extra time and costs to the search and writing processes.

7. Develop Subject Headings

You should develop a subject-headings list and keep it current throughout the research process. Include in this list all possible headings related to the topic that you may use when consulting the library catalog, bibliographies, indexes, and abstracts. For example, information on the topic "Audiovisual Aids" may be found under many headings (see Figure 3). The more topical categories you include in the subject-headings list, the more likely it is that you will find most of the possible references to that topic.

As you have probably discovered, though, not all reference sources use the same subject headings for indexing. However, there is one useful source that identifies many subject-headings alternatives, the *Library of Congress Subject Headings*:

> Library of Congress. (1910–). *Library of Congress Subject Headings* (4 vols.). Washington, DC: Author.

This four-volume work provides quite a few of the headings used in the catalogs of most libraries. This source is an ideal place to begin the subject-headings list for your own research project. You can add new headings as the research progresses. Figure 4 shows a Library of Congress heading for one topic.

The *precise subject head* in this example is "Communication in management." The information listed directly below it (in this example, *May Subd Geog* and *HD30.3*) is of interest primarily to librarians who catalog library materials. Several abbreviations are

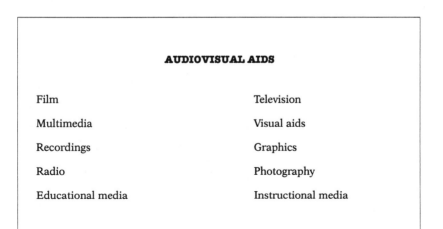

AUDIOVISUAL AIDS

Film	Television
Multimedia	Visual aids
Recordings	Graphics
Radio	Photography
Educational media	Instructional media

Figure 3. Subject-headings list.

Communication in management
  (May Subd Geog)
    [HD30.3]
    Here are entered works on the role of communica-
    tion in effective management. Works on the various
    forms of oral and written messages used by a business
    in the conduct of its affairs are entered under Busi-
    ness communication.

    UF   Communication Industry
    BT   Management
    NT   Automatic data collection systems
          Management—Comunication systems

Figure 4. Library of Congress subject heading.

used to refer library users to related headings and synonymous terms. *UF*, which stands for *use for*, tells the researcher that the terms listed after it are synonymous with the precise subject heading but are *not* Library of Congress subject headings. Thus, they will not be used in library catalogs, although they might appear in periodical indexes or abstracts. Next, *related headings* are listed. These are either *broader terms* (BT) or *narrower terms* (NT). These terms are **Library of Congress classification** subject headings and are used in library catalogs.

By looking at the library's subject catalog under "Communication in Management," you could find an entry like the one shown in Figure 5.

The call number of the book, along with other information that might be useful in compiling the subject-headings list or a bibliography card, is included. The publication date (after the *c* for copyright) indicates how current the book is. The entry also notes that this book contains an index and bibliographic references (the page numbers of the bibliography are also sometimes provided). You should examine books with bibliographies carefully to obtain references to other useful sources on the topic. Be sure to include all this information on the bibliography card or record you prepare for this book.

The subject **tracings** at the bottom of the catalog entry inform researchers of the subject headings under which a particular book is listed in the subject section of the catalog. You can then consult these subject headings for other related sources. The subject tracings are

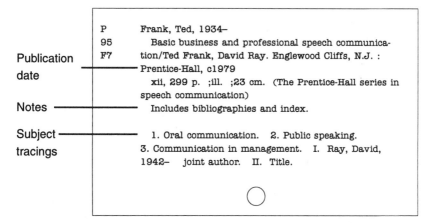

Figure 5. Catalog record.

also important subject-headings to add to your subject-headings list. The example in Figure 5 is from a card catalog. The format of entries in on-line catalogs is not standardized but most will include information very similar to what is found on a catalog card.

8. Use Search Records

When undertaking lengthy research projects, it is wise to note all sources you've consulted to prevent redoing research work or missing valuable sources. Search records indicate which finding tools or sources (indexes, abstracts, bibliographies, and so forth) you have already examined and what portions of these sources you inspected. Index cards are most convenient for this purpose, although search records can also be entered in notebook computers. One card, which includes relevant subject headings and dates searched, should be used for each source. Figure 6 is an example of such a search record.

In addition, a general search record card, which lists all sources that have been examined, should be prepared for quick reference (Figure 7).

Evaluating and Summarizing Information

Scholarship is not of uniform quality. Some research studies and books are of greater substance than others. Not all authors engage in flawless research. The scholar who is conducting a literature

COMMUNICATION ABSTRACTS

volumes searched: Vol. 1 no.1 (1978) to Vol. 10, no. 3 (1987)
Topic: Television violence
Headings used:
  Aggression   Newscast effects
  Aggressive behavior   Television effects
  Children and television   Television programming
  Message effects   Violence

Figure 6. Search record card.

Communication Abstracts
Topicator
Index to Journals in Communication Studies
International Encyclopedia of the Social Sciences
Communication Yearbook
Handbook of Social Psychology

Figure 7. General search record card.

review is expected to know and to evaluate the quality of the work
in addition to summarizing the findings.

To evaluate a scholarly journal article, you must understand
the research process and its conventions. There are rules that
guide research investigations, and breaking these rules can result

in research of lower quality. By conducting a systematic review process, most scholarly journals prevent publication of articles that have major or serious flaws. Occasionally, though, dubious practices are not uncovered or are overlooked in the review process and result in published articles that cause one to question the validity of the findings. As beginning scholars in the communication discipline, you must learn about research conventions and rules and be able to evaluate research articles and books with a critical eye.

9. Evaluate the Sources

Just because a book has been published and acquired by a library or an article has been published in a scholarly journal doesn't mean it is a quality source. Many complex factors determine a book or an article's worth or quality. Here are some suggested criteria for judging quality:

1. Examine the book's front matter. The preface and introduction should indicate why the work was written. Was the purpose to inform, interpret, explain, or share new discoveries? Also, determine the intended level of audience (high school students, college seniors, other researchers). Books that are intended as **secondary sources**—ones that summarize previously reported research or contain opinion essays—may help you understand the field better but may not be works you would want to cite in a literature review. Literature reviews should contain findings from **primary sources** (scholarly books and journal articles). Sometimes, authors of journal articles intend to summarize published literature in an area or to comment on that literature. Such articles mostly serve the purpose of a secondary source. Journal articles that are primary sources seek to add new knowledge or insights. Even all primary research, though, is not of equal quality. Sometimes the author's purpose is to test or to develop a new theory or research procedure. If such research is published in a top-tier national or international journal in the discipline (see Chapter 7), it is likely to be highly regarded, even if the theory is controversial. At other times, an author's purpose may be: (a) to replicate previous studies looking for similar or contrasting results, (b) to revise or to adapt a scale or other research measure, or (c) to test a small aspect of an existing theory. These studies are important and well-regarded, but will typically fall below the level of regard for research that

breaks new ground about theory and measurement. The purpose of the article or book, then, can tell you the scope of the study and its potential value.

2. Critique the book or article's methodology and data. The methodology should be clearly detailed. The data should be accurate. The work that went into producing the study should be apparent. Also, determine how recent the research is. Have environmental or social conditions changed since the data were collected in a way that might cause you to question the results? Sometimes you may not be expert enough to critique a work's validity and reliability. If not, consult reviews for others' opinions about books. Book reviews, too, are of uneven quality, but there may be agreement among several reviews about the book you're evaluating. Another indicator of quality is if the book or article has received an award from a national association; directories may contain this information.

3. Explore the author's background and qualifications. Try to check his or her publication track record. What else has the author written in the area? Who else has cited his or her writings in their own work? Authors should be experts in the area and their qualifications should tell you if they are. If their qualifications are not printed in the book, look them up in relevant directories to see if they belong to national professional organizations and their work affiliation. If authors are in communication, you can examine their research records in *ComIndex* or in the *Index to Journals in Communication Studies through 1990* (see Chapters 3 and 6). You can also look in *Social Sciences Citation Index* or *Arts and Humanities Citation Index* to see who else has cited their research (see Chapter 6).

4. Investigate the reputation of the publisher. National and international journals with high rejection rates tend to publish consistently high-quality articles. Readers can generally trust editorial boards and editors to scrutinize the articles prior to publication. Regional journals are also respected, although often below the level of the national or international journal. State and local journals, and those with lower rates of rejection, often have somewhat lower standards and publish articles that may have some minor flaws or are of interest to a specific population. Book-publishing companies also have reputations. Some have editors and editorial boards in charge of reviewing texts or scholarly books for possible publication;

these tend to have higher standards. At the other end of the continuum are publishers who are paid by authors to publish their work. "Vanity" presses tend to publish books of lower quality.

5. Examine the back matter. A book that contains an index can be used as a reference source; if it lacks an index, the use of the book may be limited. The footnotes and bibliography indicate the breadth and depth of research that went into the book and the author's authoritative knowledge of the field. It is possible, though, that innovators may not have many works to cite or may be restricted to citing their own work because of the recency of the topic. If few original books and articles are cited or if major works in the field are not mentioned, there may be reason to question the value of the book as a reputable source. Also, expect some works cited in the bibliography to be 1 or 2 years older than the copyright date of the book itself. For instance, this edition of this book was completed in early 1995, but because of the publication process, the copyright date is 1996. We have included, however, sources that were available through late 1994 (and even early 1995 in some cases). Had we not included any recent sources, you could suspect that we hadn't done our homework.

10. Read Materials Thoroughly

Some articles and books are easier to read than others. Historical, critical, and qualitative research reports (see Chapter 9 for explanations of these research forms) typically contain verbal descriptions of findings; the results are presented in everyday language or common communication jargon. Empirical research, which relies on observation or experimentation, often contains statistical data and tables, which students often skip over when reading. If you are not familiar with statistics, this may be the only way you can read the article.

Here are some pointers on how to read a research article, chapter, or book:

1. Look at the title. Often the main features can be identified from the title. Also, take a look at who the authors are and their backgrounds.

2. Read the abstract (if provided). The abstract gives you a short synopsis of the work and prepares you to read it.

3. Read the introductory material and review of research. This tells you why the study was done and what prior research led up to this present research project. This is a good time to create new bibliography cards for important sources that you may have missed.

4. Read the method section. Here you will find how the study was actually performed, who was involved in it, and what instruments or techniques were used to perform it. This section will reveal the soundness of the empirical choices made by the author.

5. Read the results. This is the meat of the research article. Most of your notes about this research report will come from this section because it contains the actual findings. Look at the tables and figures to see what was found. If the results are full of numbers and statistics that you can't understand, read past the numbers to the conclusions drawn by the authors. Don't give up!

6. Read the discussion. The authors typically summarize the results in less technical terms here. Authors sometimes inflate the actual importance of the findings, but some journal editors temper these exaggerations. Try to identify here the most important findings in the study, the meaning or implications of these findings, and the limitations of the study. Authors also offer good ideas for future research projects.

7. Scan the bibliography for sources that may be useful but you have not yet encountered.

Careful reading of research takes energy and concentration. The reading is much more difficult than textbook prose, and you should be prepared for it. Keep a communication, statistics, or general dictionary handy so you can look up terms you don't understand (see Chapter 8).

11. Take Careful Notes

New scholars sometimes find it difficult to take notes on what they read, either because the material contains too much information or because they are unfamiliar with the techniques of *abstracting*. Abstracting helps you synthesize the information you read and distinguish the most important parts of the article, book, or chapter. In effect, abstracting helps you become more critical of what you read because it forces you to understand the research thoroughly. We explain some of the basic steps involved in abstracting in Chapter 11.

For additional guidance, consult the following source:

Cremmins, E. T. (1982). *The art of abstracting*. Philadelphia: ISI Press.

When taking notes from books or research articles, be sure to summarize the materials in your own words, or you might fall prey to inadvertent plagiarism. If you summarize the material in your own words, you will be certain that what you will later write will be your own words, not those of the original author. If you find that certain passages are so well stated that you couldn't do justice to them yourself, copy the direct quote (using quotation marks) and the page number for future reference in a footnote or bibliographic citation. But as a rule of thumb, try to understand what the author is saying and then translate it into your own words.

Scholars who take careful notes during the literature search can proceed to the writing stage without having to reexamine sources already read. When typing the bibliography, you will find that having these citations on 3-inch by 5-inch index cards is helpful.

Tips on Searching the Literature

Keep in mind three main points when searching the literature. First, don't let yourself get bogged down. Read completely only those articles that are relevant and note other interesting articles for future reading. It is sometimes tempting to browse through a multitude of new sources, but all you will be doing is delaying the inevitable task of pursuing your research.

Second, don't entertain the illusion that you can exhaust *all* possible sources related to your topic. It is, of course, important to be as thorough as possible. It is also important to start your research early. Remember, some sources may not be in the library, and you will need to order them through an interlibrary loan. But you will *never* find all possible references.

You must set a research stopping point and at that time start writing. You will learn to realize that you've exhausted all the pertinent, available sources when newly found bibliographies list sources you've already seen and have nothing new for you to examine.

Third, remember to practice good note-taking skills when you are conducting your library research. To take notes on the content of the material, you will need to abstract, or condense, what you read. You will also need to have a complete and accurate bibliographic citation (one that is legibly written). We summarize proper format for bibliographic citations in Appendix A, "APA Style

Basics." You may want to refer to that section as you proceed through this book.

Writing

We emphasize throughout this book how essential it is that you thoroughly examine the literature *before* you start the writing process. That means all library work should be done before you begin to write. As you pursue your search, find a topic that is interesting and related to the project. Through exploratory reading of general sources, narrow the topic to a manageable size. One or more research questions should emerge at this point. These questions guide the rest of the literature search, your evaluation of what you read, and the writing process.

After exhausting all relevant sources, you will need to consider how best to organize the materials you've found into a meaningful review of the literature. Even if your research goal is something other than a research paper (for example, a speech, group discussion, broadcast script, debate case, feature article, seminar, critique, review, or exam), the process is similar. You will need to make sense of the information, organize it into a coherent pattern, and select the best method of presentation. To do this, you must keep your specific research question and the goal of your research endeavor clearly in mind.

12. Develop an Outline
Complete an initial outline at this time to help decide which specific sources to examine. An outline organizes the subtopics or subthemes found in the literature and guides the arguments you will make in your review. Once you have found all the materials you need, expand and develop your original outline. Always check your outline along the way to ensure it conforms to the thesis statement or research questions.

13. Edit
Write from the outline. Then set the written review aside for a day or two before editing and revising it into final form. We suggest you set this final form aside for another day or two, then edit again. Once the final copy is typed, proofread it carefully for typographic errors.

Details on writing, proofreading the parts of the literature review, and summarizing strategies are found in Chapters 10 and 11. Be sure to take a look at these chapters before you begin writing.

Summary

The research process, then, relies on how well you define your topic and your awareness of the many possible sources of information. Research into topic areas is necessary for most assignments communication students encounter and for many tasks communication professionals face in their daily routines. Being able to identify a research topic and to clarify specific questions for investigation are essential skills for all communication researchers. These skills simplify the research process by providing an efficient, organized direction.

Selecting a topic and defining the research problem are often the most difficult parts of searching the literature. Once a topic is chosen and a specific research question is formulated, a researcher concentrates on finding and reviewing the available literature related to that preliminary question. Often the topic must be adjusted (narrowed or broadened) during the search process.

Researchers must be familiar with the library and understand the workings of the library catalog, interlibrary loan, and systematic procedures for library searching. These procedures include bibliography cards or records, subject-headings lists, and search record cards. Tips for conducting a literature search include reading only relevant materials, setting a stopping point for the search, and practicing good note-taking strategies such as abstracting. Researchers also must understand and evaluate what they read before they begin writing.

In general, researchers must be organized and approach library or documentary research tasks systematically. Not only does having a search plan save time and energy, it results in a better, more coherent product.

References

Beasley, D. R. (1988). *How to use a research library*. New York: Oxford University Press.

Cremmins, E. T. (1982). *The art of abstracting*. Philadelphia: ISI Press.

Mann, T. (1987). *A guide to library research methods*. New York: Oxford University Press.

Roth, A. J. (1995). *The research paper: Process, form, and content* (6th ed.). Belmont, CA: Wadsworth.

U.S. Library of Congress. (1910–). *Library of Congress Subject Headings*. Washington, DC: Author.

_____

_____

_____

_____

_____

_____

_____

_____

_____

Exercises

1. Choose an area of communication that you identified as being of interest to you in Chapter 1 and describe a general research topic you would like to pursue further.

2. Formulate three specific research questions about this general research topic.

3. Complete a search strategy sheet for one of these three research questions. Examine each of these general sources and complete bibliography cards for each source you find. The bibliography should include a sufficient number of sources to support a 20-page research report. The bibliography should be listed on 3-inch by 5-inch index cards and entries should follow the style used in this chapter.

4. As your bibliography progresses, complete the following additional records:

   a. Subject-headings/key-word list. Keep a record on a 3-inch by 5-inch index card of all headings and key words that pertain to your topic.

   b. Search record cards. Keep both a general card, listing by title all sources used, plus an individual card for each finding tool (for example, index or abstract), using the format in this chapter.

5. Answer the following questions as a way of tracking your literature search progress.

Topic

- Have you selected a topic? What is it?
- Does it need to be narrowed? What is the narrowed topic?
- How can you adjust the topic to one that is manageable? What is the topic now?

Search

- Have you selected a search strategy appropriate for this topic? Which one is best? Have you completed your search strategy sheet?
- Have you toured the library? Do you know how to use the library catalog? Do you know how to order material through an interlibrary loan? Do you know where reserve materials, government documents, and statistical materials are located?
- Have you set up a system for searching the literature? Do you have a 3-inch by 5-inch bibliography card system developed? Do you have a subject-headings list? Do you have search record cards for each reference source? Do you have a general search record card for all sources?
- Have you evaluated the sources you plan to use? Are they reliable?
- Have you read the materials carefully?
- Are your notes in your own words? Did you use quotation marks around materials you had to quote, and did you record the page number for these quotes?

Writing

- Are you ready to write? What is the thesis of the work? Have you constructed an outline? What are its main points or divisions?
- After you wrote, did you revise the paper two or three times to make sure it made sense? Did you edit the manuscript and proofread carefully for typographic errors and misspellings?

Chapter 3

Using Computers to Search Electronic Databases

Libraries and their users are in the midst of truly revolutionary changes in the ways that information is produced, stored, distributed, and accessed. In 1986 when the first edition of this book was published, relatively few academic libraries had even computerized their card catalogs, let alone acquired the CD-ROM indexes that were just becoming available. By the second edition in 1990, many libraries had on-line catalogs and CD-ROM indexes, and campus networks offering access to a few electronic library resources began to appear. In 1993, the third edition found most academic libraries with on-line catalogs and CD-ROM indexes, and many were making a wide variety of indexes and other information sources available through campus networks. With the appearance of the fourth edition in 1996, we find a rapid expansion of networked information, with campus connections to the **Internet**, an international network of networks, expanding access to many additional computerized databases and opening up entirely new ways of communicating scholarly and professional information.

Today, many library catalogs and periodical indexes and abstracts are becoming available only in electronic form. A researcher who is reluctant to use computers to find information or who does not know how to do so effectively will be severely handicapped. In this chapter, we will introduce you to the different types of computerized databases and your options for accessing them, and we will provide an explanation of the process and concepts involved in searching them. In the next chapter, we will discuss the types of information available to communication researchers through the Internet and how they can be accessed.

Technological Options

The electronic environment you find on your campus might vary considerably from that at another university. This is partly because technology has provided libraries with many options for delivering electronic information. Thus, on one campus, the electronic equivalent of *Psychological Abstracts* may be offered over a campus network, searchable not only from the library but also from offices, residence halls, or any **modem**-equipped microcomputer. On another campus, it may be available only on CD-ROM work stations in the library itself. At still another it may be available only through a statewide catalog system or via the Internet. If it is available on a campus network, the searching procedures may be identical to those used to search the library's own **on-line catalog**, the same as the procedures used to search CD-ROM indexes in the library, or quite different from either.

Students often become confused by all these options. To help sort them out, visit the reference desk of your library and ask for advice and assistance. Librarians can help you find out what electronic sources are available and how you can access and use them effectively.

Varieties of Computerized Databases

A **database** is information stored in such a way that it can be retrieved. Card catalogs and periodical indexes—in fact, all the reference sources discussed in this book—are examples of databases.

They are organized so that you can easily find what you're looking for. A **computerized database** is simply information stored electronically, to be retrieved via a computer terminal or a microcomputer. Such databases greatly increase the flexibility for retrieving information.

It is important to distinguish between electronic databases, which are fully searchable, and electronic publications whose text can be retrieved, but not searched, electronically. Many resources now available, though, are a combination of the two. Databases can be categorized broadly as *bibliographic, referral,* and *source* databases.

Bibliographic Databases

Bibliographic databases, which are the focus of this chapter, consist of citations to published literature, sometimes with abstracts. They correspond to periodical indexes and abstracts. Computerized library catalogs are also examples of bibliographic databases. At the conclusion of their search, users of these databases will usually still need to locate the actual publications cited, although some periodical indexes are beginning to include on-line the full text of at least some of the publications they cite.

Most of the periodical indexes and abstracts described in Part Two of this book are now available both **on-line** and on **CD-ROM** as bibliographic databases. Those of major interest to communication researchers are *ERIC* (Educational Resources Information Center), the computerized equivalent of the printed indexes *Resources in Education* and *Current Index to Journals in Education*, *Linguistics and Language Behavior Abstracts*, *PAIS* (Public Affairs Information Service), *PsycLIT* (*Psychological Abstracts*), *Social Sciences Citation Index, Sociofile* (*Sociological Abstracts*), *Business Periodicals Index, Social Sciences Index, Humanities Index,* and *Education Index*. Most of these databases correspond closely to their print counterparts in scope and journal coverage. A major difference, however, is the number of years available for retrospective searching. Just a few databases were available on-line before the 1970s, and the coverage of most CD-ROM indexes starts after 1980.

Other bibliographic databases do not correspond to any printed index and are available only in computerized form. Those potentially useful to communication researchers, particularly those in organizational communication, include *ABI/INFORM* and *Management Contents*, which index and abstract periodical literature in business and management. More general indexes include *Academic Index* and *Periodical Abstracts*.

Most of these databases provide only selective coverage to communication publications. One bibliographic database specific to the communication discipline is *ComIndex*, which is produced by the Communication Institute for Online Scholarship (CIOS). *ComIndex* contains more than 18,500 references from all major and many other communication journals. As of 1995, it indexed 55 journals mostly from 1970. *ComIndex* can be loaded onto most personal computers and users can search by author, title, or year. Searches for authors or for titles of articles are relatively complete. Subject searching, though, is limited to cases where the word or term appears in the article's title. This results in many missed sources because titles do not contain all important subject search terms. Beginning in 1995, *ComIndex* introduced a "co-occurrence analysis," whereby it is possible to identify networks of authors or of title **keywords** (for example, concepts and theories) in a research area.

Referral Databases

Referral databases correspond to printed directories and contain references to organizations, people, grants, archives, research projects, and so on. Although some referral databases contain summaries or abstracts, researchers most often use these databases to locate a primary information source. Referral databases of possible interest to communication researchers include *CineScan*, which describes film and videotape footage available from major archives, and the *Encyclopedia of Associations*.

Source Databases

In contrast, **source databases** contain such complete information that after consulting them you may not need to continue the search for information. This category includes numeric, full-text, image, and multimedia databases.

Numeric databases consist primarily of statistical or other numerical data and are somewhat equivalent to statistical compendia such as yearbooks and almanacs. They may also contain some textual information. Many libraries now receive most of their current census data as numeric databases on CD-ROMs produced by the U.S. Bureau of the Census. The searching **protocols** for numeric databases usually allow the user to create, correlate, and retrieve personally defined sets of data that might take many hours to assemble from printed publications.

Full-text databases contain the complete text of publications such as journals, newspapers, wire service stories, court decisions, books, and encyclopedias. In true full-text databases, every word of the entire text can be searched interactively on-line. For example, if a person's name, hometown, street address, or occupation appeared as incidental information in a newspaper article, the article could be retrieved by searching for any of those words or phrases. This capability distinguishes full-text databases from electronic publications available merely for on-line perusal. Be warned, however, that the term *full text* is used loosely and may apply to one or both types of products.

It can now be assumed that major newspapers (e.g., *New York Times, Washington Post, Christian Science Monitor*) are available full text on CD-ROM, and that most newspapers from large cities are available on-line. Newspapers are generally available from one of several **vendors**, such as DIALOG, DataTimes, and Mead Data Central (*NEXIS*). Increasing numbers are also available through such services as AmericaOnline, CompuServe, and Prodigy. Unfortunately, although almost all college and university libraries offer access to databases on DIALOG through a mediated search service, many fewer subscribe to the other vendors.

Image databases consist of graphic images, such as photographs, representations of works of art, and textual material. Textual material available in this manner is simply a reproduction of the printed page and cannot be searched interactively. Many periodicals are now available as part of image databases. Examples commonly available in university libraries include the ProQuest products produced by University Microfilms International (*General Periodicals Ondisc* and *Business Periodicals Ondisc*) and the InfoTrac products produced by Information Access Corporation (*Expanded Academic Index* and *Business Index*). An advantage of image databases for reproducing text is that, in contrast to full-text databases, they include illustrations and photographs as they appeared in the printed publication.

Full-text and image databases are becoming increasingly available as more and more electronic publications are incorporated into bibliographic databases. Newspapers have led the way with true full-text databases, making many national and regional newspapers available to subscribers through such services as *NEXIS*, DIALOG, and DataTimes. A legal research service, *LEXIS*, is accessible to law students and practitioners for searching laws, court decisions, and other federal and state documents.

LEXIS provides the full text of state, federal, and foreign court cases, codes, and pending legislation. It also allows access to Shepard's Citation Service, major law school journals, and libraries in tax, securities, trade regulation, bankruptcy, labor, public contracts, environmental law, and communications. Once you select your chosen library, you can search by word, phrase, or topic. You can print out citations, look at words on either side of your search term, or examine the document in full. Documents can also be downloaded to disk. You search *NEXIS* in a similar way, but *NEXIS* is the full text of newspaper articles.

Multimedia databases include, in addition to text and graphics, audio and video components. A number of reference works on CD-ROM, such as encyclopedias, now incorporate additional media, for example.

A list of some of the major databases that are useful for communication researchers appears at the end of this chapter. However, the number and variety of computerized databases are increasing so rapidly that any inventory is incomplete and promises to be soon out of date. Directories that describe currently available databases are the *Directory of Online Databases*, which lists those available remotely from commercial vendors, and the *Directory of Portable Databases*, which lists those available on CD-ROM, magnetic tape, and computer disks.

How to Search Computerized Databases

Computerized databases can be deceptively easy to search. When novice searchers type in the first topical word or phrase that occurs to them and retrieve some articles on their topics, they may be satisfied with the results. They may not, however, realize that they have failed to identify many other, sometimes more appropriate, articles. Or they may spend hours browsing through hundreds of citations, not realizing that they could easily have narrowed their search and obtained more manageable results.

In this section, we describe some basic features of search systems. Mastering these concepts will help you search effectively, making your searches as precise or as comprehensive as you wish. Of course, it will be necessary to combine this general information with specific information about the features of the databases you are searching. Fortunately, such specific information is readily available. Most databases include on-line tutorials and ample help screens. Such tutorials are well worth the small amount of time that it takes to go through them. Manuals with sample searches and detailed information are usually available, as well.

Because companies use virtually the same search system for each of the databases they distribute, learning only a few search systems will enable you to search a wide range of sources. For example, many libraries subscribe to databases distributed by SilverPlatter and Wilsondisc. Among the databases useful to communication researchers that these two vendors offer are: SilverPlatter's *ERIC*, *PsycLIT*, *Sociofile*, and *PAIS*; and Wilsondisc's *Social Sciences Index*, *Wilson Business Abstracts*, *Humanities Index*, and *Education Index*.

Standard Search Features

The search features that we describe next are so widely used that they can be termed "standard." Their implementation varies from one system to another, but the concepts involved remain the same.

Controlled Vocabulary Versus Free-Text Searching

Most databases allow the user to enter **search statements** simply by typing in everyday words or phrases. The system then retrieves those citations whose records contain the words or phrases entered. The citations retrieved may have found matches in almost any part of the record: the title, journal title, publisher, abstract, or **subject headings**. Searching in this way, using **natural language**, is called **free-text searching**.

Free-text searching is often effective in locating citations on a topic, but it does have drawbacks. First, because language is imprecise, it is likely that at least some of the records retrieved will match the words entered but will not actually be on the topic intended. At the same time, the searcher may miss a number of citations that were about this topic but that did not happen to contain the term used. Perhaps the citation contained a synonym instead.

For these reasons, almost all databases have established a **controlled vocabulary** that is used in a systematic way to describe the subject of articles and books. The subject terms (called headings or **descriptors**) are assigned to each record and are listed in the record for each item. The example in Figure 8 is a record in the *Periodical Abstracts Ondisc* database.

Actually, you may already be familiar with the concept of a controlled vocabulary and the use of subject headings, because

91011230
Title: Notes in the History of Intercultural Communication: The Foreign
Service Institute and the Mandate for Intercultural Training
Authors: Leeds-Hurwitz, Wendy
Journal: Quarterly Journal of Speech Vol: 76 Iss: 3 Date: Aug 1990 pp:
              262–281
Abstract: Edward T. Hall's "The Silent Language" has been influential in
              establishing the agenda for the field of intercultural communi-
              cation. Knowing about the history of linguists and anthropolo-
              gists at the Foreign Service Institute from 1946–56 will help
              improve understanding of this work. References
Subjects: Language; Cultural relations; Diplomatic & consular services;
              History; Interpersonal communication; Foreign Service-US
Type: Feature
Length: Long (31+ col inches)

Figure 8. Periodical Abstracts Ondisc database record.

their use is essential for using all printed indexes and catalogs. And,
you are probably familiar with the Library of Congress subject
headings, which are used in almost all college and university
library catalogs. Computerized **database producers** usually publish lists of subject headings or descriptors (often called a **thesaurus**). Even better, many products have incorporated this
thesaurus into their search system. Thus, when searching many
SilverPlatter CD-ROM products, for example, it is possible to query
the on-line thesaurus to determine if a particular term is a descriptor. The on-line thesaurus allows the user to move easily between
cross-references, and terms may be selected and entered directly
from the screen.

Of course, some concepts are so new that they have not yet
been incorporated into the controlled vocabulary, and free-text
terms must be used. As they gain experience, searchers will find
that it is effective to use both free-text terms and descriptors. A
common and often effective strategy is to start by doing a free-text
search, then to review the displayed citations. If you find citations
on your topic, the descriptors assigned to that record are usually an
excellent source of descriptors that can be entered to make the
search more effective.

Locating descriptors in this way is sometimes called *lat-
eral* or *sideways* searching, and some search systems have added
a feature to facilitate it. For example, SilverPlatter and IAC

(InfoTrac) software both allow the user to select and then search desired subject descriptors directly from records displayed on the screen, without having to retype them.

Search systems vary in the way in which descriptors are actually designated and entered. Some typical examples are the following:

SilverPlatter: social-interaction in de

Wilsondisc: press relations (su)

UMI: su (interpersonal communication)

Operators

Operators are special words that allow searchers to connect or combine words and concepts. The most widely used operators— AND, OR, and NOT—are sometimes called **logical**, or *Boolean*, **operators**.

AND: This operator retrieves only those citations that include all of the combined search terms. In Figure 9, *television AND radio* are terms contained in bibliographic records that the computer is searching. The computer is being asked to AND the **sets** of records together. The shaded area represents those records that the computer is being asked to retrieve. It includes only those records in which both words, television AND radio, appear.

OR: When we OR the sets of records together (see Figure 10), we get all records to which at least one of these descriptors has been assigned—either *television OR radio*. They need not

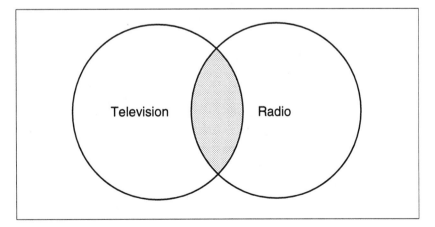

Figure 9. Television AND Radio.

necessarily both be assigned to the same document. Thus, many more records will be found with the OR operator than with the AND operator. This operator is generally used to combine synonyms, related terms, alternate spellings, and acronyms.

NOT: (or AND NOT): This operator excludes a particular term from your search results. For example, *television NOT radio* (see Figure 11) excludes all records that include the term *radio*. This operator is used much less often than AND and OR, and it should be used with care. In the example in Figure 11, we

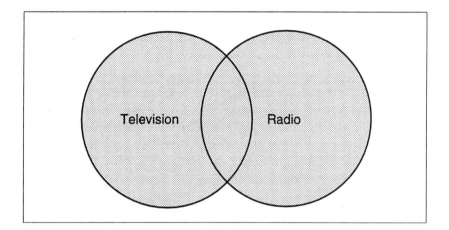

Figure 10. Television OR Radio.

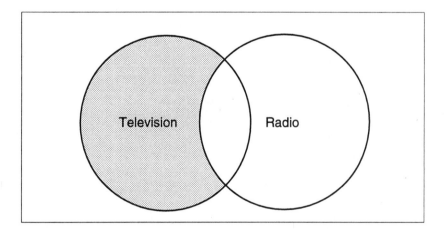

Figure 11. Television NOT Radio.

may be excluding desirable articles that contain valuable information on television, simply because they also mention radio.

In conducting searches, we often group together with the OR operator all synonyms and related terms that represent each separate concept we wish to search. The resulting sets of records, which tend to be large, are then AND-ed together to produce a much smaller set. Simply stated: Synonyms are OR-ed, then the resulting sets, representing concepts, are AND-ed. Using a form such as the one in Figure 12 when preparing a search can clarify the relationships between concepts and terms.

Other operators frequently available for use with search systems are called **proximity operators**. These operators allow the searcher to specify the physical proximity of the terms being searched. Unfortunately, not much standardization exists among search systems in terms of proximity operators. Those used in SilverPlatter products are typical and are offered as examples:

WITH: Terms connected by WITH must both be in the same field (for example, both in the title or both in the abstract).

NEAR: Terms connected by NEAR must both be in the same sentence.

Field-Specific Searching

The information in each database record is organized in fields. Fields, and the terms and abbreviations used to designate them, vary from one database to another. Some databases include many fields with a great deal of information that can be used by the searcher to narrow and broaden searches. To search most effectively, searchers should familiarize themselves with the fields used in the database they are searching. The following record from SilverPlatter's *ERIC* database illustrates the variety of fields available.

RECORD FIELDS	KEY TO FIELD ABBREVIATIONS
AN: EJ381831	Accession number
CHN: CD737111	Clearinghouse number
AU: Ting-Toomey, Stella	Author
TI: Rhetorical Sensitivity Style in Three Cultures:	Title

France, Japan, and the United States	
PY: 1988	Publication year
JN: Central-States-Speech-Journal; v39 n1 p28-36 Spr 1988	Journal citation
AV: UMI	Availability level
DT: Journal Articles (080); Reports—Research 143)	Document type
LA: English	Language
DE: Foreign-Countries; Higher-Education; Verbal-Communication	Descriptor
DE: *Cross-Cultural-Studies; *Cultural Differences; *Speech-Communication	Descriptor
ID: Communication-Styles; France-; Japan; United-States	Identifier
ID: *Rhetorical-Sensitivity; *Rhetorical-Sensitivity-Scale	Identifier
IS: CIJMAY89	Issue of abstract journal
AB: Explores cross-cultural attitudinal differences toward rhetorical sensitivity style. Finds that French subjects preferred a direct rhetorical sensitivity style; Japanese subjects expressed a moderate orientation towards the use of rhetorical sensitivity style; and United States subjects preferred an indirect rhetorical sensitivity style of communication. (MS)	Abstract
CH: CD	Clearinghouse
FI: EJ	Source file (ED or EJ)
DTN: O80; 143	Document type number

When searching computerized databases, it is possible to restrict the search to particular fields. For example, when entering descriptors in SilverPlatter databases, you normally restrict the search to the descriptor field in this way:

cross-cultural-studies in de

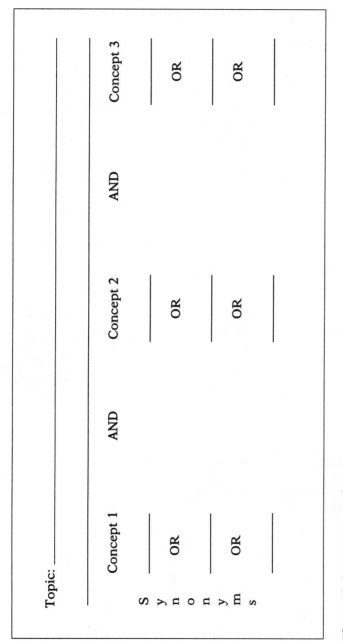

Figure 12. Search preparation form.

But when entering a free-text search statement, you can restrict your search to fields that contain subject information, for example, in the title, abstract, or identifiers:

Japan in ti

rhetorical sensitivity in ab

communication-styles in id

In this example, note that *ERIC* has a special category of controlled vocabulary, called **identifiers**. Identifiers are not in the *ERIC* thesaurus but are highly specific subjects that are useful for subject retrieval.

If you are interested only in articles written in a particular language, you can limit your search to that language:

english in la

Because *ERIC* has a document-type field, you can restrict your search to a particular type of publication. The following example uses *ERIC*'s number to designate research reports:

143 in dtn

ERIC indexes both journal articles and documents that are distributed as part of the *ERIC* microfiche collection, owned by many academic libraries. If the item is a journal article, EJ appears in the source file (FI) field. If the item is a document, ED appears in that field. This allows you to restrict your search to one or the other type of publication:

ed in fi

ej in fi

Because there is a field for publication year (PY), you can also limit your search to items published during a particular year, after a particular year, or within a range of years:

py = 1987

py > 1986

py = 1985-1990

This gives you some idea of how you can use field-specific searches to focus and narrow your searches.

Truncation

When entering free-text terms, you may find that you want to enter several words that have the same root (for example: adolescent, adolescents, adolescence). It is possible to do this simply by typing each word connected with the OR operator, but it is a bit faster to truncate (shorten) the word to its root. Most search systems allow you to use a symbol to indicate that you wish to truncate a word. Here are some examples:

> SilverPlatter: adolescen*
>
> Wilsondisc: adolescen:
>
> IAC & UMI: adolescen?

Of course, you must use truncation with caution. If you truncate to too short a root, you will retrieve many irrelevant terms. For example, *auto* would retrieve not only auto, automobile, and automotive but also automatic, autobiography, and so on. It is almost always a good idea to use truncation to search for both the singular and plural form of terms. Another way of searching for alternate forms of terms is to use the *word index* feature of your search system.

Word and Phrase Indexes

Many databases have an index feature that allows you to view and select terms from an alphabetized list of all words (and, sometimes, hyphenated phrases) contained in the database. This is an as-is list: don't be surprised when you find typos and misspellings. Use this feature to find alternate spellings for words. It is always advisable to use such an index when searching for the names of authors and other individuals, which due to the variation of first names and initials can be particularly troublesome.

Creating and Reusing Sets

As you enter search terms into most search systems, the results are displayed on the screen in numbered sets of records or **hits**. For example, if you have separately entered the terms *television*, *children*, and *violence* in a SilverPlatter database, the following results would appear:

No.	Records	Request
#1	6709	TELEVISION
#2	2171	VIOLENCE
#3	54547	CHILDREN

It is then possible to refer to these sets by set numbers and to combine them using AND, OR, and NOT operators. For example, if we AND-ed the preceding sets, we would receive the following result:

No.	Records	Request
#4	95	#1 and #2 and #3

The resulting set, #4, could then be modified and combined with other sets, as desired.

Sets can also be created using parentheses to group terms connected by operators, as they are entered:

(SEX-BIAS OR SEX-STEREOTYPES) AND (TELEVISION OR TV)

This will give us only listings of sex-bias *or* sex-stereotypes that also mention television *or* TV.

Search Strategies

A well-designed search strategy will use a variety of these search options to search efficiently and effectively. Start by investigating the controlled vocabulary to see if there are descriptors for your concepts. If you have several from which to choose, pick the most specific available, enter them as search statements, and appropriately combine them with AND and OR operators. Then review the results. Depending on your objective, you may be able to stop here. If you retrieved too few citations, you will need to broaden your search; if you have located too many, you will want to narrow it.

■ To narrow a search: (a) Use the AND operator to add additional concepts, one at a time, and/or (b) use field-specific search statements and the AND operator to limit your search (for example, by year, language, age groups, publication type, and so on.)

■ To broaden a search: (a) Consult the thesaurus and choose a broader search descriptor, and/or (b) use the OR operator to add synonyms, and/or (c) reduce the number of concepts.

As you attempt to refine your search, take full advantage of the interactive nature of computerized searching systems. By examining the records you retrieve, together with the assigned descriptors, you can determine whether you should drop or add search terms to achieve either a more precise or a more complete set of results.

As a sample search to illustrate these strategies, we'll search the *ERIC* database, using the SilverPlatter CD-ROM, to find reports dealing with the effect of television on children. If we followed our own advice, we would start by using *ERIC*'s on-line thesaurus, but to make this search closer to the way many students actually behave, we'll plunge in with a free-text search statement.

We enter:

television and children

The result:

No.	Records	Request
#1	1240	TELEVISION and CHILDREN

Wow! We don't want to look through 1,240 records, so it's time to narrow this search. Actually there are over 3,000 studies in this area, so this search—which is limited by year (to only the past 24 years) and by database (education-related journals)—is already narrow to start. Yet 1,240 records seems like a good start, so you make a mental note to search other databases and look for references older than 1983 (this version of *ERIC* was 1983 to date).

One way to narrow this search is to restrict the terms we used, *television* and *children*, to the descriptor field. This should eliminate items that are only peripherally related to the topic. We revise our search statement to:

television in de and children in de

The result:

No.	Records	Request
#2	437	(TELEVISION in DE) and (CHILDREN in DE)

That's better, but it's still far too many citations to browse through. Perhaps we can narrow one of the descriptors. There are two ways to go about this. We can either go to the on-line thesaurus, enter "television," and examine the possibilities, or we can look at some of the 437 records we retrieved to find one that's right on the topic and then see what descriptors were assigned to it. In either case, the SilverPlatter software will allow us to select our descriptor of choice right from the screen and then initiate a search.

We decide that the descriptor *television-viewing* comes closest to our intent.

We enter:

television-viewing in de and children in de

The result:

No.	Records	Request
#3	321	(TELEVISION-VIEWING) in DE and (CHILDREN in DE)

More progress, but it looks as though this topic was just too broadly conceived to begin with. It's time to do some serious thinking about how to narrow it. Some possibilities:

■ Add another concept (*academic achievement* or *violence* are possibilities).

■ Narrow the *children* concept by restricting it to *young children*.

The results of each of these options:

No.	Records	Request
#4	12	(TELEVISION-VIEWING in DE) and (CHILDREN in DE) and (ACADEMIC-ACHIEVEMENT in DE)
#5	65	(TELEVISION-VIEWING in DE) and (YOUNG-CHILDREN in DE)
#6	33	#3 and (VIOLENCE in DE)

We'll let you decide which of these options you would choose. As you can see, there are many different ways to proceed in virtually every search.

Using Your Search Results

The final product of most searches is a printed list of sources. If you have conducted your search on a microcomputer, you have another option available to you. Modem-equipped microcomputers using suitable **communications software** programs are capable of capturing the results of a remote search in their memory so that the results can be downloaded to hard drives and computer disks for storage. CD-ROM systems also offer this possibility. If you have an appropriate database management software program, you can add the citations you have retrieved to others you have located and entered in the database, either manually or through

downloading. In this way, you can create your own personal on-line database.

The software program should allow you to add your own descriptors and notes to individual records. And it should also allow you to sort your records, selectively retrieve and print them, use them with a word processing program, and so on. Of course, such downloading practices do raise questions of copyright, and database vendors and producers have varying policies about downloading, which you should explore. It also raises the possibility of plagiarism, either from the original article or from the abstract. These abstracts are written by others and are copyrighted, so you cannot use sections of the abstract without using quotation marks and citing the abstract as the source.

Citing abstracts in this manner, though, is not typically done. The abstract, itself, is incomplete and merely provides a summary and someone else's interpretation of the original publication. In other words, the abstract should help you identify a publication as being relevant to your project, but you then must locate and read the actual publication (for example, journal article) if you are going to use it in your own literature review or research project.

As with other search aids, then, the final step in using a bibliographic database is retrieving the actual documents. After exploring the resources of your library to determine which publications are readily available, you will probably want to use your library's interlibrary loan service to obtain any other sources you need that your library does not have. Many records for journals will include a special number, called an ISSN (International Standard Serial Number). This number may help your library staff quickly identify and retrieve the document you need. Citations may also provide other useful numbers. Ask the interlibrary loan staff which numbers to include on your request.

Another convenient avenue for retrieving materials is available for those library users fortunate to live in states that have created statewide on-line systems that allow users access to the on-line catalogs of all or most of that state's college and university libraries, as well as to various periodical databases. These systems may allow users to initiate transactions on-line to borrow materials from other libraries, thus eliminating the need to fill out interlibrary loan request cards. Often, materials can be delivered using these systems in a matter of days.

Many database producers and distributors offer an additional service to help you secure publications not owned by your library. Called **document delivery services**, they allow you to order publications on-line for delivery by fax or through the mail. CARL UnCover and many of **OCLC**'s (Online Computer Library Center) First Search databases provide such document delivery services. The fees charged for such services, which include a copyright charge, may often be charged to a credit card.

Mediated Searching

Although most libraries now make a variety of electronic databases available to their users to search on their own at workstations within and outside the library, hundreds more databases are available for remote searching through such vendors as DIALOG and BRS (Bibliographic Retrieval Services). Many of these databases may be used only by librarians who have been specially trained to search via the vendors' often complicated software, and libraries usually provide access through a mediated **on-line search service**. Typically, users will make an appointment with a librarian to discuss their search topics and will be present while the librarian performs the search. Students may be asked to pay some or all of the on-line fees associated with such searches. If you have questions about the availability of additional computerized databases, ask at the reference desk of your library about this service.

Summary

Methods used by communication professionals to conduct documentary research are changing rapidly and using computer-based sources has become essential. Many necessary tools for communication research are available only in electronic formats and through electronic networks. A computerized database stores information on a magnetic or optical storage medium so that the information can be retrieved via a microcomputer or a computer terminal. Databases are classified as being bibliographic, referral, or source.

To use computerized databases effectively, researchers must understand basic searching concepts and acquire skill in using controlled vocabularies, free-text terms, field-specific searching, word and phrase indexes, and logical and proximity operators.

Documentation should be used to gain familiarity with the structure of databases and the features of search systems. On-line help screens, tutorials, and printed manuals are usually available. A few minutes spent exploring such documentation will save time in the long run and help you retrieve more relevant search results.

In general, the most effective search strategy is to start with the most specific descriptors available, examine the results, and add search statements to broaden or narrow the search as necessary. To narrow a search, add additional concepts, one at a time, using the AND operator. You can also limit search results by publication year, language, document type, and so on. To broaden a search, use a less specific descriptor and/or add synonymous terms using the OR operator.

Computer databases help researchers identify pertinent publications, but the actual document must then be located and fully examined before it is used in a research project.

Selected Computerized Databases

The following databases have been selected from among those most likely to be accessible to students through libraries and campus networks. Availability through CompuServe has also been indicated in some cases, for those who might have private access to this service. Most of the databases selected are bibliographic in nature, with the exceptions to this rule noted in scope notes. Not included in this listing are the many newspapers available full-text on-line and on CD-ROM.

The time spans of particular databases vary considerably from vendor to vendor and format to format. The time spans listed reflect the earliest date the database is available from any vendor in any format.

ABI/INFORM
SCOPE: Selective coverage of over 1,400 periodicals in business and related fields; includes abstracts; since 1991 some versions include the complete text of more than one third of the publications
TIME PERIOD: 1971 to date
PRINT EQUIVALENT: None
PRODUCER: UMI
AVAILABILITY: DIALOG, CDP, FirstSearch; CD-ROM; some campus networks and consortia

Academic Index
SCOPE: Bibliographic index of over 1,500 scholarly and general periodicals, including the *New York Times*. Some versions include full text of approximately one third of the publications.
TIME PERIOD: 1976 to date (varies)
PRINT EQUIVALENT: None
PRODUCER: Information Access
AVAILABILITY: DIALOG, CompuServe; CD-ROM (*Expanded Academic Index*); some campus networks and consortia

American Statistics Index (ASI)
SCOPE: Bibliographic index and abstracts covering U.S. government statistics and statistical publications
TIME PERIOD: 1973 to date
PRINT EQUIVALENT: *American Statistics Index*
PRODUCER: Congressional Information Service
AVAILABILITY: DIALOG; CD-ROM (*Statistical Masterfile*)

Books in Print
SCOPE: Citations to in-print books published or exclusively distributed in the United States
TIME PERIOD: Current (on-line from 1979)
PRINT EQUIVALENT: *Books in Print, Forthcoming Books in Print*
PRODUCER: Bowker
AVAILABILITY: DIALOG, CDP, CompuServe; CD-ROM (*Books in Print Plus*).

Business Periodicals Index (Also see entry for *Wilson Business Abstracts)*
SCOPE: Bibliographic index covering approximately 350 business periodicals
TIME PERIOD: 1982 to date
PRINT EQUIVALENT: *Business Periodicals Index*
PRODUCER: Wilson
AVAILABILITY: Wilsonline, CDP, OCLC FirstSearch; CD-ROM; some campus networks and consortia

CENDATA (The Census Bureau Online)
SCOPE: Numeric database consisting of U.S. Census Bureau economic and demographic reports. Also includes text of press releases and new product announcements
TIME PERIOD: 1980 to date
PRINT EQUIVALENT: *Current Population Reports, County*

Business Patterns, 1990 U.S. Census of Population and Housing
PRODUCER: U.S. Bureau of the Census
AVAILABILITY: DIALOG, CompuServe

CIS
SCOPE: Indexes and abstracts publications of the U.S. Congress
TIME PERIOD: 1970 to date
PRINT EQUIVALENT: *CIS/Index to Publications of the U.S. Congress*
PRODUCER: Congressional Information Service
AVAILABILITY: DIALOG; CD-ROM (*Congressional Masterfile*)

ComIndex
SCOPE: Bibliographic index covering more than 55 journals and annuals in the field of communication. Does not include subject indexing, but permits keyword searching on words in article titles
TIME PERIOD: Varies
PRINT EQUIVALENT: None
PRODUCER: Communication Institute for Online Scholarship (CIOS)
AVAILABILITY: Computer disk

County and City Databook
SCOPE: Numeric database containing demographic, economic, and geographic data on U.S. counties and cities; data are collected from federal agencies and private organizations
TIME PERIOD: Data covers approximately 6 years previous to date of issue
PRINT EQUIVALENT: *County and City Databook*
PRODUCER: U.S. Bureau of the Census
AVAILABILITY: CD-ROM

Dissertation Abstracts Online
SCOPE: Dissertations from United States and over 200 foreign universities
TIME PERIOD: 1861 to date
PRINT EQUIVALENT: *Dissertation Abstracts International (DAI), American Doctoral Dissertations (ADD), Comprehensive Dissertation Index (CDI)*
PRODUCER: UMI
AVAILABILITY: DIALOG, CDP, CompuServe; CD-ROM; some campus networks and consortia

Education Index
SCOPE: Bibliographic index to over 375 periodicals, books, and yearbooks in the field of education
TIME PERIOD: 1983 to date
PRINT EQUIVALENT: *Education Index*
PRODUCER: Wilson
AVAILABILITY: Wilsonline, CDP, OCLC FirstSearch, CARL; CD-ROM; some campus networks and consortia

ERIC
SCOPE: Bibliographic index to articles, reports, and books in education and related areas; includes abstracts
TIME PERIOD: 1966 to date
PRINT EQUIVALENT: *Current Index to Journals in Education (CIJE)* and *Resources in Education (RIE)*
PRODUCER: U.S. Department of Education, Office of Educational Research and Improvement
AVAILABILITY: DIALOG, CDP, OCLC FirstSearch, CompuServe; CD-ROM; some campus networks and consortia

GPO Monthly Catalog
SCOPE: Bibliographic index to publications of U.S. government agencies and Congress
TIME PERIOD: 1976 to date
PRINT EQUIVALENT: *Monthly Catalog of United States Government Publications*
PRODUCER: U.S. Government Printing Office
AVAILABILITY: DIALOG, OCLC FirstSearch; CD-ROM; some campus networks and consortia

Humanities Index
SCOPE: Bibliographic index to over 350 periodicals in the humanities
TIME PERIOD: 1984 to date
PRINT EQUIVALENT: *Humanities Index*
PRODUCER: H. W. Wilson
AVAILABILITY: Wilsonline, CDP Online, OCLC FirstSearch; CD-ROM; some campus networks and consortia

Index to Legal Periodicals
SCOPE: Bibliographic index to selected articles from more than 620 periodicals in the field of law
TIME PERIOD: 1981 to date
PRINT EQUIVALENT: *Index to Legal Periodicals*
PRODUCER: H. W. Wilson

AVAILABILITY: Wilsonline, CDP, LEXIS, WESTLAW, OCLC FirstSearch; CD-ROM

Legal Resources Index (LRI)
SCOPE: Bibliographic index to more than 800 law journals, plus selected coverage of more than 3,000 additional publications; includes selected abstracts
TIME PERIOD: 1980 to date
PRINT EQUIVALENT: None
PRODUCER: Information Access
AVAILABILITY: DIALOG, CompuServe, LEXIS, WESTLAW, CARL; CD-ROM (*LegalTrac*)

LEXIS
SCOPE: Provides the full text of state, federal, and foreign court cases, codes, and pending legislation. Also allows access to *Shepard's Citation Service*, major law journals, and libraries in tax, securities, trade regulation, bankruptcy, labor, public contracts, environmental law, and communications
TIME PERIOD: Varies
PRINT EQUIVALENT: Many and varied
PRODUCER: Mead Data Central
AVAILABILITY: Mead Data Central

Linguistics and Language Behavior Abstracts (LLBA)
SCOPE: Bibliographic index with abstracts covering international journals in language, learning disabilities, and communication
TIME PERIOD: 1973 to date
PRINT EQUIVALENT: *Linguistics and Language Behavior Abstracts*
PRODUCER: Sociological Abstracts
AVAILABILITY: DIALOG, CDP, CompuServe; CD-ROM

Management Contents
SCOPE: Indexes and abstracts more than 130 international periodicals in business and public administration
TIME PERIOD: 1974 to date
PRINT EQUIVALENT: None
PRODUCER: Information Access
AVAILABILITY: DIALOG

National Newspaper Index
SCOPE: Indexes and abstracts articles, reviews, and editorials published in the *Wall Street Journal, Christian Science Monitor, New York Times*, and the *Los Angeles Times*

TIME PERIOD: Varies
PRINT EQUIVALENT: None
PRODUCER: Information Access
AVAILABILITY: DIALOG, CompuServe, CARL; CD-ROM

Newsearch
SCOPE: Includes the current 2 to 6 weeks of other
Information Access databases, including *National Newspaper
Index, Academic Index, Legal Resource Index, Management
Contents, and PR Newswire*
TIME PERIOD: Current 2 to 6 weeks
PRINT EQUIVALENT: None
PRODUCER: Information Access
AVAILABILITY: DIALOG, CompuServe

Newspaper & Periodical Indexes
SCOPE: Indexes and abstracts more than 25 major U.S. news-
papers, 1,600 general-interest, professional, and scholarly peri-
odicals, and 70 television news and current affairs programs
TIME PERIOD: 1986 to date for periodicals; 1989 to date for
newspapers
PRINT EQUIVALENT: None
PRODUCER: UMI
AVAILABILITY: DIALOG, CARL, OCLC FirstSearch

Newswire ASAP
SCOPE: Full text of items carried on Kyodo News
International, Newsbytes News Network, PR Newswire,
Agencia EFE, Comtex, TASS, UPI, and Xinhua wire services
TIME PERIOD: Varies
PRINT EQUIVALENT: None
PRODUCER: Information Access
AVAILABILITY: DIALOG

NEXIS
SCOPE: Provides indexing and full-text access to many news-
papers, news wire services, government serial publications,
and periodicals
TIME PERIOD: Varies
PRINT EQUIVALENT: None
PRODUCER: Mead Data Central
AVAILABILITY: Mead Data Central

PAIS International
SCOPE: Citations with brief abstracts to periodical articles,
pamphlets, and books on social, economic, and political issues

TIME PERIOD: 1972 to date
PRINT EQUIVALENT: *PAIS Bulletin, PAIS International*
PRODUCER: Public Affairs Information Service
AVAILABILITY: DIALOG, CompuServe, OCLC FirstSearch

PsychINFO
SCOPE: Scholarly journals, books, and book chapters in psychology and related behavioral sciences
TIME PERIOD: 1974 to date
PRINT EQUIVALENT: *Psychological Abstracts*
PRODUCER: American Psychological Association
AVAILABILITY: DIALOG, CDP, CompuServe, OCLC FirstSearch; CD-ROM (*PsycLIT*)

Social Sciences Index
SCOPE: Indexes over 415 periodicals in a broad range of the social sciences
TIME PERIOD: 1983 to date
PRINT EQUIVALENT: *Social Sciences Index*
PRODUCER: H. W. Wilson
AVAILABILITY: Wilsonline, CDP, OCLC FirstSearch; CD-ROM

Social SciSearch
SCOPE: Cited references in over 1,400 social sciences journals worldwide
TIME PERIOD: 1981 to date
PRINT EQUIVALENT: *Social Sciences Citation Index*
PRODUCER: Institute for Scientific Information
AVAILABILITY: DIALOG; CD-ROM (*Social Sciences Citation Index*)

Sociological Abstracts
SCOPE: Research, reviews, and monographs in sociology and related areas
TIME PERIOD: 1963 to date
PRINT EQUIVALENT: *Sociological Abstracts*
PRODUCER: Sociological Abstracts
AVAILABILITY: DIALOG, CDP, OCLC FirstSearch; CD-ROM (*Sociofile*)

Statistical Abstract of the United States
SCOPE: Statistical database containing summaries of social, economic, and political statistics for the United States
TIME PERIOD: Updated annually
PRINT EQUIVALENT: *Statistical Abstract of the United States*

PRODUCER: U.S. Bureau of the Census
AVAILABILITY: CD-ROM

Statistical Masterfile
SCOPE: Bibliographic database that indexes and abstracts
publications that are statistical in nature; corresponds to
these on-line databases: *American Statistics Index (ASI),
Index to International Statistics (IIS)*, and *Statistical Reference
Index (SRI)*
TIME PERIOD: *ASI* (1973–), *IIS* (1983–), *SRI* (1980-)
PRINT EQUIVALENT: *ASI, IIS,* and *SRI*
PRODUCER: Congressional Information Service
AVAILABILITY: CD-ROM

Transcript (Journal Graphics)
SCOPE: Indexes and abstracts transcripts of approximately
20,000 television news and information shows for which the
Journal Graphics company sells transcripts
TIME PERIOD: Varies by program
PRINT EQUIVALENT: *Transcript/Video Index*
PRODUCER: Journal Graphics
AVAILABILITY: CompuServe, CARL

UnCover
SCOPE: Includes the tables of contents of over 14,600 period-
icals held by libraries, searchable by author, title, keyword,
periodical title, and issue
TIME PERIOD: 1988 to date
PRINT EQUIVALENT: None
PRODUCER: UnCover
AVAILABILITY: CARL

Wilson Business Abstracts
SCOPE: Articles from more than 350 business periodicals;
corresponds to *Business Periodicals Index*, with the exception
that all entries since June 1990 include abstracts
TIME PERIOD: 1982 to date
PRINT EQUIVALENT: None
PRODUCER: H.W. Wilson
AVAILABILITY: Wilsonline; CD-ROM; some campus net-
works and consortia

Wilson Education Abstracts
SCOPE: Indexes more than 400 periodicals, books, and yearbooks in the field of education; corresponds to *Education
Index*, with the exception that entries since 1994 include
abstracts

TIME PERIOD: 1983 to date
PRINT EQUIVALENT: None
PRODUCER: H.W. Wilson
AVAILABILITY: Wilsonline; CD-ROM; some campus networks and consortia

Wilson Humanities Abstracts
SCOPE: Indexes more than 350 periodicals in the humanities; corresponds to *Humanities Index*, with the exception that entries since 1994 include abstracts
TIME PERIOD: 1984 to date
PRINT EQUIVALENT: None
PRODUCER: H.W. Wilson
AVAILABILITY: Wilsonline; CD-ROM; some campus networks and consortia

Wilson Social Science Abstracts
SCOPE: Indexes more than 400 journals in a broad range of the social sciences; corresponds to *Social Sciences Index*, with the exception that since 1994 entries include abstracts
TIME PERIOD: 1983 to date
PRINT EQUIVALENT: None
PRODUCER: H. W. Wilson
AVAILABILITY: Wilsonline; CD-ROM; some campus networks and consortia

WorldCat
SCOPE: More than 30 million records describing books, audiovisual materials, computer software, and serial publications that are held by libraries
TIME PERIOD: Unlimited
PRINT EQUIVALENT: None
PRODUCER: OCLC
AVAILABILITY: OCLC FirstSearch

1990 Census Summary Tape I
SCOPE: Numeric database offering access to the U. S. Census of Population and Housing; includes data on age, race, sex, marital status, Hispanic origin, and housing
TIME PERIOD: 1990
PRINT EQUIVALENT: *Census of Population*
PRODUCER: U.S. Bureau of the Census
AVAILABILITY: CD-ROM

References

Directory of Online Databases. (1982–). New York: Cuadra/Elsevier.

Directory of Portable Databases. (1990–1992). New York: Cuadra/Elsevier.

Gale Directory of Databases (2 vols.). (1993–). Detroit: Gale Research.

Glossbrenner, A. (1990). *The complete handbook of personal computer communications* (3rd ed.). New York: St. Martin's Press.

Hogan, K. M., & Shelton, J. H. (Eds.). (1995). *CD-ROM finder: The world of CD-ROM products for information seekers* (6th ed.). Medford, NJ: Learned Information.

Information Industry Directory. (1980–). Detroit: Gale Research.

Marcaccio, K. Y. (Ed.). (1992). *Computer-readable databases: A directory and data sourcebook* (8th ed.). Detroit: Gale Research.

Online database selection: A user's guide to the Directory of Online Databases. (1989). New York: Cuadra/Elsevier.

Exercises

1. When a descriptor is not available for your topic and free-text terms must be used, take care to find all possible alternative phrasings and spellings. For each of the following concepts, make a list of at least 10 synonymous free-text terms or phrases: role playing, executives, news media, press interviews, minorities, gender.

2. In your research paper, you want to investigate the relationship between teachers' communication styles, gender or ethnic background of students, and student performance. You have decided to limit your research to middle schools. You have entered a number of terms and now have the following sets:

#1	minorities
#2	educational performance
#3	teachers
#4	blacks
#5	females
#6	native americans
#7	junior high school
#8	communication styles
#9	hispanics
#10	gender differences
#11	student performance
#12	middle schools
#13	ethnic groups
#14	males
#15	african americans
#16	mexican americans
#17	academic achievement
#18	asian americans

Assuming that you wish to use all of these terms in your search, write a single search statement that will incorporate them all. Use set numbers to refer to each term, connecting sets as appropriate with AND and OR operators. Use parentheses to group terms, for example: (#1 or #2 or #7) and (#6 or #8) and (#11 and #15).

If you retrieve too many citations, how could you narrow this search? If you retrieve too few citations, how could you broaden it?

3. Now plan searches for the topic in Exercise 2 in each of the following databases: *PsycLIT*, *ERIC*, and *Sociofile*. Use the thesaurus for each database to identify relevant descriptors and list search statements in the order in which you would enter them.

4. Complete the following Search Preparation Form for your topic.

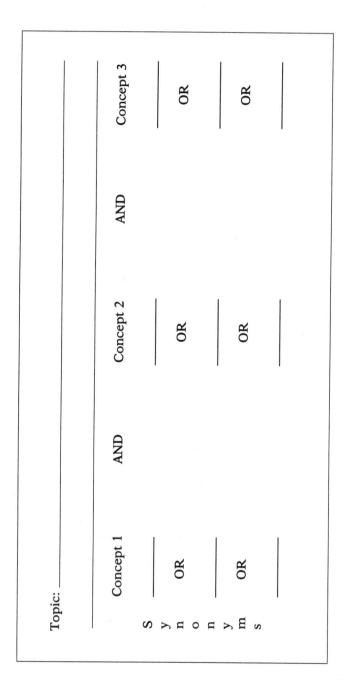

Chapter 4

Using the Internet for Communication Research

The Internet is a network that connects computer networks all around the world. It allows users to communicate with other individuals and with groups of people and to use and retrieve information from computers at remote sites. An outgrowth of networks originally established by the U.S. Department of Defense to facilitate defense-related research, the Internet now connects most colleges and universities in the United States and major ones abroad. In recent years, scholars in many fields have taken advantage of it to establish new ways of communicating with each other, and it is now opening up to the general public. Much is being written in general periodicals about this increasingly popular medium and its utility for everything from determining weather forecasts, locating subway maps worldwide, and taking language lessons, to retrieving restaurant reviews. The focus of this chapter will be on the uses of the Internet for communication researchers.

As you learn your way around the Internet, it is important to understand that there is no one person or organization in charge. In other words, no one started this enterprise by first devising an over-all organizational structure, and no one controls what is made available in terms of content, quality, or format. Amazingly, this does not mean that all is chaos and frustration for users. The exciting potential of the Internet has inspired many people and organizations to make available on it vast amounts of information and to develop tools that now make it relatively simple to navigate. In fact, the pace of development is so rapid that we can predict with certainty only that such tools will evolve considerably over the next few years. Fortunately, the trend is overwhelmingly toward making the Internet easier to use and the variety and depth of its resources richer.

Research and the Internet

What does the Internet have to offer scholars and other researchers? At its most basic level, it provides a more convenient medium than telephone lines for accessing many of the databases and document delivery services discussed in Chapter 3. But the Internet has many other uses for scholars, as well. For starters, professional and scholarly associations use the Internet to communicate with and distribute information to their members. In some cases, scholarly periodicals are published solely for Internet distribution, never appearing in paper format.

For those following politics and government, the Internet is becoming invaluable as a way of keeping up to date; many government publications that formerly appeared only in paper are now being made available much more quickly via the Internet. Electronic archives of political speeches, press releases, and historical documents are being established.

Most intriguing, perhaps, are the ways in which scholars are sharing information in areas of current research through **E-mail** (that is, electronic mail) or by participating in electronic discussion groups, or hotlines, some of which can be monitored by onlookers. Thus, already a useful source of information for scholars and researchers, the Internet's importance is growing rapidly. And, of course, as a fascinating communication phenomenon, it is being studied by communication researchers in its own right.

Gaining Access to the Internet

Most students will not have difficulty gaining access to the Internet. Students generally do so by obtaining an account, sometimes referred to as an "E-mail account," on a university computer. If you don't already have an account, ask at your computer center for information about getting one. This account will be your gateway to the Internet. If you access the Internet from a workstation that is connected directly to the campus network, it will usually provide you with a **full-Internet connection**, which should allow you to use all Internet capabilities. Another common way of accessing the Internet is by dialing into your account from off-campus, using a microcomputer equipped with a modem. This type of connection may put certain restrictions on the types of Internet services available. We'll clarify these restrictions as we discuss particular capabilities later in this chapter.

For the general public and for students who don't have access through their college or university, it is now possible to gain access through commercial services such as CompuServe, Delphi, Prodigy, and AmericaOnline. Your area may have local services (that is, freenets) that provide Internet access, as well.

Internet Tools: The Basics

Students and others do three basic things on the Internet: (a) correspond with individuals and groups using E-mail; (b) log into and use computers at remote sites, using the "telnet" command; and (c) transfer files to their computer from a remote computer using the FTP command.

To do any of these things, you will need to use Internet addresses. Your own Internet address will look something like those of the authors of this book:

Rebecca Rubin:	rrubin@kentvm.kent.edu
Alan Rubin:	arubin@kentvm.kent.edu
Linda Piele:	pielel@cs.uwp.edu

The @ symbol is used to separate the name of an individual (on the left) from his or her **domain** (to the right). In the first two cases, the domain, *kentvm.kent.edu*, refers to a mainframe computer at Kent State University. In the third, the domain is a computer at the University of Wisconsin–Parkside. You'll use addresses like these to send electronic mail to people. If you log into a remote computer, you'll use only the domain portion of the address. The extension, *edu*, means that these locations are colleges or universities in the United States.

Becoming familiar with the following extensions will give you useful information about various Internet addresses:

edu   educational sites in the United States.
com   commercial sites in the United States (companies or
       corporations); a site of the U.S. government
net   an administrative site for a network
mil   military sites
int   international organizations such as NATO
org   nonprofit organizations that don't fit elsewhere

Another piece of general information that you can glean from an Internet address is the country of the addressee. Each country has been assigned a two-letter code. For example, *.fr* refers to France, *.it* to Italy, *.ch* to Switzerland, *.us* to the United States, *.ca* to Canada, and *.de* to Germany. If there is no country designation, the location is the United States.

You may also see addresses, termed **IP** (Internet Protocol) **addresses**, that are entirely numerical. These addresses, which consist of four numbers connected by periods, are assigned to each machine on the Internet; 137.113.10.35 is a typical IP address. Each Internet domain address has a corresponding IP address, which is how the address is actually transmitted over the Internet. You may use either form of an address to send electronic mail or to log into a remote computer.

E-Mail

You'll send mail to other people, groups, or organizations, and even to yourself, using the E-mail system that your college or university provides. These systems vary so much that we won't bother to provide instructions here. Documentation is probably available either on-line or at a service desk in your computer center. Even if you are one of the few who don't become hooked on E-mail to correspond with friends or colleagues, you'll find it necessary to use E-mail for various Internet activities, such as subscribing to electronic discussion groups or retrieving documents from sources that allow you simply to mail them to yourself.

Telnet

The **telnet** command enables you to log into and use a computer at a remote site. Such a computer could be on your own campus or halfway around the world. The term, *telnet*, is often used as a verb, as in, "I'm going to telnet to Harvard's library catalog." One of the most common uses of this command by researchers is, in fact, to access library catalogs at remote libraries. Usually, all that is needed to do so is the Internet address of the remote computer. If you wish to access the Library of Congress's catalog, *LOCIS*, you could determine its address by looking in one of the many printed guides to the Internet. Such guides typically include the addresses for popular or standard Internet resources. Several guides are listed at the end of this chapter, and the reference department of your library will probably have several. After determining that the Internet address is *locis.loc.gov*, you log into your computer account as usual. At the prompt you type "telnet," space, and then the Internet address. The following prompt is for a UNIX computer system:

% telnet locis.loc.gov

This will take you to the Library of Congress's main menu, which then tells you how to proceed.

In addition to library catalogs, communication researchers might want to access other databases. Suppose you learn that the Journal Graphics database, which provides access to radio and television transcripts, is available through CARL, the Colorado Alliance of Research Libraries. Looking in a published Internet guide, you determine that CARL's Internet address is *pac.carl.org* and you telnet there (*telnet pac.carl.org*). During the log-in process, the CARL system will ask you to specify the **terminal emulation** that you are using. VT100 is the most common terminal emulation on the Internet, and that is what you should specify when you set up your communications software.

The CARL menu of "Information Databases" is shown in Figure 13. Notice that this menu offers access to several databases

---

INFORMATION DATABASES

60. Choice Book Reviews (access restricted as of 9/1/93)
61. Encyclopedia
64. School Model Programs
65. Internet Resource Guide
66. Department of Energy
67. Journal Graphics (Television/Radio Transcripts)
82. Company ProFile
88. Federal Domestic Assistance Catalog
89. Librarian's Yellow Pages
90. KnowledgeOne (Information Service)

Figure 13. CARL menu.

besides Journal Graphics. Most of these are available for use only by those affiliated with CARL (they require a password), but the Journal Graphics database is an exception, as is the *UnCover* database (which is on a different menu screen). Both of these databases (which are described in Chapter 3) have document delivery components, and there is a charge for ordering transcripts and journal articles.

Although a few bibliographic databases are freely available to Internet users, most are not. Libraries typically pay licensing fees for the databases they offer on library workstations and over campus networks. They are required by licensing agreements to restrict use to their own students and faculty. If you would like the convenience of accessing databases from home, inquire at your library's reference desk to see if you might be able to take advantage of any of the library's licensing agreements.

For example, many academic libraries have an agreement with OCLC, which provides access to a large number of databases, including *WorldCat*, through its easy-to-use FirstSearch service. Some libraries purchase and then resell to students FirstSearch access cards. These cards provide authorization numbers and passwords that are valid for a certain number of searches on any of the many FirstSearch databases. Reaching FirstSearch through the Internet is simple: telnet to *fscat.oclc.org*. Unless your library has a special licensing arrangement, you will be asked for an authorization and password before you can proceed.

File Transfer Protocol (FTP)

The *File Transfer Protocol* **(FTP)** command allows you to transfer files stored on a remote computer over the Internet to your own computer. In recent years, many information resources, such as back issues of electronic journals and other electronic texts, have been made freely available by this method. Because the files are available to anyone who logs in under the name "anonymous," the documents are said to be available via **anonymous FTP**. The basic steps in FTP-ing a document include logging in to a remote computer, listing the files available in the public directory, and then issuing a command to "get" a particular file and transfer it to your own computer.

With thousands of documents stored on computers all over the world for retrieval by anonymous FTP, how can you find out what is available and where? A special Internet finding tool, **Archie**, was created especially for this purpose. By querying an

Archie **server**, it is possible to determine where a particular file is stored.

Although it's important to be familiar with FTP concepts and terms, we're not going to provide detailed instructions for using FTP and Archie. The development of Gopher and of **World Wide Web** *browsers* such as **Mosaic**, which will be described later in this chapter, have largely automated the FTP process. Most people now use these tools when they want to retrieve files and access databases on remote computers.

Gopher

Gopher is software developed in 1991 at the University of Minnesota and freely distributed by that institution as **shareware**. Using this software, many colleges, universities, and other organizations around the world have set up **Gopher servers** making information available, using a hierarchical menu structure. For example, at many universities, Gopher has been used to develop and maintain a campus-wide information system for students and faculty.

The power of Gopher lies in the fact that any Gopher server is able to list on its own menus (or "point to") items that are actually housed on remote Gopher servers. Such pointers are transparent to the user, who may not realize that the information they are retrieving is coming from halfway around the world.

Accessing Gopher

To access a campus Gopher server (or a remote Gopher whose address you know), you use a Gopher **client** program. That program is housed on either one of your university's mainframe computers or your own microcomputer. Through this Gopher server you will be able to access and use Gophers all over the world. Gopher client programs vary, so the program you use on your Macintosh computer may look quite different from the one your friend uses on a campus IBM or Unix mainframe computer. At your college or university, you will probably find a local Gopher server listed on menus in microcomputer labs. The Gopher title may indicate that it is the campus-wide information system of your college or university. If you don't find something that looks likely, simply type "Gopher" at your system prompt to see if this connects you to a default Gopher at your university. If this doesn't work, you can: (a) ask a computer lab attendant or computer center or library staff member for advice on connecting to Gopher; or (b) log into your system and Gopher or telnet to the server at the University of Minnesota, *consultant.micro.umn.edu*:

> % gopher consultant.micro.umn.edu
> % telnet consultant.micro.umn.edu

Addresses of many other university Gopher sites should be listed in published Internet guides in your library's reference department.

If you have access to Gopher, use the following menu choices to learn more about Internet:

Internet Training and Information
  Clearinghouse for Subject-oriented Internet Resource
    Internet Training Materials (NISP)
      Networking Guides
        General Guides to Networking
        Guides to Information Services
        Guides to Networking Tools

Geographic Listings of Gopher Servers

As you explore Gopher menus, you will undoubtedly find a menu selection for "All the Gophers in the World." Selecting this will reveal an exhaustive geographic listing of Gophers, making it easy to find a Gopher server geographically. Thus, if you have heard that a Gopher server at Louisiana Tech University provides access to on-line college and university newspapers, you can locate it by first browsing the Louisiana portion of the listing to find the university, and then accessing it through that university's Gopher. Once you get to a particular Gopher, you may be able to do a keyword search of its directories to find the precise term you are looking for. Many Gopher servers offer a keyword searching capability for their menus (through a program named **Jughead**), facilitating the search through menus.

Subject Listings of Gopher Resources

Lacking a geographic starting point, how does one navigate the Gopher world (or **Gopherspace** in Internet lingo) to find resources on a given topic? Fortunately, several Gopher sites have developed useful listings of Gopher resources by subject. Notable examples include LC Marvel's Global Electronic Library (Machine-Assisted Realization of the Virtual Electronic Library) at the Library of Congress and RiceInfo's "Information by Subject Area." In many cases these and other subject listings will be listed on your campus Gopher. If not, you can always locate them geographically using the "All the Gophers in the World" menu pick. Their direct addresses are:

LC Marvel: % gopher marvel.loc.gov
RiceInfo: % gopher riceinfo.rice.edu

You'll find a wide variety of Internet resources by browsing these Gophers. For example, RiceInfo's listings under "Film & Television" and "News & Journalism" include Gophers for C-SPAN, PBS, BBC TV and radio, the Voice of America, and the Television News Archive at Vanderbilt University.

Another useful source for finding resources by subject is a series of guides collected by the Library School at the University of Michigan, the Clearinghouse for Subject-oriented Internet Resource Guides. This resource is also listed on many campus-wide information systems. To get there directly, Gopher to *lib.umich.edu*, select "What's New and Featured Resources," and then the Clearinghouse. Early in 1995, the Clearinghouse included extensive lists of Internet resources related to computer-mediated communication, film and video, and journalism.

Gopher Servers by Type of Resource

Another way of organizing Internet resources is by format. For example, wouldn't it be useful to find a listing of all library catalogs, campus-wide information systems, or electronic books and journals available? Fortunately, campus Gophers typically include such listings, complete with linkages. A listing of library catalogs available worldwide is maintained at the University of Texas at Dallas (*gopher.utdallas.edu*). Collections of electronic journals, books, and ready-reference sources (such as dictionaries) are maintained at numerous sites. The easiest way to access these is through LC Marvel (*marvel.loc.gov*), which provides access to the various collections of electronic publications available under three menu items: "Electronic Journal Collections," "Electronic Text Collections," and "Reference Collections." Campus-wide information systems are available through the University of North Carolina, Chapel Hill (*gibbs.oit.unc.edu*).

Finding devices such as these makes it much easier to use the Internet. Previously, to dial in to a library catalog, you had to identify the domain address of the library, then telnet to it. Using the listing previously cited, you need only pick the library catalog in which you are interested and the Gopher automatically arranges the telnet session. Likewise, many publications formerly available only via FTP are now more easily accessed through Gopher. Documents may simply be read on-line, or you may use your Gopher client software to save them as files on your computer or to mail them to your E-mail address.

Keyword Searching of Remote Gophers

You may need information that you can't locate with the finding tools already described, or perhaps, you simply don't have time to use the indirect approach of browsing a hierarchy of menus. It is possible to do a keyword search of Gopher servers all over the world, using a tool called **Veronica**. This tool usually can be found on the menu of your campus Gopher in the "All the Gophers of the World" menu. If not, you can Gopher to another server such as the University of Minnesota (*consultant.micro.umn.edu*), which does provide access to Veronica searching.

For example, suppose you have heard of a Gopher for communication researchers called "Comserve," but have no idea where it's located. First, you would pick Veronica from the menu. After being prompted to enter a keyword, you would enter "comserve." The system would search an index and display a listing of different menu items from directories of remote Gophers that contain that word. You would then need to pick and investigate these, one by one. Naturally, this tool works best when the keyword is a relatively unusual one.

Other Gopher Tools

Although Gopher client programs differ in many respects, they do share some handy features. For example, when you have located a file that's of interest to you, your client software will allow you to save it to a file on your host computer or to mail it to your own or someone else's E-mail address.

Another especially useful Gopher feature is the ability to create *bookmarks*. As you browse Gophers and find useful items that you would like to consult again, you can create a bookmark on your system for them. This is easily accomplished, no matter which client you are using. Using the Unix client, for example, you simply move to the menu for which you wish to create a bookmark, and press the letter *A*. This item will now be added permanently to your list of bookmarks and will remain on your list until you choose to delete it. To call up your list of bookmarks in any subsequent Gopher session, simply type the letter *v*. The bookmark feature allows you to create your own personal menu of frequently consulted resources.

World Wide Web

World Wide Web, often referred to as "WWW," "W3," or "the Web," was developed by Tim Berners-Lee at CERN, the European Laboratory for Particle Physics. Like Gopher, WWW links resources on servers around the world in a way that is largely transparent to the user. Users access these servers through client software. But the conceptual frameworks are quite different. Unlike Gopher's hierarchical menus, World Wide Web uses **hypertext** to link resources.

Hypertext is simply regular text that includes connections within the text to other documents. For instance, if we were to convert the preceding paragraph into hypertext, we might indicate all terms that are hypertext links, or **hyperlinks**, by italicizing them:

> World Wide Web, often referred to as "WWW," "W3," or "the Web," was developed by *Tim Berners-Lee* at *CERN*, the European Laboratory for Particle Physics. Like *Gopher*, WWW links resources on *servers* around the world in a way that is largely transparent to the user, and users access these servers through *client software*. But the conceptual frameworks are quite different. Unlike Gopher's hierarchical menus, World Wide Web uses *hypertext* to link resources.

In its hypertext form, the reader could click on any of the hyperlinks to go to documents containing, for example, a definition or history (*servers*, *client software*, *hypertext*), a description and background information (*CERN*), or biographical information (*Tim Berners-Lee*). If this were **hypermedia**, the *Tim Berners-Lee* link might take you to a photograph, audio, or video recording of this person. Students may be familiar with encyclopedias on CD-ROM that are now being produced with such multimedia capabilities.

World Wide Web's innovation is to make it possible for hyperlinks to take the user to resources stored on servers anyplace on the Internet. These servers might be a Gopher, a file at an FTP repository, a database stored on a remote computer accessed via telnet, another Web server, or several other types of Internet resources. When the link leads to another hypertext document, we can envision a veritable web of interconnected resources, with each user creating his or her own complex pathway.

Accessing World Wide Web

As of early 1995, many campus-wide information systems and other Gopher sites were being converted from Gopher to World Wide Web, and this trend is likely to continue and accelerate. (Existing Gopher servers are often maintained, as well, though not developed further.) Thus, most students will gain access to WWW simply by selecting the Web version of their campus information system from a computer lab menu. If you can't locate a Web *homepage* (or menu) from your campus's main menu, inquire at your computer center or library to find out what access method will work best for you.

WWW Browsers

Client programs, often called browsers, are used to access World Wide Web and exist for virtually all microcomputer platforms. By 1994, the program of choice had become Mosaic and its offspring such as Netscape. Developed at the National Center for Supercomputing Applications (NCSA) at the University of Illinois at Urbana–Champaign, Mosaic brought full hypermedia capabilities to WWW. With an easy-to-use, point-and-click interface, it allows hyperlinks to graphic images, sound, and video as well as text. In addition, Mosaic serves as an easy-to-use front end to such traditional and somewhat complex Internet tools as FTP.

Unfortunately, Mosaic and Netscape can be used only with microcomputers with a graphical user interface, such as Macintosh or Microsoft Windows. They also require a full-Internet connection. Workstations connected to a campus network will usually have such a connection, but many of those using a dial-up connection will not yet have one. Ask at your computer center to see if your connection will support Mosaic or other graphics-based WWW browsers.

If you are not able to use a graphics-based browser, you will still be able to access virtually all of the textual resources on World

Wide Web using an easy-to-use browser. For example, Lynx, a character-based browser developed at the University of Kansas, will allow you to do most of what you could do with Mosaic, but without the pictures. It doesn't require a full-Internet connection.

Like Gopher, World Wide Web offers numerous finding tools for locating information on the Internet. In fact, many of the Gopher sites previously described have a corresponding WWW server. The subject and type of source listing available on WWW often incorporate Gopher servers. Each World Wide Web browser and server opens with a **homepage**, which functions much as a Gopher main menu would, but in hypertext format. Both Mosaic and Netscape have homepages that will offer you avenues for exploring Internet resources by subject and type. One source that you may access from these homepages is the Library of Congress WWW server, which provides comprehensive access to Internet resources. It is arranged by subject and type of source. The Library of Congress's homepage is shown in Figure 14.

Universal Resource Locators

In Figure 14 below, notice the **URL** notation (*http://lcweb. loc.gov*) near the top of the screen. This URL, or **Uniform Resource**

Figure 14. Library of Congress homepage.

Locator, is the Web address of the homepage being displayed. To transport users transparently between WWW servers, the developers of World Wide Web devised URLs as a standardized way of addressing different documents, media, and network services. Nearly any file or service on the Internet can be represented by a URL. You never need actually to type a URL yourself to use WWW. Starting from a homepage and following hyperlinks will do the initial navigating for you, and maintaining a personal list of bookmarks ("hotlists" in Web jargon) will let you return repeatedly to your favorite Web sites. However, you will find that many published references to Internet resources now routinely supply their URLs. These addresses can be entered directly in your Web browser, using the "Go" command. This allows you to access interesting-sounding Internet resources directly.

Because URLs have been widely adopted as a convenient, shorthand way of indicating Internet locations, even outside the WWW environment, we'll use them in this book when we cite Internet resources. The URLs in Figure 15 provide two straightforward examples of sources we've previously described. Note that they are formatted as a single, unbroken line, with no spaces. The method of access is specified first, followed by a colon and two slashes. The slashes are followed by the address of the computer where the information or service is located.

These URLs are somewhat simplified, because the path to follow once the main menu is reached is not specified. Further parts may specify the names of files, the port to connect to, or the text to search for in a database. We'll use the simplified version for resources other than World Wide Web, but URLs for the latter are usually more complete, allowing users to go directly to a resource.

For example, the URL for the WWW version of the Clearinghouse for Subject-Oriented Internet Resource Guides follows:

http://www.lib.umich.edu/chhome.html

Library of Congress catalogs: telnet://locis.loc.gov

RiceInfo: gopher://riceinfo.rice.edu

Figure 15. URLs for two previously cited Internet resources.

Note that the basic URL for a World Wide Web hypertext resource, such as this one, includes *www* in the address and usually begins with **http** (for hypertext transport protocol) and ends with **html** (for hypertext markup language).

Electronic Discussion Groups

We have focused to this point in this chapter on the use of the Internet to locate information in files and databases. Another important way researchers use the Internet is to participate in electronic discussion groups. Depending on the context, such groups are usually called **LISTSERVs**, or **newsgroups**.

LISTSERVs are set up as mailing lists on an Internet server using special LISTSERV software. The software facilitates the sharing of E-mail messages among members by automatically forwarding to the entire LISTSERV mailing list any message addressed to the group. Messages are received by group members in their individual mailboxes, at their home E-mail sites. Such a system facilitates ongoing discussion of research and professional topics of common interest. LISTSERVs have become a popular way to share information in many fields. The LISTSERV software also makes it a simple matter to join or resign from the group.

Newsgroups are discussion groups on **UseNet News**, a network of thousands of groups available on most campus networks. Instead of receiving electronic mail in your mailbox, you use special software to read the newsgroups in which you're interested. Although many newsgroups are strictly recreational in nature, others are professional and scholarly. In fact, many LISTSERVs are also available as UseNet newsgroups, providing an alternative and convenient method for participating in them. (Users may prefer to access LISTSERVs through UseNet to avoid dealing with an overabundance of messages in their E-mail boxes.) WWW browsers such as Mosaic and Netscape provide a convenient way to access UseNet, right from their homepages. If this method isn't available to you, inquire at the computer center on your campus about the **newsreader** software used on your campus to provide access to UseNet.

To find a comprehensive listing and description of scholarly and professional LISTSERVs and newsgroups, consult the *Directory of Scholarly Electronic Conferences*. This source is widely disseminated on the Internet (*URL: gopher://gopher.usask.ca*).

Looking in this directory under "Social Sciences," you might decide to participate in the Intercultural Communication Practicum. Two addresses are listed for the group:

listserv@umrvmb.umr.edu and *xcult-x@umrvmb.umr.edu*

The first is the address you use to subscribe to the group. The second is the address you use to send a message that you want to share with the entire group. It's very important not to confuse the two, if you want to avoid clogging the mailboxes of your new electronic colleagues with extraneous and annoying messages.

To subscribe, you would send an E-mail message to the LIST-SERV address: *listserv@umrvmb.umr.edu*. Leave the subject line blank. Type a one-line message, as follows:

subscribe xcult-x FirstName LastName

For example:

subscribe xcult-x Jane Doe

This model can be used to subscribe to most LISTSERVs. You'll quickly receive a message from the LISTSERV welcoming you to the group, describing its mode of operation, and giving you instructions for, among other things, canceling your subscription. It's important to save this message, as you may decide at some point that this particular group is not for you or that you want to suspend your subscription during a vacation period. Naturally, all messages about your subscription should be sent to the LISTSERV address, not to the group address.

Communication Research and Theory Network (CRTNET) is a LISTSERV in communication, which is moderated by Tom Benson at Pennsylvania State University. CRTNET provides discussions of issues relevant to all aspects of the subject and discipline of communication. It also includes announcements posted from the national office of the Speech Communication Association, job listings, and texts of recent political speeches. To subscribe or to obtain back issues of CRTNET send a message to the LISTSERV (*listserv@psuvm.psu.edu*). For back issues ask for the index (*index CRTNET*).

Special Internet Resources for Communication

The focus of this chapter has been to familiarize you with Internet tools and resources of use to researchers. Students of communication will find much of interest by using the subject listings and format-type finding tools available for Gopher and World Wide Web. Several important Gopher servers can be of use to students interested in mass, political, and public communication, as well as other areas of the discipline:

Congressional Quarterly (*gopher.cqalert.com*): Table of contents, selected articles, election returns, and congressional votes

ACLU (*aclu.org*): ACLU Reading Room; gender, race, and sexual orientation research

C-Span (*c-span.org*): Press releases, Supreme Court and congressional information, and how-to-order transcripts

Chronicle of Higher Education (*chronicle.merit.edu*): News about higher education, job openings, and new books

Internet Wiretap (*wiretap.spies.com*): Selected government documents, speeches, historical documents

Library of Congress (*marvel.loc.gov*): Search the Library's holdings, and access to speech collections

U.S. House or Senate (*gopher.house.gov* or *ftp.senate.gov*): Information on Members, congressional committees, and recent votes

American Political Science Association (*apsa.trenton.edu*): Allows connection to other Gophers, political science discussion groups, archives of speeches, and magazines/journals/ books

Supreme Court (*ftp.cwru.edu*): Court rulings and decisions

Communication researchers and practitioners have been active in developing useful Internet resources, and pointers to these are incorporated into the subject-listings available. Two Internet resources have been developed especially to access information in the field of communication: Comserve and a WWW site devoted to communication and education resources.

Comserve

Comserve is an on-line service provided by the Communication Institute for Online Scholarship (CIOS) that provides access to news services (position announcements, new books, news, new research), electronic journals, syllabi, bibliographies, research articles, and hotlines (electronic discussion groups in the many different areas of the discipline). Communication scholars join hotlines to discuss issues relevant to many specialty interests, for example:

computer-mediated, family, gender, health, intercultural, interpersonal, mass, organizational, and political communication; history; magazine journalism; philosophy; research methods; rhetoric; speech disorders; and speech education.

Students may join ComGrads, a hotline for students to exchange ideas about graduate school, teaching, and research. Students attending universities that are affiliates of CIOS may download unlimited numbers of files and join as many hotlines as they wish, but students at nonaffiliated universities and the general public have only limited access. If the university is an affiliate, students, faculty, and others connected to the university can conduct global searches of Comserve's *Journals' Index* and do full-text searches in the resource library.

Comserve is accessible through some Gopher programs (*cios.llc.rpi.edu*) or you can send electronic messages to Comserve (*comserve@cios.llc.rpi.edu*).

Comserve is an important electronic service, one designed especially for communication scholars. It's a way to become involved in the discipline, to see what topics are of interest to faculty and fellow students, and to search the communication literature.

A World Wide Web Site for Communication

Indiana University has developed a comprehensive Web server that provides links to many Internet resources in communication:

(URL:http://alnilam.ucs.indiana.edu:1027/sources/comm.html)

The Web server attempts to cover several media (for example, radio, television, film, print, telephones, and computer-mediated communication), as well as additional resources in several information categories: bibliographies, information science, libraries and related databases, LISTSERV lists, regulation, research, social issues, and teaching. Among the organizational Web servers to which this site includes links are: the Association of America's Public Television Stations, National Association of Broadcasters' Library and Information Center, Vanderbilt Television News Archive, International Telecommunications Union, AT&T, ACLU Reading Room, and the Electronic Frontier Foundation.

This site also includes links to many communication-related resources maintained on various World Wide Web servers, including:

NetMedia: a listing of mass media that can be contacted via the Internet

Newspapers and journalism links on the Web

Electronic journals in communication

Information sources: the Internet and computer-mediated communication

Advertising Law Internet Site

Telecommunications Reading Room

The File Room Censorship Archive

The Satellite TV Page

Computer-Mediated Communication Studies Center

Communication and Mass Communication Resources: University of Iowa

Mass Media Articles Database (Penn State)

This selective list as of early 1995 provides a sense of the utility of this resource. Students wishing to keep up with what is happening on the Internet in communication should check this list regularly.

The *Journal of Communication* also announced plans to devote a special issue in 1996 to the Internet and computer-mediated networked communication. This would be a useful source to update the information in this chapter. However, keep in mind that Internet tools and resources are evolving quite rapidly. It is difficult to keep pace with the fast-changing technology of the information superhighway. There is no substitute for regular browsing of the Net to remain aware of what is available. Many Web and Gopher sites regularly feature new resources, providing a convenient means of keeping current.

Summary

The Internet is a rapidly evolving communication network that offers many resources for communication researchers. Students should become well acquainted with basic Internet tools, especially Gopher and World Wide Web, and with the subject-oriented and format-type finding aids on both that can be used for general and specialized communication research purposes. CRTNET, Comserve, and Indiana University Web server are useful Internet resources for students of communication.

References

Directory of electronic journals, newsletters and academic discussion lists. (1994). Washington, DC: Association of Research Libraries.

Gilster, P. (1994). *The Internet navigator* (2nd ed.). New York: Wiley.

Gilster, P. (1995). *The Mosaic navigator: The essential guide to the Internet interface.* New York: Wiley.

Glossbrenner, A. (1995). *Internet 101: A college student's guide.* New York: Windcrest/McGraw-Hill.

Hahn, H., & Stout, R. (1994). *The Internet complete reference.* Berkeley: Osborne McGraw-Hill.

Hoffman, P. E. (1994). *Internet instant reference.* San Francisco: Sybex.

Krol, E. (1994). *The whole Internet: User's guide & catalog* (2nd ed.). Sebastopol, CA: O'Reilly.

Levine, J. R., & Baroudi, C. (1994). *Internet for dummies* (2nd ed.). San Mateo, CA: IDG Books.

OPAC Directory: An Annual Guide to Internet-Accessible Online Public Access Catalogs. (1994 –). Westport, CT: Meckler.

Exercises

1. Find out how to access Gopher on your campus. Explore the main menus of a campus Gopher server and locate a directory that will allow you to search "All the Gophers in the World." Use this feature to locate the Gopher at the University of California at Santa Cruz. What is the name of this university's campus-wide information system?

2. Now find the campus Gopher of the University of Texas at Dallas. On this Gopher you will find a listing of library catalogs

worldwide. Go to MELVYL, the catalog of the entire University of California system, and determine how many University of California libraries own a copy of some edition of this book.

3. Find the Veronica search feature on a campus Gopher server. Do a Veronica search using the keywords *public radio*. How many Gopher directories include these keywords?

4. Telnet to the Library of Congress catalog (*locis.loc.gov*). Search this catalog to determine how many books on the Internet were published in 1995.

5. Using a World Wide Web browser such as Lynx, Mosaic, or Netscape, go to the Library of Congress's Global Electronic Library homepage (*URL: http://lcweb.loc.gov/homepage/ lchp.html/global electronic library*). Explore this Web site and locate and read an article from an electronic journal that relates to the field of communication.

PART TWO

Communication Research Sources

In the second part of this book, we try to identify current, important, and useful communication and communication-related sources in print or available through electronic databases. In the next four chapters, we discuss a variety of general and specific research sources. We describe handbooks, textbooks, encyclopedias, and annual reviews in Chapter 5. These are useful for defining, refining, and developing a research topic. The bibliographies, guides, indexes, and abstracts described in Chapter 6 can help further develop the research topic or question. In Chapter 7, we discuss the periodical literature of communication: scholarly journals and professional or trade magazines. The articles found in these publications present current conceptual and practical knowledge. Finally, in Chapter 8 we describe several specific, factual information sources such as collections, statistical sources, government publications, yearbooks, directories, dictionaries, and manuals.

In each chapter, we annotate several sources. We consider these to be some of the more important, useful, or representative sources of the type discussed. The end-of-chapter exercises refer you to some of these sources and ask you to use them. Clues to their use are found in the annotations or in the questions themselves.

The annotated sources certainly do not constitute the totality of sources of that genre. Many additional and valuable sources are listed at the end of each chapter. Several of these can help you select, refine, and develop an interesting research topic and project. Space is also available at the end of each chapter so that you can add sources you find (and don't forget to index them at the back of the book). You'll then be able to refer to these sources whenever you undertake a research project in the future.

Chapter 5

General Sources

In the preceding chapter you've become acquainted with the multi-faceted nature of communication and with systematic research search strategies to address communication topics. Now it's time to examine more closely the various communication sources that are available in or accessible from most college and university libraries.

You may be working on a literature review or research project and have not yet fully identified a specific topic or research question. To gain an understanding of topics that others find interesting or relevant, there are some general sources through which you can browse. These sources may help you formulate or develop your own research topic. If you already know the topic you wish to investigate, these general reference works often have useful bibliographies that can lead you to sources specifically related to your research question.

After you examine these sources, list them on bibliography and search record cards as a reminder that you've already searched through them for references to pertinent materials. As we have stressed, this action can save much time, especially because there will be so many sources that are potentially valuable to your research goal.

Just like many other disciplines, communication is a rapidly evolving field. New research results, new applications, and changes in professional practices often make it difficult to get a grasp of the state of generally accepted knowledge in a given field. Even the vocabulary keeps changing. To alleviate this problem, authorities in all disciplines create handbooks, subject encyclopedias, and subject dictionaries. These sources summarize generally accepted findings or practices in a field at a particular time. In so doing, they provide a useful reference point when you begin researching a subject area.

Handbooks

The term **handbook** is often used to categorize two distinctive types of publications. One type, a manual, is a compact book of facts. We will discuss manuals in Chapter 8 when we deal with other compilations of information. The other type of handbook, the scholarly or subject handbook, is more general in nature and helps orient communication scholars to current issues and topics.

Scholarly handbooks provide a comprehensive summary of past research and thematic viewpoints in a particular discipline. They are generally broad-based and treat a great number of topics. It is difficult for the editors of these volumes to keep them current because of the breadth of topics covered and the delays in publication time. Thus, handbooks are soon dated, although they provide important background information about knowledge and development of many relevant topics.

One handbook outside the communication discipline that communication researchers find valuable for background information, even though they must always look for other sources to give perspective on new developments, is *The Handbook of Social Psychology*:

Lindzey, G., & Aronson, E. (Eds.). (1985). *The handbook of social psychology* (3rd ed., 2 vols.). New York: Random House.

■ Two volumes contain independent articles (each with a lengthy bibliography) summarizing the state of the art in social psychological theory and research. Volume 1 provides a historical perspective, explains theories and models of social psychology, and reviews research methods, including attitude measurement, quantitative methods, survey methods, and program evaluation.

Volume 2 contains articles on altruism and aggression, attitudes and attitude change, sex roles, socialization, language use, attribution and social perception, personality and social behavior, interpersonal attraction, intergroup relations, leadership and power, social influence and conformity, social deviance, applied social psychology, mass-communication effects, environmental psychology, public opinion and political action, and cultural psychology. Author and detailed subject indexes appear at the end of each volume.

A slightly more recent handbook examines several aspects of the field of communication:

Berger, C. R., & Chaffee, S. H. (Eds.). (1987). *Handbook of communication science.* Newbury Park, CA: Sage.

■ This handbook synthesizes research in communication. It is divided into five sections: overviews, levels of analysis, functions, contexts, and conclusions. Topics include interpersonal, family, marital, organizational, mass, campaign, and cross-cultural communication, as well as language, nonverbal signals, persuasion, conflict, children, health care, and public opinion. The overview chapters provide an introduction to the communication field.

Similar handbooks concentrate on more specific content areas. Sometimes these handbooks are onetime works; others may be revised and reissued. One useful handbook examines organizational communication:

Jablin, F. M., Putnam, L. L., Roberts, K. H., & Porter, L. W. (Eds.). (1987). *Handbook of organizational communication: An interdisciplinary perspective.* Newbury Park, CA: Sage.

■ This handbook offers a multidisciplinary view of organizational communication issues, contexts, structures, and processes. The 19 chapters cover topics such as communication climate, culture, networks, superior/subordinate communication, conflict and negotiation, decision making, feedback, motivation, assimilation, and power. The volume contains both author and subject indexes.

Another recent handbook updates writings in political communication. It intends to move research beyond traditional ways of looking at the persuasion of voters to new contexts and views of political communication:

Swanson, D. L., & Nimmo, D. D. (Eds.). (1990). *New directions in political communication: A resource book*. Newbury Park, CA: Sage.

■ This handbook examines the role of communication in politics. Besides an introductory chapter that considers the present state and future directions of research, nine other chapters are divided into four sections: foundations of political communication, understanding political messages, the institutional perspective on political communication, and recent political communication research. Each essay contains a series of references. The last section provides a selective bibliography of research published within the last 10 years.

Handbooks have been developed for several areas of the discipline. Another communication handbook provides an overview of intercultural communication:

Asante, M. K., & Gudykunst, W. B. (Eds.). (1989). *Handbook of international and intercultural communication*. Newbury Park, CA: Sage.

■ Communication specialists, psychologists, and anthropologists review the present state of research in international and intercultural communication. They attempt to provide a framework for future work in the field. The 23 essays are arranged in three sections: overviews, processes and effects, and contexts. An index provides access to subjects and authors.

A recent addition to handbooks in the communication discipline is a revised edition of a specialized handbook in interpersonal communication:

Knapp, M. L., & Miller, G. R. (Eds.). (1994). *Handbook of interpersonal communication* (2nd ed.). Thousand Oaks, CA: Sage.

■ This handbook summarizes the development and present state of theory and research in interpersonal communication. The authors discuss approaches to basic issues in studying interpersonal communication, fundamental units, processes and functions, and contexts.

Chapters cover such topics as language, communicator characteristics, nonverbal signals, power, influence, competence, and communication in work, social, health, and family contexts. Each essay contains a lengthy list of references.

Communication researchers, particularly those in organizational communication, advertising, and public relations, often find subject handbooks from business to be useful. These handbooks usually offer a practical, rather than scholarly, approach to their subjects. Although they may lack extensive bibliographies, their concise explanations of accepted practices, procedures, and concepts in a given area are useful when you start a research paper or other communication project. Among the handbooks available in marketing, advertising, and public relations is the following:

Dilenschneider, R. L., & Forrestal, D. J. (1987). *Dartnell public relations handbook* (3rd ed., rev.). Chicago: Dartnell.

■ This handbook describes different aspects of the public relations profession, the work of public relations professionals in various fields, and methods of internal communication. A special section is devoted to hospital and medical school public relations. Many chapters offer short case studies of exemplary public relations campaigns. A detailed subject index is provided.

We list other scholarly and subject handbooks from communication and related disciplines at the end of this chapter. These handbooks are valuable for selecting and refining research topics. Their content also provides specific information for developing a literature review, research paper, or prospectus.

Textbooks

Textbooks are handy aids when defining and refining research questions. They seek to survey information about a field of study, and to present the fundamentals of a subject in an easy-to-understand manner. Some textbooks are edited collections of writings in a subject area and are quite similar to handbooks. In fact, it is sometimes not an easy task to distinguish some textbooks from scholarly handbooks. At times, instructors may even use handbooks as class texts.

In basic textbooks, the authors offer a brief summary of existing knowledge along with their conclusions about the essential points derived from communication theory and research in that area. The bibliographies at the ends of chapters can be helpful for locating useful books and articles about the subject. However, these bibliographies are often limited in scope. When using textbooks, keep in mind that, as with all printed materials, there is a gap between the time the book is written and the time it is printed. As secondary sources, it is usually best to use textbooks to acquire an overview or general orientation to a topic, and to gather a few reference sources.

Several communication-related textbooks are listed at the end of this chapter. The list is quite selective and by no means represents the multitude of communication-related textbooks published each year.

Encyclopedias

Encyclopedias are all-embracing compilations of information that provide a multifaceted approach to a subject. The essays within encyclopedias generally have bibliographies that can be used to find other general sources about the topic. These bibliographies may also identify specific sources that can give background for narrower aspects of the topic. It may not be too helpful, though, to consult general encyclopedias like the *Encyclopedia Britannica* unless you initially know very little about your topic.

Subject encyclopedias contain overview articles summarizing what is known about topics in a specific discipline. The first communication subject encyclopedia was published in 1989, but it promises to be a useful source for years to come:

Barnouw, E. (Ed.). (1989). *International encyclopedia of communications* (4 vols.). New York: Oxford University Press.

■ This encyclopedia contains over 500 articles on various facets of communication. It provides interdisciplinary and international coverage. Major topics include: advertising and public relations, animal communication, arts, communication research, computer era, education, international communication, journalism, language and linguistics, media, motion pictures, music, nonverbal communication, photography, political communication, radio, speech, television, theatre, and theories of communication. Articles are illustrated and include bibliographies of general books and textbooks. A comprehensive index lists concepts, terms, names, and titles.

A legal encyclopedia is another type of subject encyclopedia. It is a useful source when you are researching topics of communication law, freedom of speech, and debate. Legal encyclopedias are typically written in narrative form and are nonevaluative in approach. They best serve as case finders and starting points in searching the law. They generally include a statement of the applicable law, citations to appropriate cases, and analytical and subject indexes. Good encyclopedias also have frequent supplements.

The two principal legal encyclopedias of national scope are *Corpus Juris Secundum* and *American Jurisprudence Second* (second series). State and local legal encyclopedias are also available.

When first reading the literature of an academic discipline, you may encounter a whole new language. The words may be familiar, but many times the meanings seem to be different. Although we discuss most dictionaries in Chapter 8 as largely being information manuals, a **subject dictionary** can be an abbreviated type of subject encyclopedia. Subject dictionaries may help clarify your understanding of new or unique terms and lead you to important references.

Subject dictionaries list and define basic and specialized terms in a particular field. They also provide meanings for abbreviations, jargon, and slang. Most disciplines (for example, education, psychology, and political science) have comprehensive dictionaries that define terms used in those fields. One dictionary that provides broad coverage of communication terms is:

DeVito, J. A. (1986). *The communication handbook: A dictionary*. New York: Harper & Row.

■ This is perhaps the only dictionary that addresses several areas of communication. Besides providing brief definitions for communication terminology, it gives over 100 essays for major communication areas such as interpersonal communication, language, mass media, nonverbal communication, organizational communication, persuasion, public speaking, and small-group communication. The dictionary gives references to seminal articles and books for additional information.

Annual Reviews and Series

Besides handbooks and encyclopedias, other general sources will help you find information or define a research question more clearly. Communication, like many other disciplines, is experiencing a surge in research activity. This expansion is so rapid that keeping abreast of what others in the various specialty areas are researching is sometimes difficult. **Annual reviews** provide yearly summaries of current research activities. They are useful for selecting and refining a research topic or question, finding information and sources, and updating bibliographies. Because some of the sources cited in annual reviews may be outside your usual reading area, reading annual reviews helps to broaden your search strategy.

Annual reviews, then, are vehicles for gauging the level of research activity in various areas of communication. They also update research and are helpful later in the research process when you're looking for recent information and bibliographic citations.

Some annual reviews provide updates of current research and thinking in a variety of content areas. Others focus on one particular content area that changes each year. One annual review of the former type is *Communication Yearbook*. It contains current research and writings in several related content areas.

Communication Yearbook. (1977–). Thousand Oaks, CA: Sage.

■   This annual review is an official publication of the International Communication Association (ICA). Volumes prior to 1988 presented two different types of articles: *reviews and commentaries*, covering general communication topics, and *selected studies*, including research papers in each subfield (for example, interpersonal, organizational, and mass communication), competitively selected and presented at the annual meeting of the ICA. Early editions also included overviews of developments within the subfields during that year. From 1988 to 1994, the *Yearbook* offered original essays and commentaries reflecting conceptual developments across the communication discipline. Starting in 1995, the *Yearbook* refocused to feature reviews of the literature.

Reviews and research studies contain valuable bibliographic sources. You should examine the table of contents to determine the broader chapter topics and use the subject index at the back to locate references to narrower topics. There is also an index by author.

Another annual review focuses on information systems, communication uses and effects, and control of communication and information:

Progress in Communication Sciences. (1979–). Norwood, NJ: Ablex.

■ Each annual volume contains 7 to 10 review essays on topics in most subareas of communication. Over the years, essays have focused on broadcast regulations, grapevines, telephone networks, children's television, political campaigns, communication competence, gender, statistics, ethnography, and many other topics too numerous to list here. Each volume has a subject and author index.

Mass Communication Review Yearbook, which ceased publication in 1987, presented a collection of published and previously unpublished research papers and studies about developments and trends in mass communication. Although the broad divisions of the book varied from year to year, typical sections included theoretical perspectives, research strategies and methodology, information processing, political communication, mass-communication effects, and international and comparative research.

Series examine new topics each year, focus on research related to those specific subjects, and often have different titles. The articles in each volume are reports of original research or theoretical pieces. Sage Publications publishes a series (which it calls an "annual review") of communication research. These volumes are helpful in identifying recent research topics, finding contemporary information, and broadening your search strategy.

Sage Annual Reviews of Communication Research. (1972–). Thousand Oaks, CA: Sage.

■ Each volume in the series explores a different communication topic. The editors, publication years, and titles in the series follow:

Volume 1: Kline, F. G., & Tichenor, P. J. (1972). *Current perspectives in mass communication research.*

Volume 2: Clarke, P. (1973). *New models for communication research.*

Volume 3: Blumler, J. G., & Katz, E. (1974). *The uses of mass communications: Current perspectives on gratifications research.*

Volume 4: Chaffee, S. H. (1975). *Political communication: Issues and strategies for research.*

Volume 5: Miller, G. R. (1976). *Explorations in interpersonal communication.*

Volume 6: Hirsch, P. M., Miller, P. V., & Kline, F. G. (1977). *Strategies for communication research.*

Volume 7: Wartella, E. (1979). *Children communicating: Media and development of thought, speech, understanding.*

Volume 8: Roloff, M. E., & Miller, G. R. (1980). *Persuasion: New directions in theory and research.*

Volume 9: Rosengren, K. E. (1981). *Advances in content analysis.*

Volume 10: Ettema, J. S., & Whitney, D. C. (1982). *Individuals in mass media organizations: Creativity and constraint.*

Volume 11: Wiemann, J. M., & Harrison, R. P. (1983). *Nonverbal interaction.*

Volume 12: Rowland, W. D., & Watkins, B. (1984). *Interpreting television: Current research perspectives.*

Volume 13: McPhee, R. D., & Tompkins, P. K. (1985). *Organizational communication: Traditional themes and new directions.*

Volume 14: Roloff, M. E., & Miller, G. R. (1987). *Interpersonal processes: New directions in communication research.*

Volume 15: Carey, J. W. (1988). *Media, myths, and narratives: Television and the press.*

Volume 16: Hawkins, R. P., Wiemann, J. M., & Pingree, S. (1988). *Advancing communication science: Merging mass and interpersonal processes.*

Volume 17: Bradac, J. J. (1989). *Message effects in communication science.*

Volume 18: Salmon, C. T. (1989). *Information campaigns: Balancing social values and social change.*

Volume 19: Blumler, J. G., McLeod, J., & Rosengren, K. E. (1992). *Comparatively speaking: Communication and culture across space and time.*

Volume 20: Putnam, L. L., & Roloff, M. E. (1992). *Communication and negotiation.*

Volume 21: Mumby, D. K. (1993). *Narrative and social control: Critical perspectives.*

Volume 22: Ettema, J. S., & Whitney, D. C. (1994). *Audiencemaking: How the media create the audience.*

Other series that may contain helpful reference sources are listed at the end of this chapter. Several of these series, including *Sage Annual Reviews of Communication Research, Communication Arts Books,* and *People and Communication,* are known as *publishers' series.* This means volumes in the series have different titles and may not appear regularly. Because many libraries list these works only by the title of the individual volumes and not by the series title, identifying and locating the specific volumes that make up a particular series can be difficult. If you wish to find individual works in a series in order to survey current communication topics, consult the following reference book:

Books in series (5th ed.). (1989). New York: Bowker.

■ This work indexes original, in-print, and out-of-print books that are published or distributed in the United States and are in popular, scholarly, and professional series. *Books in Series* is an invaluable search aid for disciplines such as communication that rely heavily on annual reviews appearing in publishers' series. The subject index can be used to locate specific-topic annual reviews. The author and series title indexes can be used to find complete bibliographic data.

These sources, then, provide a general understanding of the communication field, as well as specific interests, concerns, and methodologies of communication researchers. They are most helpful when identifying a specific area within communication that may be of interest for a term paper, literature review, or research prospectus. In many instances, handbooks, yearbooks, and annual reviews can also serve as vehicles for widening a search strategy and locating additional and, in some cases, recent sources about a chosen communication topic.

Selected Sources

Handbooks

Arnold, C. C., & Bowers, J. W. (Eds.). (1984). *Handbook of rhetorical and communication theory.* Boston: Allyn and Bacon.

Asante, M. K., Gudykunst, W. B., & Newmark, E. (Eds.). (1989). *Handbook of international and intercultural communication*. Newbury Park, CA: Sage.

Berger, C. R., & Chaffee, S. H. (Eds.). (1987). *Handbook of communication science*. Newbury Park, CA: Sage.

Christ, W. G. (Ed.). (1994). *Assessing communication education: A handbook for media, speech, and theatre educators*. Hillsdale, NJ: Erlbaum.

Craig, R. L. (1987). *Training and development handbook* (3rd ed.). New York: McGraw-Hill.

Dervin, B., Grossberg, L., O'Keefe, B., & Wartella, E. (Eds.). (1989). *Rethinking communication* (2 vols.). Newbury Park, CA: Sage.

Dilenschneider, R. L., & Forrestal, D. J. (1987). *Dartnell public relations handbook* (3rd ed., rev.). Chicago: Dartnell.

Duck, S. (Ed.). (1988). *Handbook of personal relationships: Theory, research and interventions*. New York: Wiley.

Dunnette, M. D., & Hough, L. M. (1992). *Handbook of industrial and organizational psychology* (2nd ed., 2 vols.). Palo Alto, CA: Consulting Psychologists Press.

Gehring, W. D. (Ed.). (1988). *Handbook of American film genres*. New York: Greenwood Press.

Gerbner, G., & Siefert, M. (Eds.). (1984). *World communications: A handbook*. New York: Longman.

Giles, D., & Robinson, W. P. (1990). *Handbook of language and social psychology*. London: Wiley.

Goldhaber, G. M., & Barnett, G. A. (Eds.). (1988). *Handbook of organizational communication*. Norwood, NJ: Ablex.

Hare, A. P., Blumberg, H. H., Davies, M. F., & Kent, M. V. (1994). *Small group research: A handbook*. Norwood, NJ: Ablex.

Hess, B. B., & Ferree, M. M. (Eds.). (1987). *Analyzing gender: A handbook of social science research*. Newbury Park, CA: Sage.

Inge, M. T. (Ed.). (1989). *Handbook of American popular culture* (2nd ed., 3 vols.). New York: Greenwood Press.

Jablin, F. M., Putnam, L. L., Roberts, K. H., & Porter, L. W. (Eds.). (1987). *Handbook of organizational communication: An interdisciplinary perspective*. Newbury Park, CA: Sage.

Knapp, M. L., & Miller, G. R. (Eds.). (1994). *Handbook of interpersonal communication* (2nd ed.). Thousand Oaks, CA: Sage.

Lesly, P. (Ed.). (1991). *Lesly's handbook of public relations and communications* (2nd ed.). Chicago: Probus.

Levy, S. J., Frerichs, G. R., & Gordon, H. L. (Eds.). (1994). *The Dartnell marketing manager's handbook* (3rd ed.). Chicago: Dartnell.

Lindzey, G., & Aronson, E. (Eds.). (1985). *The handbook of social psychology* (3rd ed., 2 vols.). New York: Random House.

March, J. G., & Brief, A. P. (Eds.). (1987). *Handbook of organizations*. New York: Garland.

Nimmo, D. D., & Sanders, K. R. (Eds.). (1981). *Handbook of political communication*. Beverly Hills, CA: Sage.

Noth, W. (1990). *Handbook of semiotics*. Bloomington: Indiana University Press.

Nussbaum, J. F., & Coupland, J. (Eds.). (1995). *The handbook of communication and aging research*. Hillsdale, NJ: Erlbaum.

Phillips, G. M., & Wood, J. T. (Eds.). (1990). *Speech communication: Essays to commemorate the 75th anniversary of the Speech Communication Association*. Carbondale: Southern Illinois University Press.

Rosen, P. T. (Ed.). (1988). *International handbook of broadcasting systems*. New York: Greenwood Press.

Ruch, W. (1989). *International handbook of corporate communication*. Jefferson, NC: McFarland.

Smelser, N. J. (Ed.). (1988). *Handbook of sociology*. Newbury Park, CA: Sage.

Spitzberg, B. H., & Cupach, W. R. (1989). *Handbook of interpersonal competence research*. New York: Springer-Verlag.

Swanson, D. L., & Nimmo, D. D. (Eds.). (1990). *New directions in political communication: A resource book*. Newbury Park, CA: Sage.

Swanson, J. L., & Castle, C. L. (Eds.). (1990). *First Amendment law handbook*. New York: Clark Boardman.

van Dijk, T. A. (1985). *Handbook of discourse analysis* (4 vols.). London: Academic Press.

_____

_____

_____

_____

_____

_____

_____

_____

Textbooks

Agee, W. K., Ault, P. H., & Emery, E. (1994). *Introduction to mass communications* (11th ed.). New York: HarperCollins.

Allen, R. C. (1992). *Channels of discourse, reassembled: Television and contemporary criticism* (2nd ed.). London: Routledge.

Allen, R. C., & Gomery, D. (1993). *Film history: Theory and practice* (2nd ed.). New York: McGraw-Hill.

Barge, J. K. (1994). *Leadership: Communication skills for organizations and groups*. New York: St. Martin's Press.

Beebe, S. A., & Masterson, J. T. (1995). *Family talk: Interpersonal communication in the family* (2nd ed.). New York: McGraw-Hill.

Bettinghaus, E., & Cody, M. (1987). *Persuasive communication* (4th ed.). New York: Holt, Rinehart & Winston.

Borisoff, D., & Merrill, L. (1992). *The power to communicate: Gender differences as barriers* (2nd ed.). Prospect Heights, IL: Waveland Press.

Botan, C. H., & Hazleton, V., Jr. (Eds.). (1989). *Public relations theory.* Hillsdale, NJ: Erlbaum.

Bryant, J., & Zillmann, D. (Eds.). (1994). *Media effects: Advances in theory and research.* Hillsdale, NJ: Erlbaum.

Burgoon, J. K., Buller, D. B., & Woodall, W. G. (1994). *Nonverbal communication: The unspoken dialogue* (2nd ed.). Columbus, OH: Greyden Press.

Carbaugh, D. (Ed.). (1990). *Cultural communication and intercultural contact.* Hillsdale, NJ: Erlbaum.

Carter, T. B., Franklin, M. A., & Wright, J. B. (1994). *The First Amendment and the fourth estate* (6th ed.). Westbury, NY: Foundation Press.

Cherwitz, R. A. (Ed.). (1990). *Rhetoric and philosophy.* Hillsdale, NJ: Erlbaum.

Christians, C. G., Fackler, M., & Rotzoll, K. B. (1994). *Media ethics: Cases and moral reasoning* (4th ed.). New York: Longman.

Daly, J. A., Friedrich, G. W., & Vangelisti, A. L. (Eds.). (1990). *Teaching communication: Theory, research, and methods.* Hillsdale, NJ: Erlbaum.

Daniels, T. D., & Spiker, B. K. (1994). *Perspectives on organizational communication* (3rd ed.). Madison, WI: Brown & Benchmark.

DeFleur, M. L., & Ball-Rokeach, S. (1989). *Theories of mass communication* (5th ed.). New York: Longman.

Denton, R. E., Jr., & Woodward, G. C. (1990). *Political communication in America* (2nd ed.). Westport, CT: Praeger.

DeVito, J. A. (1995). *The interpersonal communication book* (7th ed.). New York: HarperCollins.

Donohew, L., Sypher, H. E., & Higgins, E. T. (1988). *Communication, social cognition, and affect.* Hillsdale, NJ: Erlbaum.

Eastman, S. T. (Ed.). (1993). *Broadcast/cable programming: Strategies and practices* (4th ed.). Belmont, CA: Wadsworth.

Ellis, D. G. (1992). *From language to communication.* Hillsdale, NJ: Erlbaum.

Foss, S. K., Foss, K. A., & Trapp, R. (1991). *Contemporary perspectives on rhetoric* (2nd ed.). Prospect Heights, IL: Waveland Press.

Gudykunst, W. B., & Kim, Y. Y. (1992). *Communicating with strangers: An approach to intercultural communication* (2nd ed.). New York: McGraw-Hill.

Harris, R. J. (1994). *A cognitive psychology of mass communication* (2nd ed.). Hillsdale, NJ: Erlbaum.

Head, S. W., Sterling, C. H., & Schofield, L. B. (1994). *Broadcasting in America: A survey of electronic media* (7th ed.). Boston: Houghton Mifflin.

Infante, D. A., Rancer, A. S., & Womack, D. F. (1993). *Building communication theory* (2nd ed.). Prospect Heights, IL: Waveland.

Jamieson, K., & Campbell, K. K. (1992). *The interplay of influence: The mass media and their publics in news, advertising, and politics* (3rd ed.). Belmont, CA: Wadsworth.

Jandt, F. E. (1995). *Intercultural communication: An introduction.* Thousand Oaks, CA: Sage

King, S. S. (Ed.). (1989). *Human communication as a field of study: Selected contemporary views.* Albany: State University of New York Press.

Kreps, G. L., & Thornton, B. C. (1992). *Health communication: Theory & practice* (2nd ed.). Prospect Heights, IL: Waveland.

Lavine, J. M., & Wackman, D. B. (1988). *Managing media organizations: Effective leadership of the media.* New York: Longman.

Littlejohn, S. W. (1996). *Theories of human communication* (5th ed.). Belmont, CA: Wadsworth.

Matlon, R. (1988). *Communication in the legal process.* New York: Holt, Rinehart & Winston.

Matsen, P. P., Rollinson, P. B., & Sousa, M. (Eds.). (1990). *Readings from classical rhetoric.* Carbondale: Southern Illinois Press.

Moore, R. L. (1994). *Mass communication law and ethics.* Hillsdale, NJ: Erlbaum.

Newsom, D., Scott, A., & Turk, J. V. (1993). *This is PR: The realities of public relations* (5th ed.). Belmont, CA: Wadsworth.

O'Keefe, D. J. (1990). *Persuasion: Theory and research.* Newbury Park, CA: Sage.

Pearce, W. B. (1989). *Communication and the human condition.* Carbondale: Southern Illinois University Press.

Rogers, E. M. (1995). *Diffusion of innovations* (4th ed.). New York: Free Press.

Severin, W. J., & Tankard, J. W. (1992). *Communication theories: Origins, methods, and uses in the mass media* (3rd ed.). New York: Longman.

Sherman, B. L. (1995). *Telecommunications management: Broadcasting/cable and the new technologies* (2nd ed.). New York: McGraw-Hill.

Sloan, W. D. (1991). *Perspectives on mass communication history.* Hillsdale, NJ: Erlbaum.

Smith, C. A. (1990). *Political communication.* San Diego: Harcourt Brace Jovanovich.

Sterling, C. H., & Kittross, J. M. (1990). *Stay tuned: A concise history of American broadcasting* (2nd ed.). Belmont, CA: Wadsworth.

Tedford, T. (1993). *Freedom of speech in the United States* (2nd ed.). New York: McGraw-Hill.

Teeter, D. L., Jr., & Le Duc, D. R. (1995). *Law of mass communications* (8th ed.). Westbury, NY: Foundation Press.

Trent, J. S., & Friedenberg, R. V. (1991). *Political campaign communication: Principles and practices.* New York: Praeger.

Williams, F. (1992). *The new communications* (3rd ed.). Belmont, CA: Wadsworth.

Wolvin, A. D., & Coakley, C. G. (1993). *Perspectives on listening.* Norwood, NJ: Ablex.

Wood, J. T. (1994). *Gendered lives: Communication, gender, and culture.* Belmont, CA: Wadsworth.

Yerby, J., Buerkel-Rothfuss, N., & Bochner, A. P. (1995). *Understanding family communication* (2nd ed.). Scottsdale, AZ: Gorsuch Scarisbrick.

_____

_____

_____

_____

_____

_____

_____

Encyclopedias

Alkin, M. (Ed.). (1992). *The encyclopedia of educational research* (6th ed., 4 vols.). New York: Macmillan.

American Jurisprudence Second (82 vols.). (1962–). Rochester, NY: Lawyers Co-operative.

Barnouw, E. (Ed.). (1989). *International encyclopedia of communications* (4 vols.). New York: Oxford University Press.

Borgatta, E. F., & Borgatta, M. L. (Eds.). (1992). *Encyclopedia of sociology* (4 vols.). New York: Macmillan.

Clark, B. R., & Neave, G. R. (Eds.). (1992). *The encyclopedia of higher education* (4 vols.). Oxford: Pergamon Press.

Colman, A. M. (Ed.). (1994). *Companion encyclopedia of psychology* (2 vols.). London: Routledge.

Corpus Juris Secundum (100 vols.). (1936–). St. Paul: West.

Corsini, R. J. (Ed.). (1994). *Encyclopedia of psychology* (2nd ed., 4 vols.). New York: Wiley.

DeVito, J. A. (1986). *The communication handbook: A dictionary.* New York: Harper & Row.

Duffy, B. K., & Ryan, H. R. (Eds.). (1987). *American orators before 1900: Critical studies and sources.* New York: Greenwood Press.

Duffy, B. K., & Ryan, H. R. (Eds.). (1987). *American orators of the twentieth century: Critical studies and sources.* New York: Greenwood Press.

Heyel, C. (Ed.). (1982). *The encyclopedia of management* (3rd ed.). New York: Van Nostrand Reinhold.

Hixson, R. F. (1989). *Mass media and the Constitution: An encyclopedia of Supreme Court decisions.* New York: Garland.

Hudson, R. V. (1985). *Mass media: A chronological encyclopedia of television, radio, motion pictures, magazines, newspapers, and books in the United States*. New York: Garland.

Husen, T., & Postlethwaite, T. N. (Eds.). (1994). *The international encyclopedia of education* (2nd ed., 12 vols.). Oxford, England: Pergamon Press.

Kurian, G. T. (Ed.). (1982). *World press encyclopedia* (2 vols.). New York: Facts on File.

Meyers, R. A. (Ed.). (1989). *Encyclopedia of telecommunications*. San Diego: Academic Press.

Miller, D. (1991). *The Blackwell encyclopaedia of political thought* (rev. ed.). New York: Blackwell.

Paneth, D. (1983). *The encyclopedia of American journalism*. New York: Facts on File.

Ramachandran, V. S. (Ed.). (1994). *Encyclopedia of human behavior* (4 vols.). San Diego: Academic Press.

Reed, R. M., & Reed, M. K. (1992). *The encyclopedia of television, cable, and video*. New York: Van Nostrand Reinhold.

Sills, D. L. (Ed.). (1968). *International encyclopedia of the social sciences* (19 vols.). New York: Macmillan.

Squire, L. R. (Ed.). (1992). *Encyclopedia of learning and memory*. New York: Macmillan.

Taft, W. H. (1986). *Encyclopedia of twentieth-century journalists*. New York: Garland.

Unwin, D., & McAleese, R. (Eds.). (1988). *The encyclopaedia of educational media communications and technology* (2nd ed.). New York: Greenwood Press.

_____

_____

_____

_____

_____

_____

_____

_____

_____

Annual Reviews

Advances in Experimental Social Psychology. (1964–). San Diego: Academic Press.

Advances in the Study of Behavior. (1965–). New York: Academic Press.
Advances in the Study of Communication and Affect. (1974–). New York: Plenum.
Annual Review of Anthropology. (1972–). Palo Alto, CA: Annual Reviews.
Annual Review of Applied Linguistics. (1980–). Rowley, MA: Newbury House.
Annual Review of Information Science and Technology. (1966–). Melford, NJ: Learned Information.
Annual Review of Psychology. (1950–). Palo Alto, CA: Annual Reviews.
Annual Review of Sociology. (1975–). Palo Alto, CA: Annual Reviews.
Annual Review of the Institute for Information Studies. (1990–). Falls Church, VA: Institute for Information Studies.
Communication Yearbook. (1977–). Thousand Oaks, CA: Sage.
Current Issues and Research in Advertising. (1978–1990). Ann Arbor: University of Michigan, Graduate School of Business Administration.
Current Research in Film. (1985–1991). Norwood, NJ: Ablex.
Free Speech Yearbook. (1962–). Carbondale: Southern Illinois University Press.
International and Intercultural Communication Annual. (1974–). Thousand Oaks, CA: Sage.
Mass Communication Review Yearbook. (1980–1987). Newbury Park, CA: Sage.
Progress in Communication Sciences. (1979–). Norwood, NJ: Ablex.
Research in Consumer Behavior. (1985–). Greenwich, CT: JAI Press.
Research in Marketing. (1982–). Greenwich, CT: JAI Press.
Review of Marketing. (1978–). Chicago: American Marketing Association.
Syntax and Semantics. (1972–). New York: Academic Press.
Written Communication Annual. (1986–). Newbury Park, CA: Sage.

Series

Advances in Semiotics. (1976–). Bloomington: Indiana University Press.
Books in series (5th ed.). (1989). New York: Bowker.

CommText Series. (1980–). Thousand Oaks, CA: Sage.

Communication and Behavior: An Interdisciplinary Series. (1977–1985). New York: Academic Press.

Communication and Human Values Series. (1988–). Thousand Oaks, CA: Sage.

Communication and Information Science. (1979–). Norwood, NJ: Ablex.

Communication and Society. (1994–). New York: Routledge.

Communication Concepts. (1991–). Thousand Oaks, CA: Sage.

Communication Series. (1989–). New York: Guilford.

Communication Series. (1992–). Cresskill, NJ: Hampton Press.

Communication Technology and Society. (1986–1991). New York: Free Press.

Communication Textbook Series. (1988–). Hillsdale, NJ: Erlbaum

Communications in Society Series. (1986–). Thousand Oaks, CA: Sage.

Contributions to the Study of Mass Media and Communications. (1983–). Westport, CT: Greenwood Press.

Critical Studies in Communication. (1992–). Boulder, CO: Westview.

Current Mass Communication Research. (1957–). Paris: UNESCO.

Information and Behavior. (1985–). New Brunswick, NJ: Transaction.

International Series on Communication Skills. (1990–). New York: Routledge.

LEA's Communication Series. (1985–). Hillsdale, NJ: Erlbaum.

Media and Society Series. (1987–). New York: Praeger.

Media Culture & Society Series. (1987–). Thousand Oaks, CA: Sage.

People and Communication Series. (1977–1986). Thousand Oaks, CA: Sage.

Sage Annual Reviews of Communication Research. (1972–). Thousand Oaks, CA: Sage.

Series in Interpersonal Communication. (1983–). Thousand Oaks, CA: Sage.

Series in Political Communication. (1990–). Westport, CT: Praeger.

Series in Public Communication. (1981–). New York: Longman.

Studies in Communication Processes. (1990–). Columbia: University of South Carolina Press.

Studies in Culture and Communication (1990–). New York: Routledge.

Studies in Rhetoric and Communication. (1989–). Tuscaloosa: University of Alabama Press.

Studies in Rhetoric/Communication. (1984–). Columbia: University of South Carolina Press.

SUNY Series in Human Communication. (1985–). Albany: State University of New York Press.

SUNY Series in Speech Communication. (1991–). Albany: State University of New York Press.

Exercises

1. For your Persuasion class, you have decided to write a report on some aspect of *counterattitudinal advocacy*, but you still need to narrow your topic further. To get some background on research that has been done on various aspects of this subject, you consult the *Handbook of Communication Science*. Turning to the chapter that looks most promising, you find a reference to a 1973 publication by Miller.

    a. On which page does the first reference to the Miller piece appear?

    b. By referring to the bibliography at the end of this essay, you find the Miller piece is a chapter in which edited book?

2. You are a member of a small group in your Organizational Communication class that must plan a presentation on ways of resolving conflict in organizations. Your group decides to focus on *intergroup conflict* and turns to Jablin et al.'s *Handbook of Organizational Communication* to find out more about it.

    a. On what pages would *intergroup conflict* be explained for you?

3. To begin a research paper on *propaganda*, you consult a subject encyclopedia covering all the social sciences, the *International Encyclopedia of Communications*, to find an introductory essay. You find that an essay is devoted to this topic.

    a. In what volume and on what page does the essay begin?

    b. What is the title of the first book in the bibliography at the end of the essay?

4. While researching a topic for a course in new communication technologies, you come across *subscription TV*, a term with

which you are not familiar. You turn to an appropriate dictionary, *The Communication Handbook: A Dictionary*, for help.

   a.   To what does this term refer?

   b.   What other term is related to this one?

5. You are preparing for a classroom discussion on social control and obedience in the workplace. You decide to examine one publisher's series described in this chapter, *Sage Annual Reviews of Communication Research*, for an up-to-date survey of research in this area. It appears that one recent volume might be most appropriate for your topic.

   a.   What is the title of the article in this volume that seems most closely related to your topic?

   b.   An essay by Bormann in 1983 is mentioned in this article. On which page is the first reference to this study found in the article?

   c.   In what book was the Bormann essay originally published?

6. You're doing a literature review in your advanced interpersonal communication class on interpersonal communication competence. A recent handbook, the *Handbook of Interpersonal Communication*, has a chapter that relates to your topic.

   a.   On what page does the chapter begin?

   b.   As you read through the chapter, what are three components of most definitions of competence?

7. Identify some situations in which a researcher would consult an edited textbook when doing communication research.

8. Browse though recent volumes of *Communication Yearbook*. What themes are prevalent? What questions are researchers asking?

9. List five articles from the *International Encyclopedia of Communications* that you find interesting. Skim through each and identify five potential research topics you'd like to pursue. Choose one of these for a literature review.

10. Identify sources you discovered in this chapter that would be helpful in searching a communication topic and list them on your search strategy sheet.

Chapter 6

Finding Tools

The general sources identified in Chapter 5 should help you develop a precise research topic. Do not be concerned, though, if you find that you need to reword or refine the topic as your research progresses. This is normal. The more you learn about your topic, the more precisely you can state the research question.

By this time, our example topic, "The Use of Media in Organizations," might have been narrowed to a research question: "What types of public interview training programs do organizations provide for their management personnel?" It is likely that we would once again alter this question, if only slightly, as we continue our search for additional sources of information.

In this chapter, we focus on reference materials that can lead you to additional information sources. If you are writing a research paper and have already found a bibliography pertinent to your topic in a handbook or annual review, you are well on the way to identifying sources to consult for more information on your topic. If you have not found a bibliography, this chapter should lead you to helpful ones. At this point in your research, you will want to start using your library's catalog to determine which books listed in the bibliographies you have found are owned by your library. You will also want to locate items published after these bibliographies were compiled. Note that following this search strategy will mean your first approach to the library catalog will be by the authors or titles of works you have already identified, rather than by subject.

Besides books, the bibliographies you have found may also identify several periodical or journal articles (see Chapter 7) relevant to your topic. You can update and expand these periodical sources by using indexes and abstracts.

Indexes list articles in research publications by subject area and sometimes by author. These can be extremely helpful in leading you to research reports, speeches, book reviews, and so on. We explain specialized, citation, and media indexes in this chapter. We describe other indexes (covering collections of documents and government materials) in Chapter 8.

Abstracts provide paragraph- or sentence-length summaries of original sources and give you a better idea about the content of the original work. Using abstracts, then, allows you to see whether the original source, whether it be a book, chapter, or a journal article, is relevant to your topic. This can save valuable search time.

Sources such as media indexes (covered later in this chapter) and government publications (see Chapter 8) concentrate on specialized finding tools, those dealing with original media sources (such as newspapers, television, and film) and documents of the U.S. government. Not all research topics, of course, would benefit from including the sources found using the specialized finding tools for media and government sources. For example, there would be few government publications on "Eye Contact in Initial Interactions." However, research on other topics, such as "The Effect of Television Violence on Children" or "The Impact of Government Regulation on the Operation of Cable Television," would be incomplete without these specialized sources.

By the time you have examined the sources listed in this chapter, you will have a fairly comprehensive list of sources (books, articles, and so on) that you should consult in the research process and consider including in a research paper bibliography.

Bibliographies

The idea of a **bibliography** as a list of citations to sources needs little introduction, particularly for those of you who are currently compiling such a list. Your final product will probably fit the definition of a **selective topical bibliography**. This is a carefully chosen list of materials on a given topic. Like many (but by no means all) bibliographies, yours will include several different types of sources, such as books, periodical articles, and government documents, which you have identified using many different types of references. Because each of your citations will include complete bibliographic information, another researcher could use and build upon the work you have done. You also will want to use bibliographies to take advantage of the work others have already done in selecting and compiling sources relevant to your topic. Other authors may even have provided the additional service of **annotating** their bibliographies—that is, giving a brief summary of the content of the article or book and possibly a comment on its quality.

Selective topical bibliographies, such as those compiled for research papers and literature reviews, are often found **appended**, or attached, to the end of an article, chapter, or book. The bibliographies found in encyclopedias, handbooks, and yearbooks are also examples of appended bibliographies. Such bibliographies in other publications may be more difficult to find, but the following work, a bibliography of bibliographies, provides a systematic and efficient way of locating many of them.

Bibliographic Index. (1937–). New York: Wilson.

■ This index enables researchers to locate, by topic, bibliographies that have been published in books or journals. Many of these are appended bibliographies that appear at the end of a journal article or book. Only bibliographies that contain 50 or more citations are included. There are cross-references to many communication areas under the broad headings communication, speech, and mass communication. *Bibliographic Index* is published each year in April and August with a bound **cumulation** in December. It is available on-line from November 1984.

Bibliographic Index also contains references to book-length bibliographies. Some of these are similar to appended bibliographies in that they are **topical** (devoted to one specific topic, such as nonverbal communication), whereas others are **general**. A general bibliography, such as the following one, may be more useful at the beginning of the search process, when you are still choosing and narrowing a topic.

Blum, E., & Wilhoit, F. (1990). *Mass media bibliography: An annotated, selected list of books and journals for reference and research* (3rd ed.). Urbana: University of Illinois Press.

■ This annotated bibliography of 2,100 sources in mass communication serves as a reference tool for locating research materials. The entries identify mass communication sources on such topics as theory, structure, economics, and effects. Annotated entries are arranged according to media: general (two or more media); broadcast (radio and television); print (newspapers, books, and periodicals); film; and advertising and public relations. The source includes lists of mass-communication bibliographies, annuals, journals, and indexes. There are author/title and subject indexes that refer users to entry numbers.

Many valuable topical and general book-length bibliographies are published for communication researchers. A listing of several additional bibliographies, which represent a variety of subject areas and have been published within the past 15 or so years, is at the end of this chapter.

The bibliographies described thus far are known as **retrospective bibliographies**. This means they appear at a particular point in time and are not updated. The type of bibliography that appears in *The Handbook of Social Psychology*, for example, includes sources (such as books, research articles, and government documents) that have appeared since the topic was first investigated. Retrospective bibliographies, then, lend historical perspective to the research area.

In contrast, **current bibliographies** are published regularly—monthly, **semiannually**, or yearly. Each issue lists books and sometimes articles that have been published since the previous issue. Current bibliographies lead you to contemporary investigations and writings.

Not many current bibliographies are published specifically for communication, although bibliographies appended to **review articles** on regularly recurring topics in the annual editions of *Communication Yearbook* sometimes fulfill this function. One useful current annotated bibliography, which is published monthly, is the following:

Sterling, C. H. (Ed.). (1969–). *Communication Booknotes*. Annandale, Va: Author.

■ This **bimonthly**, annotated bibliography of new publications in mass communication describes in each issue about 50 books, periodicals, reports, government documents, and reference sources from the

United States and abroad. Coverage includes communications technology, electronic media, general communication, history, international communication, journalism, law and policy, mass communication, motion pictures, popular culture, and telecommunications. Contributors periodically annotate communication sources of additional countries. The July/August issue provides an annual survey of U.S. government documents. The publication was titled *Mass Media Booknotes* from 1969 to 1981.

Communication researchers working in some subject areas may find it useful to check the current bibliographies of related disciplines. A listing of some of these is provided at the end of this chapter.

Locating satisfactory bibliographies on your topic may sometimes be difficult. An option available in this case is to seek out the most comprehensive of bibliographies—those of national libraries. The Library of Congress attempts to collect copies of all significant publications available in the United States. It formerly published these records in the *Subject Catalog: A Cumulative List of Works Represented by Library of Congress Printed Cards* (1974–1982).

Since 1982, the Library of Congress has continued to contribute its cataloging records to a *union catalog* (one that includes the holdings of more than a single library) known as the *National Union Catalog*. This catalog, published on microfiche by the Library of Congress as *N.U.C. US Books* since 1983, is available in many academic libraries. However, because it is now possible to search these records through such services as OCLC, the trend is for libraries to discontinue their subscriptions to the microfiche publication and to rely on computerized services for access to this national bibliography.

Ask at your library's reference desk to find out what type of subject access the library provides to this and other large union catalogs. Keep in mind, though, when using comprehensive bibliographies, that works are included, not because they are necessarily authoritative or important, but because they exist. Before going to some trouble (using interlibrary loan, for example) to obtain a copy of a book you have identified through this catalog, it would be wise to determine its relative worth (see Chapter 2).

Guides to the Literature

One particularly useful type of bibliography is called a guide. **Guides to the literature** are broad bibliographies made up primarily of reference works and periodicals available in a given subject field or fields. Many guides also list and describe organizations that can lead you to sources of information outside libraries. Guides describe the basic organization of the field's literature and the processes and techniques of literature searches peculiar to that field. Thus, they can orient you to the literature of fields with which you are not familiar.

As you become acquainted with different types of reference works and their uses, you will probably realize at some point in a literature search that you need a particular type of reference work—a dictionary of statistics or an annual review of psychology, for example. A guide to the literature can often help you identify such a source. A general guide that covers the literature of many subject fields is the following:

Balay, R., & Sheehy, E. P. (1992). *Guide to reference books, tenth edition.* Chicago: American Library Association.

■ You can use this work and its supplements to locate a listing and evaluation of reference works arranged under these broad headings: general reference works, the humanities, social science, history and area studies, and pure and applied sciences. Within each of these groups, the listings are broken down by narrower subject fields and by type of publication (such as bibliography or dictionary). An index provides access by title, author, and subject.

The following guide, although dated, is a good introduction to the literature of the social sciences:

Webb, W. H. (1986). *Sources of information in the social sciences: A guide to the literature* (3rd ed.). Chicago: American Library Association.

■ An introductory chapter covers general sources, and specific chapters pertain to the social science disciplines. Disciplines include history, geography, economics, business administration, sociology, anthropology, psychology, education, and political science. Each chapter is written by a subject specialist and is divided into two sections. The first section surveys and lists the basic **monographs** in the discipline. The second section contains an annotated bibliography of reference works. The numbers in the author/title/subject index refer to entry numbers rather than to page numbers.

Other guides deal with a specific field of study. For example, Cates's (1990) *Journalism: A Guide to the Reference Literature* identifies sources and writing methods helpful for those conducting research in journalism. Kaid and Wadsworth's (1985) *Political Campaign Communication* contains a guide to information about political communication. These works and a few of the guides available for disciplines related to communication are listed at the end of this chapter. In addition, the following work has several uses, one of which is to serve as a guide to research in mass communication:

Bracken, J. K., & Sterling, C. H. (1995). *Telecommunications research resources: An annotated guide.* Hillsdale, NJ: Erlbaum.

■ This work presents selected publications and research sources in telecommunications. Its eight chapters describe bibliographic and selected secondary resources in: general reference areas, including indexes and abstracts; history, including archives and libraries; technology, including patents and technical standards; industry and economics, including statistical sources and annual reports; applications/impact, including research entities and educational programs; domestic policy, including government sources and policy centers; international arenas, including the International Telecommunications Union and other United Nations agencies; and periodicals, including technology, industry, and policy. Its two appendixes describe how to find library materials and to read Library of Congress subject headings in telecommunication.

Legal Research

Legal research poses some interesting complexities to communication students. Students of debate, mass-communication policy and regulation, and freedom of speech, among others, often need to consult the legal literature in their research endeavors. Just as the field of communication is constantly changing, so are the everyday legal decisions that affect the operations of communication organizations, the expression of ideas in a society, and the formulation of public policy.

Like the literature of other fields, the legal literature consists of primary sources, secondary sources, and finding tools. **Primary**

sources include legislative statutes, court decisions, executive orders, administrative agency decisions and rules, and treaties. These are the enforceable rules of a society. **Secondary sources** include legal textbooks, dictionaries, and encyclopedias (some of which were listed at the end of Chapter 5), as well as commentaries, periodicals, restatements, and document sourcebooks. Their purpose is largely to describe and explain the law. **Finding tools** ease access to the many legal statutes and court decisions. Bibliographies, citators (citation indexes for legal cases), computerized search services such as LEXIS, indexes, law digests, loose-leaf services (see Chapter 8), and legal research guides provide the means of locating primary sources.

Although further explanation of legal research is beyond our scope, there are several legal research guides you can consult. These guides focus on primary, secondary, and finding-tool sources. They describe the legal process and the procedure of legal research, as well as standard legal and citation forms. They often include identification of legal abbreviations and a glossary of legal terms. They serve not only as guides to the literature but also as manuals for conducting legal research. Several of these guides are listed at the end of this chapter. One especially useful legal research guide is the following:

Jacobstein, J. M., Mersky, R. M., & Dunn, D. J. (1994). *Fundamentals of legal research* (6th ed.). Westbury, NY: Foundation Press.

■ The guide accomplishes three purposes. First, it explains the legal process and research procedures. Second, it details primary sources (such as federal court decisions, federal legislation, and administrative law), secondary sources (such as legal periodicals and legal encyclopedias), and finding tools (such as court report digests, annotated law reports, loose-leaf services, and citators). Third, it describes international law, English legal research, federal tax research, and computers in legal research.

Among the appendixes are a glossary of legal abbreviations, state guides to legal research, state reports, and coverage of the national reporter system. There is a subject/source index.

Indexes

You will often find references to scholarly journal articles in the bibliographies you examine. **Periodical indexes** provide a way of finding additional articles. The articles listed are usually arranged by subject heading, sometimes also by author, and occasionally by journal. The information in these listings typically includes the author, title, periodical, volume, date of publication, and page numbers. Most of you are probably familiar with the *Readers' Guide to Periodical Literature*, which lists, by subject, articles found in general-interest, popular magazines (such as *Time* and *Newsweek*). This may be a useful index for investigating current-events topics. Many libraries now make *Readers' Guide* or another comparable index available in a computerized format. Comparable indexes include *General Periodicals Index* and *General Periodicals Ondisc*.

Specialized Indexes

Specialized indexes published in various academic fields are often more useful for research papers and literature reviews because they list the articles published in the scholarly journals read by professionals in that field. Unfortunately, no one index covers all communication and communication-related journals. *ComIndex*, as an electronic bibliographic database (see Chapter 3), comes the closest to indexing the predominant communication journals. Because the communication field is so broad, communication journals are referenced in a variety of indexes. For example, *Journal of Communication* and *Communication Monographs* are referenced in *Education Index*, whereas the *Journal of Broadcasting & Electronic Media* and *Communication Research* are cited in *Humanities Index*.

Education Index. (1929–). New York: Wilson.

■ This is an author/subject index to some 350 English-language periodicals, yearbooks, and monographs relevant to those in the field of education. It includes some government publications. Among the communication topics covered are semantics, mass media, and intercultural communication. An index of book reviews by author has been included since 1970 and appears at the end of each volume. *Education Index* is published monthly, except August, with an annual bound cumulation. It is available on-line and in CD-ROM format from September 1983.

Humanities Index. (1974–). New York: Wilson.
   Social Sciences Index. (1974–). New York: Wilson.

■ These **quarterly** indexes, with annual cumulations, provide subject/author indexing of about 300 periodicals each, including several in communication. Communication students find them most useful for their broad interdisciplinary coverage. They use Library of Congress subject headings with some additions and modifications. A separate section at the end of each volume indexes book reviews.

The indexes have been published separately only since 1974, when their antecedent, *Social Sciences and Humanities Index*, was divided. They are available on-line and in CD-ROM format from 1984.

The *Index to Journals in Communication Studies through 1990* indexes most of the major journals in communication. (A discussion of major communication journals, including identification of where they are indexed, is in Chapter 7.)

Matlon, R. J. (Ed.). (1992). *Index to journals in communication studies through 1990* (2 vols.). Annandale, VA: Speech Communication Association.

■ These volumes provide a table of contents for each of 19 communication journals from their first year of publication through 1990. Volume 1 contains references to the articles in *Association for Communication Administration Bulletin, Communication Education, Communication Monographs, Communication Quarterly, Communication Research, Communication Studies, Critical Studies in Mass Communication, Human Communication Research, Journal of Applied Communication Research, Journal of Broadcasting & Electronic Media, Journal of Communication, Journal of the American Forensic Association, Journalism Quarterly, Philosophy and Rhetoric, Quarterly Journal of Speech, Southern Speech Communication Journal, Text and Performance Quarterly, Western Journal of Speech Communication,* and *Women's Studies in Communication.* Volume 2 contains author, subject-matter, and keyword indexes that provide direct access to citations in Volume 1. A new edition is expected in late 1996, and a CD-ROM version is also being planned.

Several more specialized indexes are available. You may find it useful to consult indexes from other fields that provide information on communication-related topics. *Business Periodicals Index*, for example, provides references to many articles in the area of organizational communication, as does *ABI/Inform*, a CD-ROM index found in many libraries. *Index to Legal Periodicals* indexes the major legal journals in this country and a few foreign countries by author and subject. These indexes are also listed at the end of this chapter. We identify several indexes to government publications in Chapter 8.

Locating Book Reviews

Besides listing articles, many periodical indexes perform another service by referencing book reviews. As already noted, *Education Index*, *Social Sciences Index*, and *Humanities Index* have a special section devoted to book reviews. Reviews appearing in the scholarly and professional journals covered by these and similar indexes are useful sources when you need to determine how scholars and other communication professionals have evaluated a particular work. You can find reviews of works of a more general or popular nature by using indexes that consist entirely of listings of book reviews, such as *Book Review Digest* or *Book Review Index*. Several other indexes of this type are listed at the end of the chapter. Not to be overlooked as a good source of general book reviews are such CD-ROM indexes as *Periodical Abstracts Ondisc*. Many university libraries have printed guides to book reviews available at the reference desk.

Citation Indexes

Another valuable but quite different index format is the **citation index**, which has been made possible by computers. In citation indexes, references to selected journals and books are listed by the cited author. Lists are thus created of works that have been cited in journal articles by a particular author. In this way, when you know the name of an article or a book on a specific topic or you know the name of an author who works in a specific area, you can use the citation index to find more recently published and related materials. The usual process is to choose some relevant citations from those already identified in other sources. You then look up these authors in the citation index to see who has cited them. Any important works that are identified in this manner are also looked up or "recycled."

For example, when researching political advertising you will find the following citation, which seems dated, in many bibliographies:

> Sears, D. O., & Freedman, J. L. (1967). Selective exposure to information: A critical review. *Public Opinion Quarterly, 31,* 194–213.

You look at the article and wonder what more recent information on the topic is available. It is likely that more current articles in this area will cite this work, so you consult the citation index under the first author's last name (Sears, D. O). Here you find quite a few specific citations to this work. In the 1990 Citation Index volume of the *Social Sciences Citation Index*, for instance, you find:

KENNAMER JD COMM RES 17 393 90 R

By looking up this author's last name in the Source Index, you can find enough information to create the following APA-style bibliographic citation:

> Kennamer, J. D. (1990). Self-serving biases in perceiving the opinions of others: Implications for the spiral of silence. *Communication Research, 17,* 393–404.

Thus, by using a citation index, you've updated your bibliography and, by consulting this and other recent works, can trace a variety of other pertinent references. The works located in past volumes of the citation index can, themselves, also be traced forward to broaden a search.

Two citation indexes cover most communication literature: *Social Sciences Citation Index* and *Arts and Humanities Citation Index*. Because of their similarity in format and use, we will only describe the first one here:

Social Sciences Citation Index. (1972–). Philadelphia: Institute for Scientific Information.

■ The computer-generated format of this index will require first-time users to consult the explanations found inside the front and back covers of each volume. Each issue consists of three different indexes: Citation, Permuterm Subject (article titles), and Source.

If you've already identified one or more key works on a topic and want to find more recent related works, use the Citation Index. To start, look up the known author's name and check to see which of the works cited matches the publication you are tracking in terms of year of publication, journal title, volume, and page number. Underneath this citation, you will find what current author has cited this work. The information you are given about the citing work includes author, journal title, volume, page, and year of publication. To find the title of the citing work and complete bibliographic information about it, you will need to look up the citing author in the Source Index.

Another approach to the *Social Sciences Citation Index* is through the **Permuterm Subject Index**. This index is completely generated by computer, using the significant words in the titles of articles. Because titles do not necessarily have a direct relationship to the subject of a work, this approach has some obvious hazards and frustrations, but it is, at times, very useful.

The *Social Sciences Citation Index* is issued three times per year and cumulated annually. The computerized version is available on-line from 1972 and in CD-ROM format from 1986.

Media Indexes

Media indexes help you find newspaper materials, specific media sources, and reviews. Newspapers and media such as films and videotapes can provide communication students with useful information for research endeavors. They also often serve as important working tools for communication professionals.

Newspaper Indexes

Daily and weekly newspapers publish up-to-date information on current issues of local, national, and international scope. They also contain opinion columns, editorials, and media reviews that can be useful in the research process. For example, newspaper reports of Supreme Court decisions or regulatory agency actions can have a direct bearing on research about freedom of speech, broadcast programming, advertising, media law and regulation, and the like.

Like periodical indexes, **newspaper indexes** help you identify and find pertinent articles. Newspaper indexes in paper format usually reference only one newspaper. The *New York Times*, which is generally regarded as one of the most comprehensive sources of news on a variety of topics, publishes an index to which most libraries subscribe:

New York Times Index. (1913–). New York: New York Times.

■   This index provides subject access to and brief synopses of news stories, editorials, and other features. Citations include month, date, newspaper section, page number, and sometimes a column number (preceded by a colon). When using the index, you must further check the cross-references following the subject in each entry to gain complete citations.

The *New York Times Index* is issued **semimonthly**, with quarterly and annual cumulations. The "Prior Series" section of the index provides coverage of the period 1851 to 1912.

A few other newspapers also have useful indexes published in print format. The *Wall Street Journal* and the *Christian Science Monitor*, for example, are well known for their coverage of national, international, and business and economic news. Their indexes provide ready access to their feature stories, coverage of news events, and opinion columns.

Computers have greatly improved access to the information contained in newspapers. Most college and university libraries now subscribe to a CD-ROM index that covers a number of major U.S. newspapers. Two popular indexes of this type are *Newspaper Abstracts Ondisc* and the *National Newspaper Index. Newspaper Abstracts Ondisc* indexes and abstracts eight newspapers: *New York Times, Wall Street Journal, Christian Science Monitor, Washington Post, Chicago Tribune, Atlanta Constitution/Journal, Boston Globe,* and *Los Angeles Times.* The *National Newspaper Index* covers the *New York Times, Christian Science Monitor, Wall Street Journal, Washington Post,* and *Los Angeles Times.* Coverage for both sources begins with 1985.

Access to newspapers in 450 U.S. cities is provided by the *Newsbank Electronic Index,* which includes CD-ROM indexing to a collection of 2 million articles in the *NewsBank* microfiche collection. Additional access to newspapers in many smaller communities, from the *Fresno Bee* to the *Tucson Citizen,* is available through remote searching of computerized databases provided by vendors such as DIALOG and Mead Data Central. With so many options available, the situation will vary widely from library to library. Ask the reference staff at your library what access to newspaper indexing the library provides. With more and more newspapers available electronically in a full-text format, the future in this area looks bright for communication researchers.

Retrospectively, newspaper indexing is much more limited. Few of the 1,500 daily newspapers in this country were indexed in past years. *Newspaper Indexes: A Location and Subject Guide for Researchers*, Vols. 1 and 2 (1977–1982), provides a comprehensive but dated list of newspaper indexes. Sometimes newspapers that are not indexed do have extensive library files that you can search on site. Newspapers with smaller circulations, covering city, local, or regional news, can be located by using the *Gale Directory of Publications* (see Chapter 8). Occasionally, public libraries will index their own hometown newspapers, but college and university libraries seldom have time to do this.

If you are interested in investigating "nonestablishment" opinions on topics such as social movements, you might find articles in some newspapers to be important. Some publications with smaller circulations and specialized audiences are indexed in the following:

Alternative Press Index. (1969–). Baltimore: Alternative Press Centre.

■ This index covers most of the alternative and radical publications available in the United States. News of social issues and movements, as well as opinions on issues published in these magazines, journals, and newspapers, is accessible by combined author/subject listings. The index is issued quarterly.

Broadcast Indexes

Some information on other media, such as television, is also found in the collections of most libraries. (We discuss what is found in actual collections or archives in Chapter 8.) The text of productions from CBS News through 1991 is available on microfiche for student use in libraries that subscribe to the *CBS News Index*. Similar services are provided for ABC News and public television. Broadcast indexes are useful for ascertaining perspectives on current events and for conducting content analyses of news programs. The *CBS News Index* provides guidance on where in the microfiche collection the desired transcript can be found. It remains useful for historical retrospective research.

CBS News Index. (1975–1991). Ann Arbor, MI: University Microfilms International.

■ This index catalogs all daily news broadcasts, public affairs broadcasts, and programs (such as *60 Minutes* and *Face the Nation*) produced by CBS News from 1975 to 1991. Subject headings lead to

---

descriptive phrases of the pertinent broadcasts, and locator information is given for the verbatim transcripts found in an accompanying microfiche collection.

Transcript/Video Index, begun in 1991, makes accessible over 60 news and public affairs programs including *CNN News* but excluding NBC programs and *The MacNeil/Lehrer NewsHour*. It is updated quarterly and provides information back to 1968.

Abstracts

Because communication research studies appear in many different books and journals, some of which may not even be owned by a particular library, researchers often rely on publications that summarize articles to help them decide which articles to read thoroughly. These publications, called *abstracts*, are composed of paragraph-length or longer summaries or condensations of scholarly articles published in major journals and books. These summaries provide a more comprehensive overview of the content of the article than the title alone provides. Some abstracts also include summary descriptions of books, chapters, and dissertations.

Abstracts are usually not the starting place for researching communication topics. The subject indexes in abstracts, though, help you locate sources about a particular communication problem or issue. You can often identify research sources, such as journal articles, by looking up the keywords or concepts of a research topic in a periodical index. The listings there include potentially relevant articles. You can then use the author indexes in abstracts to locate summaries of the particular articles. These abbreviated summaries will help you determine the article's relevance to your topic. If the article seems pertinent, you should examine the original article in the library or order it through interlibrary loan.

Abstracts, therefore, provide a valuable service. By supplying condensed versions of articles, they allow you to find relevant sources efficiently. It is important, though, *not* to rely on abstracts at the expense of the original works. The original sources contain essential information about the research problem, procedures, findings, and conclusions. You need to read and review these fully, especially if you are going to list these sources in bibliographies, literature reviews, or research reports.

Since its initial publication in 1978, *Communication Abstracts* has become the most widely used abstracting source in the field. Most of the major communication journals, related periodicals of allied fields, and books are represented in these volumes.

Communication Abstracts. (1978–). Thousand Oaks, CA: Sage.

■ This bimonthly source comprehensively inspects the worldwide literature of communication and abstracts selected communication-related articles from over 200 periodicals, as well as relevant monographs, books, and research reports. *Communication Abstracts* includes paragraph-length summaries of journal articles or books, usually within the last year. More recent articles are not available in abstract form and must be located in the journals.

Each abstract is listed alphabetically under the author's last name. A complete subject guide (referring to abstract numbers employed in the volume) is included in each issue. Among the many subjects covered are advertising, attitudes, broadcasting, broadcast regulation, communication technology, communication theory, consumer behavior, economic issues, group communication, health communication, information processing, intercultural communication, interpersonal communication, law, media effects, national development, news, organizational communication, political communication, public opinion, research methods, speech communication, and telecommunications.

Communication Abstracts is published six times per year, in February, April, June, August, October, and December, with an annual bound cumulation. Cumulative subject and author indexes for each year appear in the December issue.

Because communication is an interdisciplinary field, you should also use abstracts that concentrate on the journals of other disciplines but selectively include several communication journals. Researchers in psychology and sociology often publish communication-related articles, so the following are also essential sources for communication researchers:

Psychological Abstracts. (1927–). Arlington, VA: American Psychological Association.

■ One of the oldest information services in the social and behavioral sciences, *Psychological Abstracts* surveys the world's literature in

Psychology and, selectively, related disciplines including communication. Journals, books, conference papers, dissertations, and other materials are abstracted. To facilitate browsing, monthly issues are divided into 17 broad subject areas, with some additional subdivisions.

As is the case with most **abstracting services**, using *Psychological Abstracts* to research a topic is a three-step process. First, use the American Psychological Association's *Thesaurus of Psychological Index Terms* to determine the correct subject heading or headings for your topic. Second, look up these headings in the Subject Index and, using the keywords offered, choose relevant articles and note their abstract numbers. Third, look up these abstract numbers in the Abstracts section to find bibliographic information and a summary, or abstract, of the publications.

The subject headings used to index *Psychological Abstracts* are taken from the *Thesaurus of Psychological Index Terms*, which is usually shelved next to the *Abstracts*. Consult this list before you begin a search. The *Thesaurus* includes two sections: the Relationship section and the Rotated Alphabetical Terms section, which arranges all significant words in the subject headings in alphabetical order. Thus, if you look up the word *communication* in this section, you will find all subject headings in which *communication* appears anywhere in the heading. After choosing relevant terms, turn to the Relationship section to find related (R), broader (B), and narrower (N) terms that might also be of interest.

Psychological Abstracts is published monthly. Cumulative subject and author indexes are issued yearly. It is available on-line, as *PsycINFO*, from 1967 and in CD-ROM format, as *PsycLIT*, from 1974.

Sociological Abstracts. (1952–). San Diego: Sociological Abstracts.

■ This interdisciplinary source indexes and abstracts more than 9,000 books and journal articles a year. Abstracts are arranged alphabetically by author within broad areas, such as mass phenomena. Each entry is numbered and provides basic bibliographic information and a brief summary of the contents.

This abstracting service has undergone significant changes over the years. Beginning in 1979, each issue contains in-depth subject, author, and source publication indexes. In 1986 the indexing terms used underwent a complete revision and a *Thesaurus of Sociological Indexing Terms*, similar to the *Thesaurus of Psychological Index Terms*, was first published. One of the useful features of the *Thesaurus* is the History Notes (HN), which link new headings with the indexing terms used before 1986. Scope Notes (SN) define the terms and tell how

Sociological Abstracts uses them.

To use *Sociological Abstracts*, follow the three-step process outlined for *Psychological Abstracts*. *Sociological Abstracts* is published five times per year. It is available on-line from 1963 and in CD-ROM format, as *Sociofile*, from 1974.

Despite the broad coverage of these sources, you may still miss some important references if you rely exclusively on these three abstracting services. Two other tools, often used by communication researchers interested in education and related areas, are *Current Index to Journals in Education* (*CIJE*) and *Resources in Education* (*RIE*). These sources are produced with the aid of the Educational Resources Information Center (ERIC), a national system of clearinghouses, funded by the U.S. Office of Education.

Current Index to Journals in Education. (1969–). Phoenix: Oryx Press.

■ *CIJE* indexes 780 periodicals, compared to *Education Index*'s 350. Research journals such as *Human Communication Research* and *Communication Research* are more likely to be covered by *CIJE* than by *Education Index*, although *CIJE*'s coverage of a particular journal is often selective rather than cover to cover. As with other abstracting services, using *CIJE* involves several steps:

First, select relevant subject headings from the *Thesaurus of ERIC Descriptors*; next, select promising article titles (and their corresponding EJ accession numbers) from the subject index; and, finally, locate a description of the article in the main entry section. *CIJE* supplies complete bibliographic information, a brief two-sentence annotation, and a list of other descriptors assigned to each article.

CIJE appears monthly and is cumulated every 6 months. It is available on-line as part of *ERIC* from 1969 and on CD-ROM, as *ERIC*, from 1983.

Resources in Education. (1966–). Washington, DC: U.S. Government Printing Office.

■ *RIE* indexes and abstracts documents that are generally locally published and available only through the ERIC system. These documents include research and project reports, bibliographies, curriculum materials, conference papers, and a variety of other materials. As with *CIJE*, using *RIE* involves several steps, moving from the *Thesaurus of ERIC Descriptors* to the subject index and finally to the document resumes.

> *RIE* is published monthly with annual cumulative indexes. It is available on-line as part of *ERIC* from 1966 and on CD-ROM, as *ERIC*, from 1983.

There are, in addition, abstracts on more specific topics. *Journalism & Mass Communication Abstracts* (1963–) is an example of a more narrowly focused abstracting service. It is a collection of abstracts of dissertations produced in departments of journalism or mass communication. You may find this source helpful when researching mass-communication topics. *Organizational Communication: Abstracts, Analysis, and Overview* (1976–1985) was another specialized publication that included abstracts of the annual literature pertinent to that subfield of communication through the mid-1980s. Other specialized abstracts are noted in the list that follows.

Selected Sources

Bibliographies

Aimiller, K., Lohr, P., & Meyer, M. (1989). *Television and young people: A bibliography of international literature, 1969–1989*. Munich: Saur.

Austin, B. A. (1983). *The film audience: An international bibliography of research*. Metuchen, NJ: Scarecrow Press.

Blum, E., & Wilhoit, F. (1990). *Mass media bibliography: An annotated, selected list of books and journals for reference and research* (3rd ed.). Urbana: University of Illinois Press.

Carothers, D.F. (1991). *Radio broadcasting from 1920 to 1990: An annotated bibliography*. New York: Garland.

Catalog of Current Law Titles. (1989–). Ann Arbor, MI: Ward.

Cooper, T. W. (1988). *Television & ethics: A bibliography*. Boston: Hall.

Flannery, G. V. (1989). *Mass media: Marconi to MTV: A select bibliography of New York Times Sunday Magazine articles on communication 1900–1988*. Lanham, MD: University Press of America.

Gillmor, D. M. (1990). *Mass media law: A selected bibliography* (2nd ed.). Minneapolis: University of Minnesota.

Gray, J. (1990). *Blacks in film and television: A Pan-African bibliography of films, filmmakers, and performers*. New York: Greenwood Press.

Hill, G. H., & Hill, S. S. (1985). *Blacks on television: A selectively annotated bibliography*. Metuchen, NJ: Scarecrow Press.

Horak, J. (Ed.). (1987). *Bibliography of film bibliographies*. New York: Saur.

Kaid, L. L., Sanders, K. R., & Hirsch, R. O. (1974). *Political campaign communication: A bibliography and guide to the literature*. Metuchen, NJ: Scarecrow Press.

Kaid, L. L., & Wadsworth, A. J. (1985). *Political campaign communication: A bibliography and guide to the literature, 1973–1982*. Metuchen, NJ: Scarecrow Press.

Langham, J., & Chrichley, J. (Comps.). (1990). *Radio research: An annotated bibliography 1975–1988* (2nd ed.). Brookfield, VT: Gower.

Lent, J. A. (Comp.). (1991). *Women and mass communications: An international annotated bibliography*. Westport, CT: Greenwood Press.

McCoy, R. E. (1968). *Freedom of the press: An annotated bibliography*. Carbondale: Southern Illinois University Press.

McCoy, R. E. (1979). *Freedom of the press, a bibliocyclopedia: Ten-year supplement, 1967–1977*. Carbondale: Southern Illinois University Press.

McCoy, R. E. (1993). *Freedom of the press: An annotated bibliography. Second supplement, 1978–1992*. Carbondale: Southern Illinois University Press.

N.U.C. US Books. (1983–). Washington, DC: Library of Congress.

Performing arts books: 1876–1981. (1981). New York: Bowker.

Pringle, P. K., & Clinton, H. H. (1989). *Radio and television: A selected, annotated bibliography, supplement two: 1982–1986*. Metuchen, NJ: Scarecrow Press.

Signorielli, N. (Ed.). (1985). *Role portrayal and stereotyping on television: An annotated bibliography of studies relating to women, minorities, aging, sexual behavior, health, and handicaps*. Westport, CT: Greenwood Press.

Sloan, W. D. (Comp.). (1989). *American journalism history: An annotated bibliography*. New York: Greenwood Press.

Sterling, C. H. (Ed.). (1969–). *Communication Booknotes*. Annandale, VA: Author.

Sterling, C. H. (1994). *Telecommunications, electronic media, and global communications: A survey bibliography*. Washington, DC: George Washington University.

Subject Catalog: A Cumulative List of Works Represented by Library of Congress Printed Cards. (1950–1982). Washington, DC: U.S. Library of Congress.

Guides to the Literature

Aby, S. H. (1987). *Sociology: A guide to reference and information sources.* Littleton, CO: Libraries Unlimited.

Balay, R., & Sheehy, E. P. (1992). *Guide to reference books, tenth edition.* Chicago: American Library Association.

Block, E. S., & Bracken, J. K. (1991). *Communication and mass media: A guide to the reference literature.* Littleton, CO: Libraries Unlimited.

Bracken, J. K., & Sterling, C. H. (1995). *Telecommunications research resources: An annotated guide.* Hillsdale, NJ: Erlbaum.

Buttlar, L. (1989). *Education: A guide to reference and information sources.* Englewood, CO: Libraries Unlimited.

Cassata, M., & Skill, T. (1985). *Television: A guide to the literature.* Phoenix: Oryx Press.

Caswell, L. S. (1989). *Guide to sources in American journalism history.* New York: Greenwood Press.

Cates, J. A. (1990). *Journalism: A guide to the reference literature.* Littleton, CO: Libraries Unlimited.

Cohen, M. L., Berring, R. C., & Olson, K. C. (1989). *How to find the law* (9th ed.). St. Paul: West.

Daniells, L. M. (1985). *Business information sources* (2nd ed.). Berkeley: University of California Press.

Day, A., & Harvey, J. (Eds.) (1994). *Walford's guide to reference material, Volume 2: Social and historical sciences, philosophy, and religion* (6th ed.). Lanham, MD: Unipub.

Dunn, G. W., & Cooper, D. W. (1981). A guide to mass communication sources. *Journalism Monographs, 74.*

Edgerton, G. R. (Ed.). (1988). *Film and the arts in symbiosis: A resource guide.* New York: Greenwood Press.

Fisher, K. N. (1986). *On the screen: A film, television, and video research guide.* Littleton, CO: Libraries Unlimited.

Garay, R. (1988). *Cable television: A reference guide to information.* New York: Greenwood Press.

Goehlert, R., & Martin, F. S. (1989). *Congress and law-making: Researching the legislative process* (2nd ed.). Santa Barbara, CA: ABC-Clio.

Greenfield, T. A. (1989). *Radio: A reference guide.* Westport, CT: Greenwood Press.

Herron, N. L., & Faries, C. (1989). *The social sciences: A cross-disciplinary guide to selected sources.* Littleton, CO: Libraries Unlimited.

Hill, S. M. (Ed.). (1989). *Broadcasting bibliography: A guide to the literature of radio & television* (3rd ed.). Washington, DC: National Association of Broadcasters.

Holler, F. L. (1986). *Information sources of political science* (4th ed.). Santa Barbara, CA: ABC-Clio.

Jacobstein, J. M., Mersky, R. M., & Dunn, D. J. (1994). *Fundamentals of legal research* (6th ed.). Westbury, NY: Foundation Press.

National Association of Broadcasters. (1994). *Legal guide to broadcast law and regulation.* Washington, DC: Author.

Passarelli, A. B. (1989). *Public relations in business, government, and society: A bibliographic guide.* Littleton, CO: Libraries Unlimited.

Rose, B. G. (Ed.). (1985). *TV genres: A handbook and reference guide.* Westport, CT: Greenwood Press.

Rose, B. G. (1986). *Television and the performing arts: A handbook and reference guide to American cultural programming.* New York: Greenwood Press.

Schwarzlose, R. A. (1987). *Newspapers: A reference guide.* New York: Greenwood Press.

Signorielli, N. (1991). *A sourcebook on children and television.* New York: Greenwood Press.

Slavens, T. P. (1985). *The literary adviser: Selected reference sources in literature, speech, language, theater, and film.* Phoenix: Oryx Press.

Slide, A. (Ed.). (1985). *International film, radio, and television journals.* Westport, CT: Greenwood Press.

Smith, M. J. (1984). *U.S. television network news: A guide to sources in English.* Jefferson, NC: McFarland.

Strauss, D. W. (1988). *Handbook of business information: A guide for librarians, students, and researchers.* Littleton, CO: Libraries Unlimited.

Ward, J., & Hansen, K. A. (1993). *Search strategies in mass communication* (2nd ed.). White Plains, NY: Longman.

Webb, W. H. (1986). *Sources of information in the social sciences: A guide to the literature* (3rd ed.). Chicago: American Library Association.

York, H. E. (1990). *Political science: A guide to reference and information sources.* Littleton, CO: Libraries Unlimited.

Indexes: Specialized and Citation

Arts and Humanities Citation Index. (1976–). Philadelphia: Institute for Scientific Information. (Available on-line from 1980)

Bibliographic Index. (1938–). New York: Wilson. (Available on-line from 1984)

Book Review Digest. (1905–). New York: Wilson. (Available on-line from 1983)

Book Review Index. (1965–). Detroit: Gale Research.

British Humanities Index. (1962–). London: Library Association Quarterly.

Business Index. (1979–). Menlo Park, CA: Information Access. (Available on CD-ROM)

Business Periodicals Index. (1958–). New York: Wilson. (Available on-line and on CD-ROM from 1982)

ComIndex [Computer disk]. (1992-). Rochester, NY: Communication Institute for Online Scholarship.

Current Law Index. (1980–). Menlo Park, CA: Information Access.

Education Index. (1929–). New York: Wilson. (Available on-line and on CD-ROM from 1983)

Film Literature Index. (1973–). Albany: State University of New York.

Humanities Index. (1974–). New York: Wilson. (Available on-line and on CD-ROM from 1984)

Index to Journals in Mass Communication. (1988–). Riverside, CA: Carpelan. (Available on computer disk)

Index to Legal Periodicals and Books. (1908–). New York: Wilson. (Available on-line and on CD-ROM from 1981)

Journalism Quarterly, cumulative index to volumes 1–40, 1924–1963. (1964). Columbia, SC: Association for Education in Journalism.

Journalism Quarterly, cumulative index to volumes 41–50, 1964–1973. (1974). Columbia, SC: Association for Education in Journalism.

Journalism Quarterly, cumulative index to volumes 51–60, 1974–1983. (1984). Columbia, SC: Association for Education in Journalism and Mass Communication.

Journal of Broadcasting: Author and topic index to volume 1 through 25 (Winter 1956/57 through Fall 1981). (1982). Washington, DC: Broadcast Education Association.

Legal Resource Index. (1980–). Menlo Park, CA: Information Access. (Available on-line through *Newsearch*)

Matlon, R. J. (Ed.). (1992). *Index to journals in communication studies through 1990* (2 vols). Annandale, VA: Speech Communication Association.

Philosopher's Index. (1967–). Bowling Green, OH: Bowling Green State University. (Available on-line and on CD-ROM)

Public Affairs Information Service. (1915–). *Bulletin.* New York: Author. (Available on-line as *PAIS INTERNATIONAL* from 1972 and on CD-ROM from 1976)

Readers' Guide to Periodical Literature. (1901–). New York: Wilson. (Available on-line from January 1983)

Social Sciences Citation Index. (1972–). Philadelphia: Institute for Scientific Information. (Available on-line as *Social SciSearch* and on CD-ROM from 1981)

Social Sciences Index. (1974–). New York: Wilson. (Available on-line and on CD-ROM from 1983)

Speech Index. (1935–). Metuchen, NJ: Scarecrow Press.

Topicator: Classified Article Guide to the Advertising/Communications/ Marketing/Periodical Press. (1965–). Golden, CO: Topicator.

_____

_____

_____

_____

_____

_____

_____

Media Indexes

Alternative Press Index. (1969–). Baltimore: Alternative Press Centre.

CBS News Index. (1975–1991). Ann Arbor, MI: University Microfilms International.

Hanson, P. K., & Hanson, S. L. (Eds.). (1986). *Film review index, volume 1: 1882–1949.* Phoenix: Oryx Press.

Hanson, P. K., & Hanson, S. L. (Eds.). (1987). *Film review index, volume 2: 1950–1985.* Phoenix: Oryx Press.

Magazine Index. (1977–). Belmont, CA: Information Access. (Available on-line through *Newsearch*)

Milner, A. C. (Ed.). (1977–1982). *Newspaper indexes: A location and subject guide for researchers* (3 vols.). Metuchen, NJ: Scarecrow Press.

National Newspaper Index. (1979–). Menlo Park, CA: Information Access. (Available on-line through *Newsearch* and on CD-ROM from 1979)

Newsbank Electronic Information System [CD-ROM]. (1990–). New Canaan, CT: NewsBank.

Newspaper Abstracts Ondisc [CD-ROM]. (1985–). Louisville, KY: UMI/Data Courier.

New York Times Index. (1851–). New York: New York Times.

NICEM Indexes. (1967–). Los Angeles: University of Southern California, National Information Center for Educational Media. (Available on-line as *A-V Online* from 1969 and on CD-ROM for current information only)

Public Television Transcripts. (1973–). Woodbridge, CT: Research Publications.

Riley, S., & Selnow, G. (Comp.) (1989). *Index to city and regional magazines of the United States.* Westport, CT: Greenwood Press.

Subject Index of the Christian Science Monitor. (1960–). Boston: Christian Science Monitor.

Television Program Index. (1980–). New York: Television Index.

Transcript/Video Index: A Comprehensive Guide to Television News and Public Affairs Programming. (1991–). New York: Journal Graphics.

Wall Street Journal Index. (1957–). New York: Dow Jones.

Abstracts

Child Development Abstracts and Bibliography. (1928–). Chicago: University of Chicago Press.

Communication Abstracts. (1978–). Thousand Oaks, CA: Sage.

Current Index to Journals in Education. (1969–). Phoenix: Oryx Press. (Available on-line and on CD-ROM as *ERIC* from 1983)

Dissertation Abstracts International. (1938–). Ann Arbor, MI: University Microfilms International. (Available on-line and on CD-ROM, with dissertations from 1861)

Journalism & Mass Communication Abstracts: M.A., M.S., Ph.D. Theses in Journalism and Mass Communication. (1963–). Columbia, SC: Association for Education in Journalism and Mass Communication.

Linguistics and Language Behavior Abstracts. (1967–). La Jolla, CA: Sociological Abstracts. (Available on-line from 1973)

Organizational Communication: Abstracts, Analysis, and Overview. (1976–1985). Beverly Hills, CA: Sage.

Personnel Management Abstracts. (1955–). Ann Arbor: University of Michigan, Graduate School of Business.

Psychological Abstracts. (1927–). Arlington, VA: American Psychological Association. (Available on-line as *PsycINFO* from 1967 and on CD-ROM as *PsycLIT* from 1974)

Public Administration Abstracts. (1974–). Thousand Oaks, CA: Sage.

Resources in Education. (1966–). Washington, DC: U.S. Government Printing Office. (Available on-line and on CD-ROM as *ERIC* from 1983)

Sociological Abstracts. (1952–). San Diego: Sociological Abstracts. (Available on-line from 1963 and on CD-ROM as *Sociofile* from 1974)

Women Studies Abstracts. (1972–). Rush, NY: Rush.

Work Related Abstracts. (1950–). Warren, MI: Harmonie Park Press. (Formerly titled *Labor/Personnel Index*, 1950–1958, and *Employment Relations Abstracts*, 1959–1972)

_____

_____

_____

_____

_____

_____

_____

_____

_____

Exercises

1. You are not having much luck with your literature search and notice that the few articles you have managed to find on your topic have appeared in journals in allied disciplines, mostly sociology. You turn to a guide to the literature of the social sciences, *Sources of Information in the Social Sciences*, to identify sources in that discipline that may help you in your search. Use the subject index to:

   a. Find the entry number of the first literature guide listed under this discipline.

   b. Give the title of this guide.

2. By using the bibliographies of subject encyclopedias and other standard texts, you have found several references to a 1972 article by M. E. McCombs and D. Shaw published in *Public Opinion Quarterly*. It appears to be a key piece of research on your topic. Unfortunately, this study is several years old. To identify research done at a later time that you hope will update it, you turn to the *Social Sciences Citation Index*. You find what you are looking for in the 1993 volume of the Citation Index.

   a. Who is the author of the last article listed that cites your key article?

   b. In what journal and year did this appear?

   c. What is the title of this article? (You will have to use a different volume to determine this.)

3. You are doing research on interpersonal communication. Subject bibliographies have been useful, but you wish to find other sources for your literature search. To find summaries of research on your topic, you are now using *Communication Abstracts*. Locate the heading for your topic in the Cumulative Subject Index of the 1994 volume.

   a. What is the third entry number listed?

   b. Locate the abstract for this item and supply the complete citation in APA format (see Appendix A).

4. When doing research for a term paper in an intercultural communication class, you have been fortunate to find plenty of background information on your topic, *multicultural training*, but nothing about research done in this area since 1980. Because you feel the topic of interviewing is likely to be of interest to educators, you believe *CIJE* would be a good finding tool.

   a. Turning first to the *Thesaurus of ERIC Descriptors*, what descriptor do you find used for your topic? In other words, to what descriptor are you referred? (Note that the *Thesaurus* is alphabetized letter-by-letter, rather than word-by-word.)

   b. Locate the entry in the *Thesaurus* for this descriptor. In what year did this term first enter the ERIC vocabulary?

   c. Locate the first entry listed under the descriptor for your topic in the subject index of the July–December 1993 Semiannual Cumulation. What is the EJ accession number of this item?

   d. Locate the entry for this term in the Main Entry section. Who is the first author?

5. Complete your search strategy sheet by adding sources from this chapter that will help lead you to primary sources. Have your instructor check your list before you begin examining each source for your topic.

6. Examine issues of *Communication Abstracts* in class and read some of the abstracts. Is your topic area a key term? If not, what key terms lead you to articles in this area?

7. List the steps necessary for searching Matlon's *Index to Journals in Communication Studies through 1990*. Try locating sources for your topic.

Chapter 7

Communication Periodicals

Previous chapters have identified important books for researching communication topics and suggested how a book might be judged a standard or viable work. We've also described the tools used to identify periodical articles. In this chapter, we focus on the periodicals containing these original research reports, articles on communication industry practices, and other original information.

We first discuss the major **scholarly journals** in the communication field, and then identify the places where the journals are indexed and abstracted. Any research study, literature review, or prospectus in communication typically references a number of the articles in these journals.

Articles found in professional and trade magazines are less "scholarly" in nature in that they are usually not original research studies. These periodicals contain data on industry trends along with industry news, opinion, and thought essays. They allow industry professionals to keep abreast of developments in their field. They contain useful information for communication students. For example, we could turn to them to find out about organizational management-training programs for dealing with the media.

Periodicals are publications with distinctive titles that are published on a regular basis. Communication periodicals are useful when researching any communication topic. Examine these sources during the research process and consider including them in research paper assignments. Be aware of their potential value in the future. In many careers, knowledge of these sources provides a means of networking and gives professionals a deeper understanding of the issues and research in the field.

Scholarly Journals

Scholarly journals are the major vehicles for reporting current studies conducted by academic and professional researchers. These journals are usually edited and published by a learned society, a professional association, an academic institution, or a commercial publishing firm. The **articles** are written by specialists and usually are critically evaluated by other scholars before being accepted for publication. They often represent well-designed, important, and current research efforts. A scholarly journal article may examine a topic that has not yet been studied and may never be treated in a book-length publication, or it may contain new information about a subject that has been researched and reported in the past.

Although editorial practices differ, scholarly journals primarily publish unsolicited reports of research endeavors. This means that the researcher conducts an investigation and submits the report or manuscript to a journal editor. The editor then sends the manuscript to other communication researchers, who are specialists in a given area, typically for a blind review. Thus, the quality of unsolicited research articles is scrutinized before publication, and reviewers of the work are usually unaware of the author's identity. Articles that withstand this review process are generally rewritten once or twice before publication. Such revised manuscripts are often re-reviewed before a publication decision. Most quality journals have a rather hefty manuscript-rejection rate.

Sometimes scholarly journal editors solicit specific articles or opinion pieces from communication scholars. These pieces may also be reviewed by editorial board members to ensure their quality. Book reviews, notices of other publications, bibliographies, and general news about people in the field and announcements or summaries of scholarly meetings may also appear. But scholarly journals concentrate on publishing original theory and research articles.

As you examine scholarly journal articles, you will note that they are fairly standardized, especially the quantitative research articles. They begin with an introductory section analyzing past research about the conceptual issue or problem. This introduction includes a summary of previous related research, an explanation of gaps or contradictions found in studying the problem, an identification of the significance of the research problem, and the positing of research hypotheses or questions. The second section details the method of the investigation and how the information was observed or collected. It includes a description of the people, objects, or events studied. For survey research or experimental studies, for example, it would contain a summary of sample size, sample selection, and the devices used to measure the variables. Next, the results of the analysis are presented along with other findings. In quantitative research, this section describes the application of appropriate statistical tests to interpret the collected data. Finally, the last section presents a discussion of the meaning or implications of the results, the limitations of the study, and the future research needs in the problem area.

A several-sentence summary or paragraph-length abstract is usually found at the beginning of each article or in the journal's table of contents. These brief abstracts are often the basis of the synopses published in collections such as *Communication Abstracts*. They can be helpful in determining the article's utility for your own research project.

The references cited in footnotes or in the bibliography at the end of each article are usually the most up-to-date sources of material for that particular area of study at that time. Thus, both the content of the article and the references cited are valuable research aids. It is important to emphasize, though, that there are varied periods of delay between the time when the research study is initially conducted, when it is submitted for publication consideration, when it is eventually accepted for publication, and when the journal issue that contains the report is finally published. This lag time is often 2 to 3 years or even longer.

An annotated list of some of the scholarly journals often used by communication students and researchers follows. These journals represent a selection of many major national scholarly journals in the communication field. We include within the annotations references to some of the volumes where the articles contained in these journals are abstracted and indexed. (The key to the abbreviations used is on page 164.)

Communication Education. (1952–). Annandale, VA: Speech Communication Association.

■ This quarterly journal publishes research and pedagogy articles about elementary, secondary, and higher education, primarily in speech communication. It has occasionally included reports that focus on organizational training or mass-communication instruction. Earlier volumes contained sections on innovative instructional practices, ERIC reports on specific communication topics, and reviews of print and nonprint resources for educators. Volumes contain reviews of books and other resources.

Communication Education (formerly *Speech Teacher*) is published in January, April, July, and October, and an annual index appears in the October issue. Articles are abstracted or indexed in CA, CC, CI, CIJE, EI, IJCS, LLBA, MLA, SA, SSCI, and elsewhere.

Communication Monographs. (1934–). Annandale, VA: Speech Communication Association.

■ *Communication Monographs* publishes research reports and new theories about the processes of communication in several contexts. In general, the journal contains quantitative empirical research articles focusing on message, source, and receiver variables in interpersonal, group, organizational, and public communication. It is published quarterly in March, June, September, and December. An annual index appears in the year's final issue. (Volumes 1 through 42 were published under the title *Speech Monographs*.) Articles are abstracted or indexed in AHL, CA, CI, CIJE, EI, HA, IJCS, LLBA, MLA, PA, SA, SSCI, and elsewhere.

Communication Research. (1974–). Thousand Oaks, CA: Sage.

■ This bimonthly journal focuses on models that explain communication processes and outcomes. Published articles report research in mass, international, political, organizational, and interpersonal communication. Some articles integrate interdisciplinary interests in human communication. There also are research and book review essays.

Communication Research is published in February, April, June, August, October, and December. Two of these issues each year are devoted to different themes. A yearly cumulative author index appears in the December issue. Articles are abstracted or indexed in ASCA, CA, CC, CI, CIJE, EAI, ETA, HI, HIF, HRA, IJMC, LLBA, PA, PAA, SA, SPPD, SSCI, and SSI.

Critical Studies in Mass Communication. (1984–). Annandale, VA: Speech Communication Association.

■ *Critical Studies* publishes theoretical and critical essays about the evolution, economics, and organization of mass-communication systems, the form and structure of media content, the relationship between culture and mass communication, models of media processes, and mass-media criticism. There are review and criticism and booknotes sections.

The journal is published quarterly in March, June, September, and December. A yearly cumulative article index appears in the December issue. Articles are abstracted or indexed in CA, CI, CIJE, IJCS, and elsewhere.

Human Communication Research. (1974–). Austin, TX: International Communication Association.

■ *HCR* offers a behavioral science approach to the study of human communication. Articles report original research, offer new methodological approaches, synthesize research literature, and present new theoretical perspectives on human interaction. The journal publishes research in interpersonal, organizational, and mass communication, as well as in methodology, information systems, and persuasion. Early volumes contained state-of-the-art pieces and a colloquy section presenting alternative ways of looking at communication issues.

This quarterly journal is published in the fall, winter, spring, and summer. An annual index appears in the summer issue. Articles are indexed or abstracted in ASCA, CA, CC, CI, CIJE, EAI, HIF, IJCS, LLBA, PA, SA, SPPD, SSCI, and elsewhere.

Journal of Broadcasting & Electronic Media. (1956/1957–). Washington, DC: Broadcast Education Association.

■ This quarterly journal, formerly the *Journal of Broadcasting*, publishes research articles about communication and the electronic media. Subject matter includes audience and media-effects research, communication policy and regulation, new technologies, broadcast history, international communication, media criticism, media content and programming, and economics. It also contains brief reports of research and book reviews.

The journal is published in the winter, spring, summer, and fall, and yearly author and title indexes appear in the fall issue. Articles are abstracted or indexed in AHCI, CA, CC, CI, CIJE, CLI, HI, IJCS, PA, PAIS, SA, SPPD, SSCI, and elsewhere.

Journal of Communication. (1952–). Austin, TX: International Communication Association.

■ This quarterly journal focuses on the interdisciplinary study of communication theory, practice, and policy. Articles concentrate on mass-communication processes and the societal impact of communication. Also included are book reviews and review essays.

The journal returned to being a publication of the International Communication Association in 1992. It is published in winter, spring, summer, and autumn. Title and author indexes appear annually in the autumn issue. Articles are indexed or abstracted in CA, CC, CI, CIJE, EI, FLI, FSA, HA, IJCS, IJMC, LLBA, MLA, PA, PAA, SA, SSCI, T, and elsewhere.

Journalism & Mass Communication Quarterly. (1924–). Columbia, SC: Association for Education in Journalism and Mass Communication.

■ This journal focuses on research in journalism and mass communication. Articles report on the conduct of news, mass-media effects, international communication, historical treatments of issues, and social and legal dimensions of the media. Also included are brief research reports, book reviews, mass-communication bibliographies, and annual convention summaries.

It is published quarterly in the spring, summer, autumn, and winter. Articles are abstracted or indexed in AHL, BRI, CA, CC, CI, HA, IJCS, LLBA, MLA, PA, PAA, PAIS, SA, SSCI, and elsewhere.

Quarterly Journal of Speech. (1915–). Annandale, VA: Speech Communication Association.

■ *QJS* is the oldest journal in speech communication. Articles are generally historical or critical in nature, with an emphasis on rhetorical theory and criticism. The goal of the journal is to broaden awareness and understanding of speech communication from a humanistic viewpoint. Book review and forum sections are included.

The journal is published in February, May, August, and November. (Volumes 1 through 3 were published under the title *Quarterly Journal of Public Speaking*, and Volumes 4 through 13 were titled *Quarterly Journal of Speech Education.*) Articles are abstracted or indexed in AHL, BRI, CI, CIJE, HA, HI, IJCS, MLA, SA, SPPD, and elsewhere.

Several other journals are also frequently consulted by communication researchers. Among these are journals published by different communication associations, such as the *Journal of Applied Communication Research* and *Text and Performance Quarterly* (Speech Communication Association); *Journalism & Mass Communication Educator* and *Journalism & Mass Communication Monographs* (Association for Education in Journalism and Mass Communication); *Communication Theory* (International Communication Association); *Communication Reports* (Western States Communication Association); *Communication Research Reports* (Eastern Communication Association); and *World Communication* (World Communication Association).

Besides the journals of several state associations, four journals are published quarterly by regional communication associations. Selected indexes and abstracts, which cite the articles contained in these regional journals, are abbreviated in parentheses in the citations that follow:

> *Communication Quarterly* (formerly *Today's Speech*). (1953–). Eastern Communication Association. (*CA, CI, CIJE, EI, HI, IJCS, LLBA, SA*)
>
> *Communication Studies* (formerly *Central States Speech Journal*). (1949–). Central States Communication Association. (*CA, CC, CI, CIJE, IJCS, LLBA, PA, SSCI*)
>
> *Southern Communication Journal* (formerly *Southern Speech Communication Journal* and *Southern Speech Journal*). (1935–). Southern States Communication Association. (*CA, CI, CIJE, HA, IJCS, LLBA*)
>
> *Western Journal of Communication* (formerly *Western Journal of Speech Communication* and *Western Speech*). (1937–). Western States Communication Association. (*AHL, CA, CI, CIJE, HA, IJCS, LLBA, PA, SA*)

In addition to these scholarly communication journals, there are several related journals, such as *Public Opinion Quarterly* and the *Journal of Personality and Social Psychology*, that you may find useful. A list of scholarly journals is at the end of this chapter. Consult the library's serials list to determine whether these scholarly journals are available. Descriptions of many of these journals can be found in the following:

> Katz, B., & Katz, L. S. (1986). *Magazines for libraries* (5th ed.). New York: Bowker.

In addition, copies of the tables of contents of scholarly journals are available in the following:

Current Contents: Social and Behavioral Sciences. (1961–). Philadelphia: Institute for Scientific Information.

■ This is a weekly publication of more than 1,300 tables of contents. Each issue has a keyword subject index, author index, address directory, and publishers' addresses. Volumes related to the arts and humanities are also available.

Professional and Trade Magazines

Professional and **trade magazines** are often important sources of information and insight into the communication field. They are used to lend perspective to practical applications of communication theory and research or to detail the issues, events, and trends facing the communication industry. Generally, research reports are not the mainstay of professional and trade magazines, although the results of a study may sometimes be capsulized. These publications emphasize news of events, issues, and innovations in the field.

For example, they publish articles on new audio and video technologies, advertising campaigns, marketing and management strategies, communication training programs in industry, public relations techniques, and in-house organizational publications. In addition, they often present news about people in the industry, upcoming professional events, and employment opportunities.

The following four publications are often consulted by students looking for information related to the professions of advertising, broadcasting, journalism, and public relations.

Advertising Age. (1930–). Chicago: Crain Communications.

■ This weekly magazine provides an extended review of news related to advertising and marketing. It includes summaries of national and international advertising news; marketing and media technology reports; editorials and commentaries; announcements about advertising professionals and businesses; analyses of marketing issues; data about products, market shares, companies, and ads in consumer magazines; summaries of advertising agency and market research activities; letters to the editor; classified advertising; and a calendar of events.

Broadcasting & Cable. (1931–). New York: Cahners.

■ This weekly trade publication offers broadcast industry news and special in-depth reports on major issues and developments in radio, television, and cable. It covers broadcast news, programming, radio, government actions, regulation, technology, and business. Regular departments include brief broadcast news summaries, a calendar of industry-related meetings and events, commentaries, industry developments, station license approvals and transfers, classified advertising, news about broadcast professionals, and a profile of an industry practitioner.

Columbia Journalism Review. (1962–). New York: Columbia University, Graduate School of Journalism.

■ This bimonthly magazine critically assesses the performance of the press. Articles focus on news professionals, journalistic practices, journalism education, press treatment of government and contemporary issues, and the operation of news organizations. Current issues and events in journalism are chronicled. It also includes editorials, comments on industry events, press treatment of news stories, book reviews, letters to the editor, classified advertising, and a graphic presentation of errors in newspaper headlines and stories.

Public Relations Journal. (1945–). New York: Public Relations Society of America.

■ This magazine is published eight times per year. It assesses trends, issues, and developments in public relations for practitioners, educators, and managers. Feature articles focus on such aspects as research and evaluation, management, marketing, new technologies, crisis management, employee relations, advertising, and professionalism. It also includes summaries of news affecting public relations activities, feedback from readers, career opportunities, book reviews, and editorials. An annual index appears in the October/November issue. It is available on *NEXIS*.

Additional professional and trade magazines related to the communication field are listed in "Selected Sources," which follows. The articles in these publications are sometimes indexed in the *Readers' Guide to Periodical Literature* and may occasionally be listed in some indexes and abstracts discussed in Chapter 6. In the listings, we include the earlier titles of scholarly journals in parentheses.

Selected Sources

Scholarly Journals

Communication
Argumentation and Advocacy (*Journal of the American Forensic Association*). (1964–). American Forensic Association.
Communication Education (*Speech Teacher*). (1952–). Speech Communication Association.
Communication Monographs (*Speech Monographs*). (1934–). Speech Communication Association.
Communication Quarterly (*Today's Speech*). (1953–). Eastern Communication Association.
Communication Reports. (1988–). Western States Communication Association.
Communication Research. (1974–). Sage.

Communication Research Reports. (1984–). Eastern Communication Association.

Communication Studies (Central States Speech Journal). (1949–). Central States Communication Association.

Communication Theory. (1991–). International Communication Association.

Health Communication. (1989–). Erlbaum.

Howard Journal of Communications. (1988–). Howard University.

Human Communication Research. (1974–). International Communication Association.

Journal-National Forensic League. (1991–). National Forensic League.

Journal of Applied Communication Research. (1973–). Speech Communication Association.

Journal of Communication and Religion (Religious Communication Today). (1978–). Religious Speech Communication Association.

Journal of Communication Inquiry. (1974–). University of Iowa Center for Communication Study.

Journal of the Association for Communication Administration (Bulletin of the Association for Communication Administration, ACA Bulletin, Bulletin of the Association of Departments and Administrators in Speech Communication). (1972–). Association for Communication Administration.

Journal of the International Listening Association. (1987–). International Listening Association.

National Forensic Journal. (1983–). National Forensic Association.

Philosophy and Rhetoric. (1968–). Pennsylvania State University Press.

Political Communication (Political Communication and Persuasion). (1980–). American Political Science Association and International Communication Association, Political Communication Divisions.

Quarterly Journal of Speech (Quarterly Journal of Public Speaking, Quarterly Journal of Speech Education). (1915–). Speech Communication Association.

Rhetoric Society Quarterly. (1971–). Rhetoric Society of America.

Southern Communication Journal (Southern Speech Communication Journal, Southern Speech Journal). (1935–). Southern States Communication Association.

Western Journal of Communication (Western Journal of Speech Communication, Western Speech). (1937–). Western States Communication Association.

Women's Studies in Communication. (1977–). Organization for Research on Women and Communication.

World Communication (Communication). (1972–). World Communication Association.

_____

_____

_____

_____

_____

Mass Communication

American Journalism. (1983–). American Journalism Historians Association.

Cinema Journal. (1966–). Society for Cinema Studies.

Communication Law and Policy. (1996–). Association for Education in Journalism and Mass Communication, Law Division.

Communications and the Law. (1978–). Meckler.

Critical Studies in Mass Communication. (1984–). Speech Communication Association.

Educational Technology Research and Development (Educational Communication and Technology Journal). (1953–). Association for Educational Communication and Technology.

European Journal of Communication. (1986–). Sage.

Federal Communications Law Journal. (1948–). University of California, Los Angeles, School of Law, and Federal Communications Bar Association.

Feedback. (1959–). Broadcast Education Association.

Film History. (1987–). Taylor & Francis.

Film Journal. (1934–). Pubson.

Film Quarterly. (1945–). University of California Press.

Gazette. (1955–). Institute of the Science of the Press.

Hastings Communications and Entertainment Law Journal (COMM/ENT: A Journal of Communications and Entertainment Law). (1977–). University of California, San Francisco, Hastings College of Law.

International Journal of Public Opinion Research. (1989–). World Association for Public Opinion Research.

Journal of Broadcasting & Electronic Media (Journal of Broadcasting). (1956/1957–). Broadcast Education Association.

Journal of Communication. (1951–). International Communication Association.

Journal of Film and Video. (1949–). University Film and Video Association.

Journal of Mass Media Ethics. (1985–). Erlbaum.

Journal of Media Economics. (1988–). Erlbaum.

Journal of Newspaper and Periodical History (Journal of Newspaper History). (1984–1992). Meckler.

Journal of Popular Culture. (1967–). Bowling Green State University Popular Press.

Journal of Popular Film and Television (Journal of Popular Film). (1972–). Popular Culture Association.

Journal of Radio Studies. (1992–). Washburn University.

Journalism & Mass Communication Educator. (1946–). Association for Education in Journalism and Mass Communication.

Journalism & Mass Communication Monographs. (1966–). Association for Education in Journalism and Mass Communication.

Journalism & Mass Communication Quarterly. (1924–). Association for Education in Journalism and Mass Communication.

Journalism History. (1974–). California State University Foundation.

Mass Comm Review. (1973–). Association for Education in Journalism and Mass Communication, Mass Communications and Society Division.

Media, Culture & Society. (1979–). Sage.

Media Management Review. (1995–). Erlbaum.

Newspaper Research Journal. (1979–). Association for Education in Journalism and Mass Communication, Newspaper Division.

Nordicom Review of Nordic Research on Media & Communication. (1981–). Nordic Documentation Center for Mass Communication Research.

Public Opinion Quarterly. (1937–). American Association for Public Opinion Research.

Quarterly Review of Film and Video (Quarterly Review of Film Studies). (1976–). Harwood Academic Publishers.

Science Communication (Knowledge). (1979–). Sage.

Telecommunications Policy. (1976–). Butterworth Scientific.

Telecommunications Policy and Regulation. (1986–). Practising Law Institute.

Speech and Language

American Journal of Speech-Language Pathology. (1991–). American Speech-Language-Hearing Association.

American Speech. (1925–). University of Alabama Press.

Applied Psycholinguistics. (1980–). Cambridge University Press.

Discourse & Society. (1990–). Sage.

Discourse Processes. (1978–). Ablex.

ETC.: A Review of General Semantics. (1943–). International Society for General Semantics.

Human Development. (1958–). Karger.
International Journal of American Linguistics. (1917–). University of Chicago Press.
Journal of Communication Disorders. (1967–). Elsevier Science Publishing.
Journal of Language and Social Psychology. (1982–). Sage.
Journal of Linguistics. (1965–). Cambridge University Press.
Journal of Memory and Language (Journal of Verbal Learning and Verbal Behavior). (1962–). Academic Press.
Journal of Psycholinguistic Research. (1971–). Plenum.
Journal of Speech and Hearing Research. (1958–). American Speech-Language-Hearing Association.
Language & Communication. (1981–). Pergamon Press.
Research on Language and Social Interaction. (1968–). Erlbaum.
Text and Performance Quarterly (Literature in Performance). (1980–). Speech Communication Association.
Written Communication. (1984–). Sage.

_____

_____

_____

_____

_____

_____

_____

_____

Advertising, Business, Marketing, and Public Relations

Academy of Management Review (Academy of Management Journal). (1957–). Academy of Management.
Administrative Science Quarterly. (1956–). Cornell University.
Business Communication Quarterly (Bulletin of the Association for Business Communication, ABCA Bulletin). (1969–). Association for Business Communication.
Industrial & Labor Relations Review. (1947–). Cornell University.
Information Economics and Policy. (1984–). International Telecommunications Society.
International Journal of Advertising. (1982–). Advertising Association.
Journal of Advertising. (1972–). American Academy of Advertising.
Journal of Advertising History. (1977–). M. C. B. University Press.
Journal of Advertising Research. (1960–). Advertising Research Foundation.
Journal of Business. (1928–). University of Chicago Press.
Journal of Business and Technical Communication. (1988–). Sage.
Journal of Consumer Research. (1974–). University of California, Los Angeles, Graduate School of Management.

Journal of Current Issues and Research in Advertising. (1992–). CtC Press.
Journal of Marketing. (1936–). American Marketing Association.
Journal of Marketing Research. (1964–). American Marketing Association.
Journal of Public Relations Research. (1989–). Association for Education in Journalism and Mass Communication, Public Relations Division.
Management Communication Quarterly. (1987–). Sage.
Organizational Behavior and Human Decision Processes (Organizational Behavior and Human Performance). (1966–). Academic Press.
Personnel Psychology. (1948–). Personnel Psychology.
Public Relations Quarterly (Quarterly Review of Public Relations). (1955–). Public Relations Quarterly.
Public Relations Review. (1975–). JAI Press.

Psychology, Sociology, and Social Psychology

American Behavioral Scientist. (1957–). Sage.
American Journal of Psychology. (1887–). University of Illinois Press.
American Journal of Sociology. (1895–). University of Chicago Press.
American Sociological Review. (1936–). American Sociological Association.
Child Development. (1930–). University of Chicago Press.
Cognitive Psychology. (1970–). Academic Press.
Cultural Studies. (1987–). Routledge.
Developmental Psychology. (1969–). American Psychological Association.
Family Relations (The Family Coordinator). (1952–). National Council on Family Relations.
Group & Organization Management (Group & Organization Studies). (1976–). Eastern Academy of Management.
Human Organization. (1941–). Society for Applied Anthropology.
International Journal of Intercultural Relations. (1977–). Society for Intercultural Education, Training, and Research.
Journal of Applied Psychology. (1917–). American Psychological Association.
Journal of Applied Social Psychology. (1971–). Winston.
Journal of Cross-Cultural Psychology. (1970–). Sage.
Journal of Educational Psychology. (1910–). American Psychological Association.

Journal of Experimental Social Psychology. (1965–). Academic Press.

Journal of Humanistic Psychology. (1961–). Association for Humanistic Psychology.

Journal of Marriage and the Family. (1939–). National Council on Family Relations.

Journal of Nonverbal Behavior (Environmental Psychology and Nonverbal Behavior). (1976–). Human Sciences Press.

Journal of Personality (Character and Personality). (1932–). Duke University Press.

Journal of Personality and Social Psychology (Journal of Abnormal and Social Psychology). (1925–). American Psychological Association.

Journal of Personality Assessment (Journal of Projective Techniques & Personality Assessment). (1936–). Society for Personality Assessment.

Journal of Research in Personality (Journal of Experimental Research in Personality). (1965–). Academic Press.

Journal of Sex Research. (1965–). Society for the Scientific Study of Sex.

Journal of Social and Personal Relationships. (1984–). Sage.

Personality & Social Psychology Bulletin. (1974–). Society for Personality and Social Psychology.

Personal Relationships. (1994–). International Society for the Study of Personal Relationships.

Small Group Research (Small Group Behavior). (1970–). Sage.

Social Forces. (1922–). University of North Carolina Press.

Social Psychology Quarterly (Sociometry). (1956–). American Sociological Association.

Symbolic Interaction. (1977–). JAI Press.

History and Political Science

American Historical Review. (1895–). American Historical Association.

American Journal of Political Science (Midwest Journal of Political Science). (1957–). Midwest Political Science Association.

American Political Science Review. (1906–). American Political Science Association.

American Politics Quarterly. (1973–). Sage.

Comparative Political Studies. (1968–). Sage.
Comparative Politics. (1968–). University of Chicago Press.
International Journal of Oral History. (1980–). Meckler.
Journal of American History. (1914–). Organization of American Historians.
Journal of Conflict Resolution (Conflict Resolution). (1957–). Sage.
Journal of Politics. (1939–). Southern Political Science Association.
Journal of Social Issues. (1945–). Society for the Psychological Study of Social Issues.
Political Behavior. (1979–). Agathon Press.
Political Science Quarterly. (1886–). Academy of Political Science.

Professional and Trade Periodicals

Advertising Age. (1930–). Crain Communications.
Adweek. (1979–). Adweek.
American Cinematographer. (1920–). American Society of Cinematographers.
American Journalism Review (Washington Journalism Review). (1977–). University of Maryland, College of Journalism.
Audio-Visual Communications. (1967–). Media Horizons.
Billboard. (1894–). Billboard.
BPME Image. (1985–). Broadcast Promotion and Marketing Executives.
Broadcasting & Cable. (1931–). Cahners.
Broadcasting and the Law. (1970–). L & S Publications.
Broadcast Management/Engineering. (1965–). Mactier.
Bulletin of the American Society of Newspaper Editors. (1970–). American Society of Newspaper Editors.
Business Horizons. (1958–). Indiana University, Graduate School of Business.
Columbia Journalism Review. (1962–). Columbia University, Graduate School of Journalism.
Corporate Television: The Official Magazine of the International Television Association. (1986–). Media Horizons.
Daily Variety. (1933–). Daily Variety.

Editor & Publisher. (1901–). Editor & Publisher.

Educational Technology. (1970–). Educational Technology.

Electronic Media. (1982–). Crain Communications.

Film Comment. (1962–). Film Society of Lincoln Center.

Film Quarterly. (1945–). University of California Press.

Folio: The Magazine for Magazine Management. (1972–). Folio.

Harvard Business Review. (1922–). Harvard University, Graduate School of Business Administration.

Hollywood Reporter. (1930–). Hollywood Reporter.

Inside PR. (1990–). Editorial Media Marketing.

Journal of Business Communication. (1963–). American Business Communication Association.

Journal of Technical Writing and Communication. (1971–). Baywood.

Marketing News. (1967–). American Marketing Association.

Media & Methods. (1964–). Society of Educators.

Media Week (Marketing & Media Decisions). (1966–). A/S/M Communications.

Presstime. (1979–). American Newspaper Publishers Association.

Public Communication Review. (1981–). Boston University.

Public Relations Journal. (1945–). Public Relations Society of America.

Quill. (1912–). Society of Professional Journalists.

RTNDA Communicator. (1946–). Radio–Television News Directors Association.

Sight and Sound. (1932–). British Film Institute.

Technical Communication. (1954–). Society for Technical Communication.

Television Quarterly. (1962–). National Academy of Television Arts and Sciences.

Television/Radio Age. (1953–). Television Editorial Corporation.

Transactional Analysis Journal. (1962–). International Transactional Analysis Association.

Variety. (1905–). Variety.

Writer's Digest. (1920–). Writer's Digest.

Abstract and Index Abbreviations

AHCI	*Arts & Humanities Citation Index*
AHL	*America: History and Life*
APC	*Abstracts of Popular Culture*
ASCA	*Automatic Subject Citation Alert*
BRI	*Book Review Index*
CA	*Communication Abstracts*
CC	*Current Contents*
CI	*ComIndex*
CIJE	*Current Index to Journals in Education/ERIC*
CLI	*Current Law Index*
EAI	*Expanded Academic Index*
EI	*Education Index*
ETA	*Education Technology Abstracts*
FLI	*Film Literature Index*
FSA	*Family Studies Abstracts*
HA	*Historical Abstracts*
HI	*Humanities Index*
HIF	*Health Instrument File*
HRA	*Human Resources Abstracts*
IJCS	*Index to Journals in Communication Studies through 1990*
IJMC	*Index to Journals in Mass Communication*
LLBA	*Linguistics and Language Behavior Abstracts*
MLA	*MLA International Bibliography of Books and Articles on the Modern Languages and Literatures*
PA	*Psychological Abstracts/PsychInfo*
PAA	*Public Administration Abstracts*
PAIS	*Public Affairs Information Service Bulletin*
SA	*Sociological Abstracts/Sociofile*
SPPD	*Social Planning/Policy & Development Abstracts*
SSCI	*Social Sciences Citation Index*
SSI	*Social Sciences Index*
T	*Topicator*

Exercises

1. During a literature search for a paper for your Communication Theory and Research class, you've examined bibliographies and indexes and found references to several scholarly journal articles. The abstracts indicate that these articles are pertinent to your topic, so you search for them. You want to read them thoroughly to determine whether they lend insight to the paper and whether their references and footnotes can offer further help in your literature search.

   a. The first abstract leads you to *Human Communication Research*:

   Saunders, C. S., Robey, D., & Vaverek, K. A. (1994). The persistence of status differentials in computer conferencing. *Human Communication Research, 20*, 443–472.

   What is the first hypothesis (H1) this study attempts to test? Was the hypothesis supported (confirmed) or rejected (not confirmed)?

   b. The second article is found in *Communication Monographs*:

   Fitch, K. L. (1994). A cross-cultural study of directive sequences and some implications for compliance-gaining research. *Communication Monographs, 61*, 185–209.

   A study by Ruth Ann Clark is referred to on the second page of the article. In what journal can this study be found?

   c. The third article is in the *Journal of Broadcasting & Electronic Media*:

   Austin, E. W., & Meili, H. K. (1994). Effects of interpretations of televised alcohol portrayals on children's alcohol beliefs. *Journal of Broadcasting & Electronic Media, 38*, 417–435.

   What is the title of Table 1?

   d. The fourth article leads you to *Communication Research*:

   Newhagen, J. E. (1994). Self-efficacy and call-in political television show use. *Communication Research, 21*, 366–379.

What was the purpose of this study? Where was the survey conducted?

e. The fifth study is in *Communication Education*:

Roach, K. D. (1995). Teaching assistant argumentativeness: Effects on affective learning and student perceptions of power use. *Communication Education, 44,* 15–29.

On what page is Table 1 found? Which type of TA power is used most often?

2. You are now working on a class report for your Media Law class and want to find recent developments in broadcast regulation. Starting with the most recent issue, you check the "Top-of-the-Week" news items in *Broadcasting & Cable* magazine and continue backward until you reach the January 30, 1995, issue. In one sentence, summarize the subject of the second Top-of-the-Week news item.

3. In your Public Relations class, your instructor suggests that you can find out about innovations in the field by examining *Public Relations Journal*. You pick up the October/November 1994 issue and scan the table of contents for interesting articles.

a. What is the title of the feature article in that issue?

b. You find that this issue contains the 1994 PRJ Editorial Index. What is the first article listed under Research in this index, and in what month was it published?

4. Identify journals that might have articles on your topic. Look at the table of contents to be sure the topic is related.

5. Examine recently published issues of these journals in your library's current periodicals section. Be sure to look at reference lists of articles on your topic.

6. Form topic-related discussion groups and talk about interesting articles found or sources valuable in searching the literature. Identify different facets of the topic so all of you will not be attempting to find the same sources.

Chapter 8

Information Compilations

You will often need to find recent facts to use in research reports, speeches, news stories, or presentations on current topics. For example, you might be preparing a public relations campaign and may need information on the cost of advertising in specific newspapers or magazines. Or the status of recent broadcast regulations may be required for a paper or television script on trends in broadcast law. Or you may have to lead a group discussion and want to consult a source about parliamentary procedure.

Several factual, quick-reference research sources can help with these and other related purposes. In addition, there are several collections and official publications of primary documents that are sometimes essential factual sources. In this chapter, we focus on methods of finding facts to support viewpoints, finding sources of information outside the library, and locating other current information related to communication.

Collections and archives lead you to the text of speeches, editorials, television programs, communication regulations, and so on, which may be the focus of your analysis or may be used as supporting information for research reports or other projects. Statistical sources identify reference works where census and other government and media statistics are reported. Because the statistical data cited in books and in journal articles are often not the most current, you should know where to turn to update such information.

Government documents are helpful when searching for up-to-date information on what is happening in Congress, the Supreme Court, or federal agencies such as the Federal Communications Commission. The U.S. government publishes so much information that a first-time user of government documents can be overwhelmed with the amount of available material. Many smaller libraries do not house all these documents, so you must find out how to request specific materials that you may need.

Yearbooks, directories, dictionaries, and manuals are also usually current. Yearbooks and directories are generally revised each year so that information is up-to-date. These sources provide names, addresses, and factual information about people, businesses, and clients, and are vital tools for many types of communication professionals. They can be especially useful when you do not find needed information within library resources. These reference works can point the way to other information sources such as trade and professional organizations. If contacted directly, these organizations may be able to supply useful information to meet your particular needs. Dictionaries and manuals are desktop reference sources, helpful when you need quick, practical information.

Collections and Archives

Collections are compilations of documents of a similar type that either are gathered together in one location or published in periodical, book, or microform format. Materials such as speeches, editorials, historical documents, and media transcripts are often not easily accessible by the typical researcher, even though they may have appeared elsewhere in book, periodical, or original form. Thus, published collections of these materials allow you to examine important original materials to learn more about the content of the subject. They also enable you to use the materials as examples of communication events when supporting arguments in a position paper, research investigation, or other project. One reference source that allows the user to determine where collections and archives are located is Ash and Miller's (1993) *Subject Collections*.

Speech Collections

If you are conducting critical or historical research, you may be interested in locating speeches given by important people or on newsworthy topics. Major newspapers such as the *New York Times* publish many newsworthy speeches shortly after they're given, but published collections make it easier to consult the original text of the speech without searching through back issues of these newspapers. They are especially helpful when the speech is old or when the newspaper account of the speech is not the original text, but an edited version. Collections also contain speeches that are not published elsewhere. The collection of speeches used most often is the following:

Vital Speeches of the Day. (1934–). New York: City News.

■ This collection of important recent speeches by government, industry, and other societal leaders usually includes the complete texts, but occasionally edited versions are presented. The many sides of issues are represented in the speeches selected for publication.

Vital Speeches is published twice per month. Annual author and subject indexes appear in the November issue. Speeches in this collection are referenced in the *Readers' Guide to Periodical Literature.*

Speeches of the President of the United States are published in the *Weekly Compilation of Presidential Documents* (1965–). This source makes the speeches and other presidential documents accessible in a relatively short period of time. An article by K. J. Turner (in the July 1986 issue of *Communication Education*, pp. 243–253) explains how to use presidential libraries to do research.

Collections of past presidential speeches are found in the following presidential libraries:

George Bush Presidential Library, College Station, TX

Jimmy Carter Library, Atlanta, GA

Dwight D. Eisenhower Library, Abilene, KS

Gerald R. Ford Museum, Grand Rapids, MI

Herbert Hoover Library, West Branch, IA

Lyndon B. Johnson Library, Austin, TX

John F. Kennedy Library, Boston, MA

Richard M. Nixon Library, Yorba Linda, CA

Ronald Reagan Library, Simi Valley, CA

Franklin D. Roosevelt Library, Hyde Park, NY

Harry S. Truman Library, Independence, MO

These libraries contain speeches, other documents, and media accounts of events during each particular presidency. Most require you to visit the library to use the materials.

State of the Union addresses for presidents Washington through Jackson are available on a WWW page:

http://www.let.rug.nl/~welling/usa/presidents/addresses.html.

Those delivered from 1946 to the present are available on the American Politics gopher: *toby.scott.mwu.edu.*

Other collections of speeches are listed at the end of this chapter. It is possible to locate in what collection the text of a speech appears by using the *Speech Index* (see Chapter 6).

Media Collections

In addition to speeches, other media materials, such as those published in newspapers, are often compiled into collections. These are useful when you are interested in learning what journalists have said about a topic. *Editorials on File*, for example, is composed of newspaper editorials.

Editorials on File. (1969–). New York: Facts on File.

■ Editorials for this collection are selected from more than 140 newspapers in the United States and Canada. Published twice per month, each issue includes the text of about 200 editorials chosen to represent newspaper positions on current issues. A cumulative subject index appears at the end of each annual volume. *Editorials on File* is indexed in the *Readers' Guide to Periodical Literature.*

Viewpoint (1976–), a similar type of periodical, brings together the work of newspaper and radio columnists with that of political cartoonists. A more complete microform edition is also available.

Facts on File (1940–) differs from these works in that it is a weekly digest of national and foreign news prepared from the accounts published in selected major newspapers, periodicals, and other standard news sources.

The ability to publish in **microform (microfiche** or **microfilm)** has made it possible to assemble and make easily accessible collections of materials that would otherwise not be widely available. Articles from regional newspapers in all areas of the United States are made available in microfiche and are indexed through *NewsBank* (1970–). In addition, coverage of selected topics in specialized print media is provided by two microform collections, *Underground Newspaper Microfilm Collection* (Alternative Press Syndicate, 1963–1977) and *Herstory: Microfilm Collection* (Women's History Research Center, 1972–). The *Alternative Press Index* (described in Chapter 6) provides limited information on tapping these two sources.

Several historical collections of U.S. and British newspapers and periodicals are also available in microform. Many libraries are likely to own one or more of these collections. Because they may not be listed in library catalogs or periodical lists and their contents may be reviewed only by using special indexes, you'll need to ask a reference librarian about their availability.

Even though most of the collections just described consist of print media, electronic media collections are also available. Researchers often need to examine original broadcasts or their scripts, for example, to analyze their content or to conduct historical or critical research. Media professionals also consult archival materials when preparing news programs or documentaries. For example, the Television Script Archive at the University of Pennsylvania contains more than 24,000 television scripts from 1976 to the present.

In addition, printed transcripts in microformat are a convenient way to access some broadcasts. For example, many libraries subscribe to the *CBS News Television Broadcasts in Microform* (1975–). To use this source most efficiently, consult the *CBS News Index* (described in Chapter 6) for the listing of broadcasts. The National Archives will lend (for a fee) the CBS videotapes through interlibrary loan. These videotapes are also available for use at 13 regional archives.

As with the CBS broadcasts, actual collections of electronic media programs are generally available only in a few **archives** in the United States, such as the Museum of Television and Radio in New York City and the Museum of Broadcast Communications in Chicago. Some are open to the general public. If they are, you'll still need to visit the archive to view or listen to the materials. Two exceptions are the Vanderbilt Television News Archive at Vanderbilt University (Nashville, TN) and the Public Affairs Video Archives at Purdue University (West Lafayette, IN); both rent videotapes and audiotapes. Vanderbilt lists its holdings in the *Television News Index and Abstracts* (1968–). This collection and others are described in the Television News Study Center's (1981–) *Television News Resources: A Guide to Collections*.

C-SPAN (Cable-Satellite Public Affairs Network) programs are archived in the Purdue University Public Affairs Video Archives. C-SPAN airs programs on Washington politics, proceedings of Congress, national events, world legislatures, conferences, and special topics that deal with communication, such as talk radio, and political campaign commercials. These programs are cataloged, indexed, and distributed on videotape (about $30/hour) or through printed transcript (about $15/hour). Archive affiliates may borrow tapes and search the index online. Transcripts of Federal News Service materials (presidential speeches, daily briefings, congressional news conferences, Supreme Court decisions) are also available. For information, contact:

> Public Affairs Video Archives
> Purdue University
> 1000 Stewart Center
> West Lafayette, IN 47907-1000
> Phone: (800) 423-9630
> Internet: *pava@vm.cc.purdue.edu*

The Political Commercial Archive at the University of Oklahoma archives radio and television political advertisements. The archive includes commercials of candidates for political office, as well as those sponsored by political action committees, corporations, and special interest groups. Presidential debates, conventions, and significant televised speeches are also archived. You can use OCLC to locate these materials, but archive staff must retrieve materials for users. For information, contact:

> Political Commercial Archive
> University of Oklahoma
> 610 Elm Avenue
> Norman, OK 73019-0335
> Phone: (405) 325-3114

Political speeches are also available in the SUNSITE Internet archive at the University of North Carolina in Chapel Hill. By telneting *sunsite.unc.edu* or using Gopher (see North Carolina), you can read speech texts or mail them to your E-mail address for downloading to your personal computer.

Other archives are identified in the Review and Criticism section of the March 1984 issue of *Critical Studies in Mass Communication* (see Chapter 7), where archives in mass communication, film, television, photography, and newspapers are described. Other indexes and directories of archive collections, including Godfrey's (1983) *A Directory of Broadcast Archives*, are listed at the end of this chapter. Note that these sources are useful in a historical sense, but are now dated. Bracken and Sterling's (1995) recent guide to the literature, *Telecommunications Research Resources* (see Chapter 6), also identifies more current electronic media archives.

Other useful source materials are primary documents relating to the regulation of the electronic media industries. A useful compilation of such documents for those working in the area of broadcast law and freedom of expression is the following:

Kahn, F. J. (Ed.). (1984). *Documents of American broadcasting* (4th ed.). Englewood Cliffs, NJ: Prentice Hall.

■ This sourcebook collects 43 primary documents about public policy, history, and issues in U.S. broadcasting. Documents include federal laws, commission regulations and notices, congressional reports and actions, court decisions, speeches, letters, and other documents from parts of the U.S. Constitution to cable access and radio deregulation.

The book includes chronological and thematic tables of contents. The broad subject areas of these documents are broadcast-regulation development, freedom of expression, competition regulation, public broadcasting, and the public interest. Brief commentaries provide background, explanation, and interpretation. A few related readings follow each document. Also included are a glossary of legal terms, a brief identification of legal citations, an index to legal decisions, and a general index.

Legal Collections

Loose-leaf reporting services assemble, organize, and digest topical legal reports on a single subject. These materials are collected in a binder, and regular supplements are distributed, often weekly. The major goal of these services is to keep the legal profession abreast of constantly evolving areas of law. These services are valuable for communication students interested in studying questions about policy, regulation, and freedom of speech. In particular, two of these services provide the text of legislative actions and court decisions that are significant for the mass media.

Pike & Fischer Radio Regulation. (1946–). Bethesda, MD: Pike & Fischer.

■ This service consists of Current Service, Digest, and Decision (Cases) volumes. The Current Service volumes contain the text of current laws and regulations that affect broadcasting, including statutes, congressional committee reports, treatises, and international agreements, as well as rules and regulations of the Federal Communications Commission (FCC) for radio, television, and cable television.

The Digest volumes contain all FCC decisions, as well as selected Federal Radio Commission and federal and state court decisions, through July 1963. The Decision volumes contain FCC decisions and reports and court decisions prior to July 1963 in the first series and after that date in the second series. There also is a volume that provides a master index, finding aids, and FCC forms.

Media Law Reporter. (1977–). Washington, DC: Bureau of National Affairs.

■ This weekly service provides indexed coverage of all decisions of the U.S. Supreme Court and selected decisions of federal and state courts and administrative agencies that affect the electronic and print media. The full text is published for most opinions, including concurrences and dissents. Summary opinions are presented for some cases.

Decisions are classified in four major divisions: regulation of media content, regulation of media distribution, newsgathering, and media ownership. There is a topical index arranged alphabetically by major subjects (such as broadcast media or commercial speech) and subheads (such as regulation of advertising content). Also provided are tables of cases by plaintiff/defendant and by jurisprudence (such as U.S. Supreme Court or First Circuit Court of Appeals) and an index digest. There is an annual cumulation.

Besides the official report of the U.S. Supreme Court decisions, *United States Supreme Court Reports* (1790–), there are two useful and privately published editions of the Supreme Court's decisions, *United States Supreme Court Reports: Lawyers' Edition, Second Series* (1956–) and the *Supreme Court Reporter* (1882–). These unofficial reporting services reproduce the same text of the decisions as the official reports and include their own summary of cases and annotations written by the publishers' editorial staffs.

These official and unofficial reports of Supreme Court decisions can be useful when you are studying communication law, debate, or freedom of speech. They are available in law libraries and many university libraries. West Publishing also produces a National Reporter System of seven regional and two state *Reporters* that includes most of the decisions issued by the appellate courts of the 50 states each year. These are also available in law libraries.

Measurement Collections

One other type of collection is a compilation of measures of communication attitudes and personality. Researchers find these collections useful when planning descriptive and experimental research studies. Robinson, Shaver, Wrightsman, and Andrews' (1991) *Measures of Personality and Social Psychological Attitudes* and McReynolds' (1968–1975) *Advances in Psychological Assessment* are often helpful to students conducting their own research projects. One additional work, Chun, Cobb, and French's (1975) *Measures for Psychological Assessment* indexes by author and subject the original sources and applications of 3,000 psychological measures. For communication, consult the following:

Rubin, R. B., Palmgreen, P., & Sypher, H. E. (Eds.). (1994). *Communication research measures: A sourcebook.* New York: Guilford Press.

■ This volume profiles over 60 often-used research measures in instructional, interpersonal, mass, and organizational communication. Besides presenting the actual measure and pertinent references to its use, each profile highlights the purpose, development, reliability, and validity of the measure. In addition, the editors and associate editors discuss measurement trends and issues within the four areas of communication research.

A table of contents and an index provide ready access to each measure that is profiled.

Collections of measures are helpful for researchers conducting investigations because they provide not only the measure but information on the validity and reliability of the instrument.

Statistical Sources

You will often need to locate statistical data to document research for a wide variety of projects, such as finding facts to support a debate case on social welfare, developing background material for a newspaper article on unemployment in a local area, doing research for a term paper on the history of broadcasting, or preparing for a speech or group discussion on trends in American television. Or when you are conducting research on a topic, you may find that the author of a book or article has cited data that are germane to your research but are now several years out of date. Thus, an important step in the research process is attempting to update such references by using **statistical sources**.

A major activity of governments at all levels is the collection, compilation, and publication of a wide variety of statistical data. The following statistical yearbook is often a good first place to check for data about the United States:

U.S. Department of Commerce, Bureau of the Census. (1879–). *Statistical Abstract of the United States*. Washington, DC: U.S. Government Printing Office.

■ This annual compendium contains summaries of social, economic, and political statistics for the United States. Communications and Information Technology is one section of the *Abstract*. Population, Vital Statistics, Education, and Elections are also included among the *Abstract*'s 30 sections. The source notes given for each table and the bibliography of sources at the end of the volume make this a handy guide to many statistics published by the U.S. government.

A detailed subject index helps locate statistics on a specific topic. The table of contents is useful for researching broad subjects. This source is also available on CD-ROM.

The *American Statistics Index (ASI)* indexes statistical publications produced by all departments and agencies of the U.S. government, including the FCC and the Census Bureau. It can be quite helpful when conducting statistical research.

American Statistics Index: A Comprehensive Guide and Index to the Statistical Publications of the U.S. Government. (1973–). Bethesda, MD: Congressional Information Service.

■ This commercially produced indexing and abstracting service provides comprehensive coverage of statistical publications of the federal government. It is issued monthly in two sections (indexes and abstracts) and is cumulated annually. Besides the index by subjects and names, the source contains indexes by title, by agency report numbers, and by geographic, economic, and demographic categories. The latter index is useful for researchers who are interested in statistics that are broken down in a particular way, such as by age, city, and so forth. Documents abstracted in *ASI* are available on microfiche in some libraries. *ASI* is available on-line and on CD-ROM as part of *Statistical Masterfile.*

Because *ASI* provides excellent access to almost all statistical information published by the federal government, we won't cite all statistical publications that might be of interest to communication researchers. Some selected publications are listed at the end of this chapter, along with several statistical sources on the international level that are published by the United Nations. Later in this chapter, we discuss other U.S. government publications.

Governments and agencies are not, of course, the only sources of useful statistics. Many of the publications described or identified later in this chapter—in particular, the *Gale Directory of Publications and Broadcast Media*, the *Broadcasting & Cable Yearbook*, the *International Television and Video Almanac*, and the *Statesman's Yearbook*—include substantial amounts of statistical data drawn from a variety of sources.

Other important sources of statistical data include trade and professional associations such as the American Association of Advertising Agencies, the American Newspaper Publishers Association, the Association of American Publishers, the Electronic Industries Association, the National Association of Broadcasters, the Radio Advertising Bureau, and the Television Bureau of Advertising. These associations gather and report a variety of statistical data and materials about their respective industries. For example, the research department of the National Association of Broadcasters produces various booklets and reports about trends and developments in broadcasting.

Sources for some subject areas include several companies whose business it is to gather and market data, such as the Arbitron Ratings Company, the A. C. Nielsen Company, Standard Rate and Data, and the Gallup, Harris, and Roper polling organizations. These data are often summarized in separate publications, a few of which are listed at the end of this chapter. The Arbitron and Nielsen organizations produce a variety of materials such as detailed ratings reports for their client stations in radio and television markets, studies of the reliability of broadcast ratings, and pamphlets that detail trends in the electronic media or report specialty studies such as investigations of cable television and videocassette recorders.

One reference work that has compiled data from many of these sources provides a historical perspective on trends in the electronic media:

Sterling, C. H. (1984). *Electronic media: A guide to trends in broadcasting and newer technologies 1920–1983*. New York: Praeger.

■ Data about quantitative trends in the electronic media industry since 1920 have been compiled from a variety of sources. About 150 tables are included in the book's eight sections: electronic media growth, ownership, economics, employment, content trends, audience, international aspects, and regulation. Each set of tables is accompanied by a narrative interpretation and by a discussion of the sources, reliability, and validity of the data. These features, as well as the additional references listed for each topic, make this a useful reference.

A detailed table of contents lists each table included. The end of the volume contains a description of sources and references.

U.S. Government Publications

The U.S. government publishes periodicals, directories, handbooks, and bibliographies. You are probably already familiar with many of these documents. However, you may be less familiar with other common types of **government documents**, such as federal statutes, congressional hearings and reports, census materials, and government agency regulations and reports. This section describes some of these publications and special finding tools that can be used to identify and locate them. Many are listed on pp. 193–195.

Several government sources detail the rules and regulations of the United States. These sources help students and professionals keep abreast of changes in the law. For example, this information is important for preparing debate cases, analyzing media policy, understanding political campaign regulations, comparing the demographic composition of a sample, and the like. These materials are generally available in the government documents section of many libraries. The general and permanent laws of the United States are codified in the *United States Code*.

U.S. Congress, House of Representatives. (1994). *United States code* (1988 ed.). Washington, DC: U.S. Government Printing Office.

■ The *Code* includes the federal laws of this country. The text of the multitude of laws that existed in this country as of January 1989 are provided in the 50 titles or content areas of this 11th edition of the *Code*. For example, selected chapters of title 17, *Copyrights*, include

Subject Matter and Scope of Copyrights, Copyright Ownership and Transfer, Duration of Copyrights, and the Copyright Office. Title 47 of the *Code—Telegraphs, Telephones, and Radiotelegraphs*—includes the Communications Act of 1934, as amended. Other titles include *Census, Commerce and Trade, Education, Labor,* and *Money and Finance.*

A new edition of the *Code* has been published every 6 years since 1926 by the Law Revision Counsel of the House of Representatives. A supplement is issued after each session of Congress. The *Code* is also available through the Internet at *http://www.house.gov.*

The *Federal Register* publishes daily, on weekdays, regulations and legal notices issued by the executive branch and federal agencies.

U.S. General Services Administration, Office of the Federal Register. (1936–). *Federal Register.* Washington, DC: U.S. Government Printing Office.

■ The purpose of the *Federal Register* is to make regulations and notices, including presidential proclamations, executive orders, and federal agency documents and activities, available to the public. It is divided into several sections: rules and regulations, proposed rules, notices, and Sunshine Act meetings. For each of the rules or proposed rules, the agency, action, rule summary, effective dates, addresses, and supplementary information are included. Each notice announces hearings and investigations, committee meetings, delegations of authority, agency decisions and rulings, and agency statements of organization and function. For example, rule-making proceedings and hearings of the FCC and the Federal Trade Commission (FTC) are announced in the *Register.*

The regulatory documents contained in the *Federal Register* are keyed to and codified in the *Code of Federal Regulations.* This publication of the U.S. General Services Administration contains the general and permanent rules of executive departments and federal agencies that are published in the *Federal Register.* The *Code of Federal Regulations* is indexed in the *Code of Federal Regulations: CFR Index and Finding Aids.*

The FCC can be a particularly useful source of information if you are researching communication policy and regulation. Three of its publications are especially helpful. *FCC Rules and Regulations* contains the text of FCC rules in such matters as commission operation, frequency allocations, broadcast services, satellite communications, and cable television services. The weekly *Federal Communications Commission Reports* incorporates the Commission's current decisions, orders, policy statements, and public notices of hearings and rule-making proceedings. The *Reports* are cumulated yearly, and these volumes have a list of commission actions and documents. They also contain a subject digest that summarizes pertinent information on such topics as fairness, issues and program lists, and cellular communication systems. The *Annual Report of the Federal Communications Commission* provides a yearly comprehensive review of significant events in all areas of communication regulation, including broadcasting, cable television, common carriers (for example, satellites), spectrum management, and frequency allocations.

Also useful are the various reports of congressional committees, executive agencies, and other regulatory commissions such as the FTC. For example, if you are researching the topic of television violence, you might find references to the report of the Surgeon General's Advisory Committee (1972), *Television and Social Behavior*, to the congressional report of the House Committee on Interstate and Foreign Commerce (1977), *Violence on Television*, or to the report by the National Institutes of Mental Health (1982), *Television and Behavior*. These reports are widely cited, and because they sometimes contain the testimony of expert witnesses in addition to well-researched background material, they are useful resources for a research project.

One problem with locating government publications is that they are not included in some library catalogs. Many libraries shelve government publications in a special section, so they might be overlooked. You will need to investigate how such documents are handled in the library you are using. If they have not been included in the library catalog, you will need to discover what local access tools are available, and how they are shelved and arranged. A reference librarian will be able to answer these questions for you.

Another difficulty in locating government publications is that they are also not included in most periodical indexes. The Public Affairs Information Service *Bulletin* (listed under "Indexes" at the end of Chapter 6) indexes some government publications. But even this source lists only about 1% of the federal documents published. Another source, though, the *U.S. Government Periodicals Index*, does index the publications of more than 100 agencies of the U.S. government. This source is also available on CD-ROM in some libraries.

In any library setting, the basic all-around tool used to identify the availability of U.S. government publications on a given topic, by a given author, or published by a given agency is the following:

U.S. Superintendent of Documents. (1895–). *Monthly Catalog of United States Government Publications*. Washington, DC: U.S. Government Printing Office.

■ The *Monthly Catalog* is the most complete catalog of publications of all branches of the federal government. It has semiannual and annual cumulative indexes by title, author/agency, and subject. Documents are listed only in the year they are published, so it is often necessary to search through several volumes to find information about a particular document.

Library of Congress subject headings have been used in the subject index since July 1976. The catalog is arranged alphabetically by issuing agency, with each entry assigned a number. It is to this number that the index refers. Information given in entries is similar to that found in most library catalog records, with the addition of the Superintendent of Documents number. This number is a classification number similar in function to a Library of Congress or Dewey decimal call number, and it is used in many libraries to arrange government documents on the shelf.

You should refer to the user's guide at the front of each volume to help identify the elements of each entry and decipher the abbreviations. The *Cumulative Subject Index to the Monthly Catalog of U.S. Government Publications, 1900–1971* should be used for retrospective searches.

The monthly catalog is available on-line as *GPO Monthly Catalog*. Many libraries with government document collections subscribe to a CD-ROM version of this database.

One disadvantage of the *Monthly Catalog* as a tool for identifying relevant materials is that it does not include annotations or abstracts. However, such abstracts for two important types of government publications are available. For those published by Congress, consult the *CIS/Index to Publications of the United States Congress* (see below), and, as you recall, for those that are statistical in nature, the *American Statistics Index* is helpful.

The various committees of the U.S. Congress and their staffs investigate many current social, economic, and political issues and publish the results of these investigations either as hearings, committee prints, or reports. A *hearing* is simply a transcript of the testimony of witnesses before a committee or subcommittee. Because many of these witnesses are experts in their fields and collectively represent a broad range of views, hearings are often excellent resource materials for researching controversial topics, such as the effects of television on children. *Committee prints* are reports of background research done either by committee staffs or by the Congressional Research Service of the Library of Congress. House and Senate *reports* are the official committee reports to the entire House or Senate summarizing the results of investigations or hearings and making recommendations.

All these publications, as well as the legislation that results from committee hearings and the like, are indexed and abstracted in the following:

CIS/Index to Publications of the United States Congress. (1970–). Washington, DC: Congressional Information Service.

■ This service provides complete indexing and abstracting for all the working papers of Congress, including committee hearings, prints, and reports. *CIS* appears monthly and is cumulated quarterly and annually. It is published in two parts, an index section and an abstract section. Entries in the index volume refer users to relevant abstracts by means of an entry number. Included in both the index and abstracts are entries for individual witnesses at hearings. The history of individual pieces of legislation is covered in annual cumulations. Some libraries own the complete microfiche collection of all documents that are abstracted. Access to this collection is by the entry number of the abstract.

This index is also available for on-line computer searching and on CD-ROM in some libraries.

Other useful publications for following current congressional deliberations are: *Congressional Index*; *Congressional Quarterly Almanac*; *Congressional Record: Proceedings and Debates of Congress*; *Congressional Record, Index to Daily Proceedings*; and *Congressional Quarterly Weekly Report*. Congressional Quarterly also produces useful guides for understanding the history and workings of Congress, the Supreme Court, and U.S. elections. These are listed at the end of this chapter.

The tools just described are useful only for finding publications of the U.S. government and for only a relatively recent time period. If you need to identify earlier documents or those at the local, state, or international levels, consult one or more of the finding aids for government materials listed at the end of this chapter, such as *Shepard's Acts and Cases by Popular Names: Federal and State* (1992).

Yearbooks

Yearbooks and **annuals** contain current information on yearly developments in a specific field. They also provide excellent background information, statistics, narrative explanations, and listings, much like that found in directories and manuals. An excellent research tool for students in mass communication is the following:

Broadcasting & Cable Yearbook (2 vols.). (1935–). New Providence, NJ: Bowker.

■ This comprehensive reference tool contains information about various elements of the radio, television, and cable industries. Volume I includes a summary of relevant law and regulation; breakdowns of important data for every television and radio station, cable system, and satellite operator in the United States and Canada; Arbitron's ADI (Area of Dominant Influence) Television Market Atlas; directories of advertising and marketing services, programming services, and equipment and professional suppliers; and listings of associations, education programs, and books, periodicals, and media relating to broadcasting.

Volume II presents the Yellow Pages of radio, television, and cable. It contains an alphabetical listing of stations/companies and industry personnel.

The *Yearbook* was originally issued as an annual supplement to *Broadcasting* magazine, and then in two separate publications, *Broadcasting Yearbook* (1944–1979) and *Cable Sourcebook* (1972–1979). In 1980 the two were combined in the *Broadcasting/Cable Yearbook* (from 1982 to 1988 it was titled *Broadcasting/Cablecasting Yearbook*) and later called *Broadcasting Yearbook*, until 1992 when the R.R. Bowker Company began publishing it as *Broadcasting & Cable Marketplace* until 1994.

Other useful yearbooks, such as *Editor & Publisher International Year Book* (1959–), are listed at the end of this chapter.

Directories

Directories provide basic information about people, companies, organizations, and publications. One directory that students in journalism and communication find helpful is the following:

Gale Directory of Publications and Broadcast Media (3 vols.). (1869–).
Detroit: Gale Research.

■ Volumes 1 and 2 of this directory list newspapers and periodicals
published four or more times yearly in the United States, Canada, the
Virgin Islands, the Bahamas, Panama, and the Philippines. Also
included are economic descriptions of the states, provinces, cities,
and towns in which the newspapers and periodicals are published.

The main section lists publications by location. For newspapers,
the information includes circulation, frequency of publication, date
of establishment, political affiliation, advertising rates, and the names
of the editor and publisher.

There are also sections listing publications by type and subject. The
most important of these for communication researchers are journalism, advertising and marketing, motion pictures, and industry. These
lists and the alphabetical list at the end of the volume refer users to the
main section for more detailed information about the publication.

Volume 3 contains maps, a list of newspaper feature editors, and
cross-referenced indexes to specific types of publications (for example, women's, Jewish, and college).

Before 1987 this directory was known as the *Ayer Directory of
Publications* and from 1987 to 1989, *Gale Directory of Publications*.

Aside from the need to locate materials from newspapers and
news programs, communication researchers occasionally need to
find educational media when pursuing research projects dealing
with the media—for example, historical or critical studies of film.

Educational or instructional media, including films, filmstrips, audiotapes, and videotapes, can be located in several reference
sources. *The Video Source Book* is a handy way to find videotapes.

The Video Source Book (2 vols.). (1979–). Detroit: Gale Research.

■ This comprehensive annual lists videotapes available for purchase,
rent/lease, off-air taping, free loan, or duplication. Coverage includes
business and industry, entertainment, and instruction. Each entry contains a short description, credits, producer, audience/purpose, permissi-
ble uses (for example, broadcast television, in-home viewing), terms of
availability (for example, loan, purchase, off-air record), television standards (for example, NTSC, PAL), distributor, and often, price. This
source provides subject and credit indexes and a section on distributors.

A useful source for locating reviews assessing the content and
quality of educational media is the following:

Media Review Digest. (1973–). Ann Arbor, MI: Pierian.

■ This annual publication indexes reviews of feature films and educational media such as educational films, videotapes, filmstrips, records, audiotapes, and miscellaneous productions. Items are arranged alphabetically by title within sections devoted to each form of media (for example, films and videotapes). Entries include a brief description of the item, followed by a listing of reviews that have appeared in periodicals. Among the indexes are a subject index by Library of Congress subject headings and an index of reviewers. The *Digest* also includes lists of film awards and prizes, bibliographies of media materials, and book reviews. From 1970 to 1972 this index was known as *Multi Media Reviews Index.*

Another type of media directory compiles facts about and synopses of television and radio programs. These are helpful when doing research about programming trends and the antecedents of contemporary programming. Descriptions usually include dates of airing, cast members, and brief summaries of program content. One such directory is:

Brooks, T., & Marsh, E. (1992). *The complete directory to prime time network TV shows 1946–present* (5th ed.). New York: Ballantine Books.

■ This volume lists and describes every regular television series (lasting 4 or more weeks) aired by the commercial networks during the 6 p.m. to sign-off period, as well as the top syndicated evening programs from 1946. News, sports, and movies are also included. Each entry provides the dates of the first and last telecasts, along with a history of the series, a list of cast members, and a synopsis of the program. Appendixes include the season ratings, season network schedules, major television awards, and other information. There is also a comprehensive index to cast members.

A general directory that may be useful to students of organizational or mass communication is the following:

Standard & Poor's Register of Corporations, Directors & Executives. (1928–). New York: Standard & Poor's.

■ This work, in three volumes, is issued annually and contains information on location, telephone number, offices, products, sales, and number of employees of more than 37,000 U.S. and Canadian corporations.

A more specialized directory of corporations is *Working Press of the Nation* (1945–).

Some other directories of interest to communication students are at the end of this chapter. *Directories in Print* can help you find directories not given here. It lists more than 10,000 industrial, trade, and professional directories.

Dictionaries

Academic disciplines use language and jargon that might confuse readers. The words may seem familiar, but often, the meanings are not what we expect. There are sources that can help clarify your understanding of new or unique terms.

Dictionaries are usually thought of simply as alphabetical arrangements of words and their meanings. Although the denotative meaning of a word is typically sought when a dictionary is consulted, other information is available. This information often includes pronunciation, spelling, hyphenation, word etymology, syllabication, and synonyms.

There are four basic types of dictionaries. General dictionaries are the abridged and unabridged versions with which you are most familiar. You consult these when you need to find out the meaning of a word, how to pronounce a word, or where to divide a word into syllables. Language dictionaries give more attention to slang terms, the root and history of a word, and synonyms and antonyms. Foreign-language dictionaries translate words from one language to another and often provide a guide to pronunciation. Subject dictionaries, which are much more specialized, concentrating on one specific topic or discipline, will be our focus here.

Subject dictionaries list and define basic and specialized terms in a particular field. They also provide meanings for abbreviations, jargon, and slang. At times, subject dictionaries may resemble encyclopedias in that they give lengthy descriptions of and bibliographic references for terms. This is why we included one subject dictionary in Chapter 5 with encyclopedias.

Less inclusive and more specialized dictionaries may be helpful when you encounter unfamiliar terms in communication and related areas. Two such dictionaries that define words and terms pertinent to the study of mass communication are the following:

Diamant, L. (Ed.). (1992). *Dictionary of broadcast communications* (new 3rd rev. ed.). Lincolnwood, IL: NTC Business Books.

■ This dictionary contains over 5,000 technical, common, and slang words used by broadcasting, advertising, and communication professionals in Great Britain and the United States. Included are terms currently used in radio and television production and programming, network and station operations, broadcast engineering, audiotaping and videotaping, performing, advertising, research, and trade and government media. Definitions are not highly technical, and cross-references to comparable terms are given.

Urdang, L. (Ed.). (1992). *The dictionary of advertising*. Lincolnwood, IL: NTC Business Books.

■ This dictionary presents words and terms used in marketing, writing copy, art direction, graphics, media planning, research analysis and buying, consumer research, promotion, and public relations. Over 4,000 entries explain special meanings of ordinary words, names of devices, services, organizations, and specialized initials and abbreviations. This is the sixth printing of a 1977 version published by Tatham-Laird & Kudner.

The dictionaries listed at the end of this chapter will help you find precise meanings for communication and research terms. The law dictionaries that we list will help when you need to know the legal sense or use of words. They are handy, quick-reference books, helpful in learning the language of a discipline.

Manuals

A **manual**, or fact book, is a quick-reference handbook about a broad subject area. Usually, manuals present generally accepted data, rather than the most recent information as in yearbooks and directories. They often provide statistical tables, bibliographies, glossaries, and limited directories. We list some examples of useful manuals in various facets of communication at the end of this chapter.

Students interested in publishing, writing, and editing also have several manuals and directories available for their use. The manuals provide tips on writing style and selling one's work. The directories reference publishing companies and other markets where work can be submitted. We also cite a few of these works in the list of "Selected Sources."

Selected Sources

Collections

Advances in Psychological Assessment. (1968–). San Francisco: Jossey-Bass.

Alternative Press Centre. (1963–). *Underground Press Collection.* Ann Arbor, MI: University Microfilms International.

American Periodicals Series. (1970–1975). Ann Arbor, MI: University Microfilms International.

Bearden, W. O., Netemeyer, R. G., & Mobley, M. F. (1993). *Handbook of marketing scales: Multi-item measures for marketing and consumer behavior research.* Newbury Park, CA: Sage.

Brewer, D. J. (1900). *The world's best orations from the earliest period to the present times* (10 vols.). St. Louis: Kaiser.

CBS News Television Broadcasts in Microform. (1975–). Ann Arbor, MI: University Microfilms International.

Early American newspapers, 1704–1820. (1983). New York: Readex Microprint Corporation.

Editorials on File. (1970–). New York: Facts on File.

Facts on File. (1940–). New York: Facts on File. (Available on CD-ROM from 1980)

Federal Reporter. (1880–). St. Paul, MN: West.

Historic Documents. (1972–). Washington, DC: Congressional Quarterly.

Kahn, F. J. (Ed.). (1984). *Documents of American broadcasting* (4th ed.). Englewood Cliffs, NJ: Prentice Hall.

Media Law Reporter. (1977–). Washington, DC: Bureau of National Affairs.

National Reporter System. (1879–). St. Paul: West. (Includes the *New York Supplement* and the following *Reporters*: *Atlantic, California, North Eastern, North Western, Pacific, South Eastern, Southern,* and *South Western*)

NewsBank. (1970–). New Canaan, CT: NewsBank. (Available on CD-ROM from 1980)

Ozer, J. S. (Ed.). (1981–). *Film Review Annual.* Englewood, NJ: Author.

Pike & Fischer Radio Regulation. (1946–). Bethesda, MD: Pike & Fischer.

Podell, J., & Anzovin, S. (1988). *Speeches of the American presidents.* New York: Wilson.

Public Affairs Video Archives: The Education and Research Archives of C-SPAN Programming. (1987–). West Lafayette, IN: Purdue University.

Representative American Speeches. (1938–). New York: Wilson.

Robinson, J. P., Shaver, P. R., Wrightsman, L. S., & Andrews, F. M. (1991). *Measures of personality and social psychological attitudes: Vol. 1, Measures of social psychological attitudes.* San Diego: Academic Press.

Rubin, R. B., Palmgreen, P., & Sypher, H. E. (Eds.). (1994). *Communication research measures: A sourcebook.* New York: Guilford Press.

Salem, J. M. (Ed.). (1971–). *A Guide to Critical Reviews.* Metuchen, NJ: Scarecrow Press.

Shapiro, M. E. (1989). *Television network prime-time programming, 1948–1988.* Jefferson, NC: McFarland.

Shapiro, M. E. (1990). *Television network daytime and late-night programming, 1959–1989.* Jefferson, NC: McFarland.

Shepard's United States citations (8th ed.). (1994). Colorado Springs, CO: Shepard's/McGraw-Hill.

Steinberg, C. (1985). *TV facts* (rev. ed.). New York: Facts on File.

Supreme Court Reporter. (1882–). St. Paul: West. (Available on CD-ROM from 1993)

Television & Cable Factbook (3 vols.). (1983–). Washington, DC: Warren.

TV Facts, Figures & Film. (1986–). Syosset, NY: Broadcast Information Bureau.

United States Supreme Court Reports: Lawyers' Edition, Second Series. (1956–). Rochester, NY: Lawyers Co-Operative.

Viewpoint. (1976–). Glen Rock, NJ: Microfilming Corporation of America.

Vital Speeches of the Day. (1934–). New York: City News.

Weekly Compilation of Presidential Documents. (1965–). Washington, DC: U.S. Government Printing Office.

Weiner, E. (1992). *The TV Guide tv book.* New York: HarperPerennial.

West's General Digest: A Digest of All Current Decisions of the American Courts as Reported in the National Reporter System and Other Standard Reports. (1936–). St. Paul, MN: West.

What They Said. (1969–). Beverly Hills, CA: Monitor.

Women's History Research Center. (1972-). *Herstory: Microfilm Collection.* Berkeley, CA: Author.

Finding Tools for Collections

Ash, L., & Miller, W. G. (Comps.). (1993). *Subject collections* (7th ed., rev. & enl., 2 vols.). New Providence, NJ: Bowker.

Balkansky, A. (1980). Through the electronic looking glass: Television programs in the Library of Congress. *Quarterly Journal of the Library of Congress, 37*, 458–475.

Black, S. (1990). *Thesaurus of subject headings for television: A vocabulary for indexing script collections*. Phoenix: Oryx Press.

Black, S., & Moersh, E. S. (Eds.). (1990). *Index to the Annenberg Television Script Archive: Volume 1, 1976–1977*. Phoenix: Oryx Press.

Brady, A., Wall, R., & Weiner, C. N. (1984). *Union list of film periodicals: Holdings of selected American collections*. Westport, CT: Greenwood Press.

Catalog of Copyright Entries. (1980–). Washington, DC: Library of Congress, Copyright Office.

CBS News Index. (1975–1991). Ann Arbor, MI: University Microfilms International.

Chun, K., Cobb, S., & French, J. R. P., Jr. (1975). *Measures for psychological assessment*. Ann Arbor: University of Michigan, Institute for Social Research.

Film and Television Index. (1975–). New Canaan, CT: NewsBank.

Godfrey, D. G. (Comp.) (1983). *A directory of broadcast archives*. Washington, DC: Broadcast Education Association.

Heintze, J. R. (1985). *Scholars' guide to Washington, D.C., for audio resources*. Washington, DC: Smithsonian Institution Press.

Historic Documents: Cumulative Index. (1973–). Washington, DC: Congressional Quarterly.

Hoornstra, J. (1979). *American periodicals, 1741–1900: An index to the microfilm collections*. Ann Arbor, MI: University Microfilms International.

Index to American Periodicals of the 1700's and 1800's. (1992–). Indianapolis: Computer Indexed Systems.

Kellerman, L. S., & Wilson, R. A. (1990). *Index to Readex microfilm collection of early American newspapers*. New Canaan, CT: Readex.

Mehr, L. (Ed.). (1977). *Motion pictures, television and radio: A union catalogue of manuscript and special collections in the western United States*. Boston: Hall.

NewsBank Electronic Index. (1986–). New Canaan, CT: NewsBank.

Oral History Index. (1994–). Westport, CT: Meckler.

Oral History Sources. (1990–). Alexandria, VA: Chadwyck-Healey.

Rivers, W. L., Thompson, W., & Nyhan, M. J. (1977). *Aspen handbook on the media 1977–79 edition: A selective guide to research, organizations and publications in communications*. New York: Aspen Institute for Humanistic Studies/Praeger.

Rouse, S., & Loughney, K. (Comps.). (1989). *3 decades of television: A catalog of television programs acquired by the Library of Congress 1949–1979*. Washington, DC: Library of Congress, Motion Picture, Broadcasting, & Recorded Sound Division.

Rowan, B. G., & Wood, C. J. (1994). *Scholars' guide to Washington, D.C., media collections.* Washington, DC: Johns Hopkins University Press.

Schreibman, F. C. (1983). *Broadcast television: A research guide.* Los Angeles: American Film Institute.

Shamley, S. L. (Comp.). (1991). *Television interviews, 1951–1955: A catalog of Longine's Chronoscope interviews in the National Archives.* Washington, DC: U.S. National Archives and Records Administration.

Smart, J. R. (Comp.). (1982). *Radio broadcasts in the Library of Congress, 1924–1941: A catalog of recordings.* Washington, DC: Library of Congress.

Television News Index and Abstracts: Annual Index. (1968–). Nashville, TN: Vanderbilt Television News Archive.

Television News Study Center. (1981). *Television news resources: A guide to collections.* Washington, DC: George Washington University, Gelman Library.

Vanden Heuvel, J. (1991). *Untapped sources: America's newspaper archives and histories.* New York: Gannett Foundation Media Center.

Statistical Sources

A. C. Nielsen. (1955–). *Nielsen Report on Television.* Northbrook, IL: Author.

A. C. Nielsen. (1988–). *Nielsen Television Index.* New York: Author.

American Statistics Index: A Comprehensive Guide and Index to the Statistical Publications of the U.S. Government. (1973–). Bethesda, MD: Congressional Information Service. (Available on-line and on CD-ROM as part of *Statistical Masterfile*)

Arbitron Radio. (1992). *Arbitron Radio market report reference guide: A guide to understanding and using radio audience estimates.* New York: Author.

Dodd, D. (1991). *Historical statistics of the United States, 1790–1990* (4 vols.). University: University of Alabama Press.

Hastings, E. H., & Hastings, P. K. (Eds.). (1978/1979–). *Index to International Public Opinion.* New York: Greenwood Press.

Index to International Statistics. (1983–). Washington, DC: Congressional Information Service. (Available on-line and on CD-ROM)

Kurian, G. (1994). *Datapedia of the United States, 1790–2000: America year by year*. Lanham, MD: Bernan Press.

Radio Advertising Bureau. (1989–). *Radio Facts for Advertisers*. New York: Author.

Roper Organization. (1983). *Trends in attitudes toward television and other media: A twenty-four year review*. New York: Television Information Office.

Roper Organization. (1991). *America's watching: Public attitudes toward television*. New York: Network Television Association.

Simmons Market Research Bureau. (1979–). *Target Group Index*. New York: Author.

Standard Rate & Data Service. (1993–). *Consumer Magazine and Agri-Media Source*. Wilmette, IL: Author.

Standard Rate & Data Service. (1993–). *Newspaper Advertising Source*. Wilmette, IL: Author.

Standard Rate & Data Service. (1993–). *Radio Advertising Source*. Wilmette, IL: Author.

Standard Rate & Data Service. (1994–). *TV and Cable Source*. Wilmette, IL: Author.

Statistical Reference Index. (1980–). Washington, DC: Congressional Information Service. (Available on-line and on CD-ROM)

Statistical Yearbook. (1963–). Paris: UNESCO.

Sterling, C. H. (1984). *Electronic media: A guide to trends in broadcasting and newer technologies 1920–1983*. New York: Praeger.

Television Bureau of Advertising. (1959–). *TV Basics*. New York: Author.

U.S. Department of Commerce, Bureau of the Census. (1879–). *Statistical Abstract of the United States*. Washington, DC: U.S. Government Printing Office.

U.S. Department of Commerce, Bureau of the Census. (1949–). *County and City Data Book*. Washington, DC: U.S. Government Printing Office.

U.S. Department of Commerce, Bureau of the Census. (1963–). *Census Catalog and Guide*. Washington, DC: U.S. Government Printing Office. (Formerly *Bureau of the Census Catalog*)

U.S. Department of Commerce, Bureau of the Census. (1980). *Social indicators III*. Washington, DC: U.S. Government Printing Office.

U.S. Department of Commerce, Bureau of the Census. (1993). *Population profile of the United States*. Washington, DC: U.S. Government Printing Office.

U.S. Government Publications

Federal Communications Commission. (1934/1935–). *Federal Communications Commission Reports.* Washington, DC: U.S. Government Printing Office.

Federal Communications Commission. (1935–). *Annual Report of the Federal Communications Commission.* Washington, DC: U.S. Government Printing Office.

Federal Communications Commission. (1982–). *FCC Rules and Regulations* (rev. ed.). Washington, DC: U.S. Government Printing Office.

U.S. Administrative Office of the United States Courts. (1993–). *United States Courts: Selected Reports.* Washington, DC: Author.

U.S. Congress. (1873–). *Congressional Record: Proceedings and Debates of the Congress.* Washington, DC: U.S. Government Printing Office.

U.S. Congress, House of Representatives. (1994). *United States code* (1988 ed.). Washington, DC: U.S. Government Printing Office. (Available through the Internet at **http://www.house.gov**)

U.S. General Services Administration, Office of the Federal Register. (1936–). *Federal Register.* Washington, DC: U.S. Government Printing Office.

U.S. General Services Administration, Office of the Federal Register. (1938–). *Code of Federal Regulations.* Washington, DC: U.S. Government Printing Office.

U.S. Supreme Court. (1790–). *United States Supreme Court Reports.* Rochester, NY: Lawyers Cooperative Publishing.

Finding Tools for Government Publications

Barrett, R. E. (1994). *Using the 1990 U.S. Census for research.* Thousand Oaks, CA: Sage.

Brightbill, G.D. (1978). *Communications and the United States Congress: A selectively annotated bibliography of committee hearings, 1870–1976.* Washington, DC: Broadcast Education Association.

CIS/Index to Publications of the United States Congress. (1970–). Washington, DC: Congressional Information Service. (Available online and on CD-ROM)

Congressional Index. (1938–). Chicago: Commerce Clearing House.

Congressional Quarterly Almanac. (1945–). Washington, DC: Congressional Quarterly.

Congressional Quarterly's guide to Congress (4th ed.). (1991). Washington, DC: Congressional Quarterly.

Congressional Quarterly's guide to U.S. elections (3rd ed.). (1994). Washington, DC: Congressional Quarterly.

Congressional Quarterly's guide to the U.S. Supreme Court (2nd ed.). (1990). Washington, DC: Congressional Quarterly.

Congressional Quarterly Weekly Report. (1943–). Washington, DC: Congressional Quarterly.

Cumulative subject index of the monthly catalog of U.S. government publications, 1900–1971 (15 vols.). (1973–1975). Washington, DC: Carrolton.

Declassified Documents Catalog. (1975–). Woodbridge, CT: Research Publications.

Government Publications and Periodicals [Computer Disk]. (1987–). New York: Wilson.

Guide to United States Supreme Court Reports, Lawyers' Edition. (1994). Rochester, NY: Lawyers Cooperative Publishing.

Index to United Nations Documents and Publications [CD-ROM and Computer Disk]. (1990–). New Canaan, CT: NewsBank/Readex.

Index to U.S. Government Periodicals. (1970–1987). Chicago: Infordata International.

Lesko, M., & Capretta, C. (Eds.). (1990). *Federal data base finder: A directory of free and fee-based data bases and files available from the federal government* (3rd ed.). Kensington, MD: Information USA.

Morehead, J. (1983). *Introduction to United States public documents* (3rd ed.). Littleton, CO: Libraries Unlimited.

Rubin, M. R. (1978). *FCC decisions—interpreting the Communications Act of 1934: An index* (2 vols.). Washington, DC: U.S. Government Printing Office.

Sears, J. L., & Moody, M. K. (1994). *Using government information sources: Print and electronic* (2nd ed., 2 vols.). Phoenix: Oryx Press.

Shepard's acts and cases by popular names: Federal and state (4th ed., 3 vols.). (1992). Colorado Springs, CO: Shepard's/McGraw-Hill.

U.S. Congress. (1981–). *Congressional Record, Index to Daily Proceedings.* Washington, DC: U.S. Government Printing Office.

U.S. General Services Administration, Office of the Federal Register. (1963–). *Code of Federal Regulations: CFR Index and Finding Aids.* Washington, DC: U.S. Government Printing Office.

U.S. Government Periodicals Index. (1993–). Bethesda, MD: Congressional Information Service. (Available on CD-ROM from 1993)

U.S. Library of Congress. (1910–). *Monthly Checklist of State Publications.* Washington, DC: U.S. Government Printing Office.

U.S. Library of Congress. (1984). *Popular names of U.S. government reports* (4th ed.). Washington, DC: U.S. Government Printing Office.

U.S. Superintendent of Documents. (1895–). *Monthly Catalog of United States Government Publications.* Washington, DC: U.S. Government Printing Office. (Available on-line as *GPO Monthly Catalog* and on CD-ROM)

_____

_____

_____

_____

_____

_____

_____

Yearbooks

Barone, M. (1972–). *The Almanac of American Politics.* Washington, DC: National Journal.

Broadcasting & Cable Yearbook (2 vols.). (1935–). New Providence, NJ: Bowker.

Cook, C. (Comp.). (1992). *Facts on File world political almanac.* New York: Facts on File.

Editor & Publisher International Year Book. (1959–). New York: Editor & Publisher.

Facts on File World Political Almanac. (1989–). New York: Facts on File.

Facts on File Yearbook. (1941–). New York: Facts on File.

Information Please Almanac, Atlas and Yearbook. (1947–). Boston: Houghton Mifflin.

International Motion Picture Almanac. (1929–). New York: Quigley.

International Television and Video Almanac. (1956–). New York: Quigley.

Miller, E. E., & Mosley, M. L. (Eds.). (1973–). *Educational Media and Technology Yearbook.* Littleton, CO: Libraries Unlimited.

Statesman's Yearbook. (1864–). New York: St. Martin's Press.

World Almanac and Book of Facts. (1868–). New York: World Almanac.

_____

_____

_____

_____

_____

Directories

Media

Andrew, G. (1990). *The film handbook*. Boston: Hall.

Audio Video Review Digest: A Guide to Reviews of Audio and Video Materials Appearing in General and Specialized Periodicals. (1989–). Detroit: Gale Research.

AV Market Place. (1984–). New York: Bowker. (Formerly *Audiovisual Market Place*, 1969–1983, and *Audio Video Market Place*, 1984–1988)

Broadcast Information Bureau. (1974–). *TV Series, Serials & Packages*. Syosset, NY: Author.

Brooks, T., & Marsh, E. (1992). *The complete directory to prime time network TV shows 1946–present* (5th ed.). New York: Ballantine Books.

Brown, L. (1992). *Les Brown's encyclopedia of television* (3rd ed.). Detroit: Gale Research.

Cable Advertising Directory. (1980–). Washington, DC: National Cable Television Association.

DWM: A Directory of Women's Media. (1972–). New York: National Council for Research on Women.

Educational film & video locator (4th ed., 2 vols.). (1990–1991). New York: Bowker.

Eisner, J., & Krinsky, D. (1984). *Television comedy series: An episode guide to 153 TV sitcoms in syndication*. Jefferson, NC: McFarland.

Gale Directory of Publications and Broadcast Media (3 vols.). (1869–). Detroit: Gale Research.

Gianakos, L. J. (1978–). *Television Drama Series Programming: A Comprehensive Chronicle*. Metuchen, NJ: Scarecrow Press.

Hammond, C. M. (1981). *The image decade: Television documentary, 1965–1975*. New York: Hastings House.

International Film Guide. (1964–). London: Tantivy Press.

Kreamer, J. T. (Ed.) (1991–). *The Video Annual*. Denver: ABC-Clio.

Kurian, G. T. (Ed.). (1982). *World press encyclopedia* (2 vols.). New York: Facts on File.

Literary Market Place: The Directory of the American Book Publishing Industry with Industry Yellow Pages. (1940–). New Providence, NJ: Bowker.

The MacNeil/Lehrer News Hour: Broadcast Review and Index. (1979–). Sanford, NC: Microfilming Corporation of America.

Maltin, L. (1983). *The whole film sourcebook.* New York: New American Library.

Mayer, I. (Ed.). (1987). *The Knowledge Industry 200: America's two hundred largest media and information companies* (3rd ed.). Detroit: Gale Research.

McNeil, A. (1991). *Total television: A comprehensive guide to programming from 1948 to the present* (3rd ed.). New York: Penguin Books.

Media Review Digest. (1973–). Ann Arbor, MI: Pierian. (Formerly *Multi Media Reviews Index,* 1970–1972.)

News Media Yellow Book: Who's Who Among Reporters, Writers, Editors, and Producers in the Leading National News Media. (1989–). Washington, DC: Monitor.

PBS Video: Program Catalog. (1974–). Washington, DC: Public Broadcasting Service.

Reed, M. K., & Reed, R. M. (1990). *Career opportunities in television, cable, and video* (3rd ed.). New York: Facts on File.

Slide, A., Hanson, P. K., & Hanson, S. L. (Comps.). (1988). *Sourcebook for the performing arts: A directory of collections, resources, scholars, and critics in theatre, film, and television.* New York: Greenwood Press.

Terrace, V. (1981). *Radio's golden years: The encyclopedia of radio programs, 1930–1960.* San Diego, CA: Barnes.

Terrace, V. (1986). *Encyclopedia of television: Series, pilots, and specials* (3 vols.). New York: Zoetrope.

Terrace, V. (1991). *Fifty years of television: A guide to series and pilots, 1937–1988.* New York: Cornwall.

The Video Source Book (2 vols.). (1979–). Detroit: Gale Research.

Wasserman, S. R. (Ed.). (1985). *The lively arts information directory: A guide to the fields of music, dance, theatre, film, radio and television, for the United States and Canada, covering national, international, state and regional organizations, government grant sources, foundations, consultants, special libraries, research and information centers, education programs, journals and periodical festivals and awards* (2nd ed.). Detroit: Gale Research.

Woolery, G. W. (1983). *Children's television: The first thirty-five years, 1946–1981, part I: Animated cartoon series.* Metuchen, NJ: Scarecrow Press.

Woolery, G. W. (1985). *Children's television: The first thirty-five years, 1946–1981, part II: Live, film, and tape series.* Metuchen, NJ: Scarecrow Press.

Working Press of the Nation (4 vols.) (1945–). New Providence, NJ: National Register.

World Guide to Television & Film. (1994–). Philadelphia: North American.

World Radio TV Handbook. (1947–). New York: Billboard.

Writer's and Artist's Yearbook: A Directory for Writers, Artists, Playwrights, Writers for Film, Radio and Television, Photographers, and Composers. (1906–). London: Black.

Writer's Market: Where and How to Sell What You Write. (1930–). Cincinnati: Writer's Digest.

_____

_____

_____

_____

_____

_____

_____

_____

General

Directories in Print (2 vols). (1980–). Detroit: Gale Research. (Formerly *Directory of Directories*)

Directory of Research Grants. (1975–). Phoenix: Oryx Press.

Federal Regulatory Directory. (1956–). Washington, DC: Congressional Quarterly.

Guide to American Directories. (1954–). Coral Springs, FL: Klein.

Information Industry Directory: An International Guide to Organizations, Systems, and Services Involved in the Production and Distribution of Information in Electronic Form (2 vols.). (1971–). Detroit: Gale Research.

International Who's Who. (1935–). London: Europa.

Martindale-Hubbell Law Directory (21 vols.). (1931–). Summit, NJ: Martindale-Hubbell. (Available on CD-ROM from 1993).

Standard & Poor's Register of Corporations, Directors & Executives. (1928–). New York: Standard & Poor's.

United States Government Manual. (1974–). Washington, DC: U.S. Government Printing Office.

Washington Information Directory. (1975–). Washington, DC: Congressional Quarterly.

Who's Who in Advertising. (1990/1991–). Wilmette, IL: Marquis Who's Who.

Who's Who in America (3 vols.). (1899/1900–). New Providence, NJ: Marquis Who's Who.

Worldbook of IABC Communicators. (1900–). San Francisco: International Association of Business Communicators.

_____

_____

_____

_____

_____

_____

Dictionaries

Black's law dictionary (6th ed.). (1991). St. Paul: West.

Bryant, D. C., Smith, R. W., Arnott, P. D., Holtsmark, E. B., & Rowe, G. O. (1968). *Ancient Greek and Roman rhetoricians: A bibliographical dictionary.* Columbia, MO: Artcraft Press.

Connors, T. D. (1982). *Longman dictionary of mass media and communication.* New York: Longman.

Delson, D., & Jacob, S. (1990). *Delson's dictionary of motion picture marketing terms* (2nd ed.). Westlake Village, CA: Bradson Press.

Diamant, L. (Ed.). (1992). *Dictionary of broadcast communications* (new 3rd rev. ed.). Lincolnwood, IL: NTC Business Books.

Ellmore, R. T. (1991). *NTC's mass media dictionary.* Lincolnwood, IL: National Textbook.

Eyseneck, M. (Ed.). (1991). *The Blackwell dictionary of cognitive psychology.* Cambridge, MA: Blackwell.

Fletcher, J. (1988). *Broadcast research definitions.* Washington, DC: National Association of Broadcasters.

Gregory, R. L. (Ed.). (1987). *The Oxford companion to the mind.* New York: Oxford University Press.

Hurwitz, L. (1985). *Historical dictionary of censorship in the United States.* Westport, CT: Greenwood Press.

Jary, D., & Jary, J. (Eds.). (1991). *HarperCollins dictionary of sociology.* New York: HarperPerennial.

Marriott, F. H., & Kendall, M. G. (1990). *A dictionary of statistical terms* (5th ed.). New York: Longman.

Marshall, G. (1994). *The concise Oxford dictionary of sociology.* Oxford: Oxford University Press.

McKerns, J. (Ed.). (1989). *Biographical dictionary of American journalism.* New York: Greenwood Press.

Meadows, A. J. (1987). *Dictionary of computing and new information technology* (3rd ed.). New York: Nichols.

Penney, E. F. (1991). *The Facts on File dictionary of film and broadcast terms.* New York: Facts on File.

Plano, J. C., & Greenberg, M. (1993). *The American political dictionary* (9th ed.). Fort Worth, TX: Harcourt Brace Jovanovich.

Platt, S. (Ed.). (1989). *Respectfully quoted: A dictionary of quotations requested from the Congressional Research Service.* Washington, DC: Library of Congress.

Reed, R. M. (1994). *The Facts on File dictionary of television, cable, and video.* New York: Facts on File.

Rosenberg, J. M. (1987). *Dictionary of computers, information processing and telecommunications* (2nd ed.). New York: Wiley.

Rosenberg, J. M. (1995). *Dictionary of marketing and advertising.* New York: Wiley.

Safire, W. (1993). *Safire's new political dictionary* (rev. 3rd ed.). New York: Random House.

Shafritz, J. M. (1993). *The HarperCollins dictionary of American government and politics*. New York: HarperCollins.

Slide, A. (1991). *The television industry: A historical dictionary*. New York: Greenwood Press.

Urdang, L. (Ed.). (1992). *The dictionary of advertising*. Lincolnwood, IL: NTC Business Books.

Vogt, W. P. (1993). *Dictionary of statistics and methodology*. Thousand Oaks, CA: Sage.

Watson, J., & Hill, A. (1993). *A dictionary of communication and media studies* (3rd ed.). London: Edward Arnold.

Weik, M. H. (1989). *Communications standard dictionary* (2nd ed.). New York: Van Nostrand Reinhold.

Weiner, R. (1990). *Webster's New World dictionary of media and communications*. New York: Webster's New World.

Wolman, B. B. (Ed.). (1988). *Dictionary of behavioral science* (2nd ed.). San Diego: Academic Press.

Words and Phrases (45 vols.). (1940–). St. Paul: West.

Manuals

Baudot, B. S. (1989). *International advertising handbook: A user's guide to rules and regulations*. Lexington, MA: Lexington Books.

Belanger, S. E. (Comp.). (1989). *Better said and clearly written: An annotated guide to business communication sources, skills, and samples*. New York: Greenwood Press.

Berger, A. A. (1990). *Scripts: Writing for radio and television*. Newbury Park, CA: Sage.

Block, M. (1994). *Broadcast newswriting: The RTNDA reference guide*. Chicago: RTNDA/Bonus Books.

Caruso, D., & McKay, G. (1992). *The screenwriter's handbook*. New York: Penguin Books.

Crawford, M. G. (1990). *The journalist's legal guide* (2nd ed.). Toronto: Carswell.

Ehrlich, E. H., & Hand, R., Jr. (1991). *NBC handbook of pronunciation* (4th ed., rev.). New York: HarperPerennial.

Goldstein, N. (1994). *Associated Press stylebook and libel manual* (rev. & updated ed.). Reading, MA: Addison-Wesley.

Henn, H. G. (1991). *Henn on copyright law: A practitioner's guide* (3rd ed). New York: Practicing Law Institute.

Henson, K. T. (1991). *Writing for successful publication*. Bloomington, IN: ERIC/RCS.

Hood, J. R. (1982). *AP broadcast news handbook*. New York: Associated Press.

Kessler, L., & MacDonald, D. (1992). *When words collide: A media writer's guide to grammar and style* (3rd ed.). Belmont, CA: Wadsworth.

Lippman, T. W. (Ed.). (1989). *The Washington Post deskbook on style* (2nd ed.). New York: McGraw-Hill.

MacDonald, R. H. (1994). *A broadcast news manual of style* (2nd ed.). New York: Longman.

Paiva, B. (1983). *The program director's handbook*. Blue Ridge Summit, PA: Tab.

Robert, H. M. (1990). *The Scott, Foresman Robert's rules of order newly revised* (9th ed., new & enl. ed.). Glenview, IL: Scott, Foresman.

Ullmann, J., & Colbert, J. (Eds.). (1990). *The reporter's handbook: An investigator's guide to documents and techniques* (2nd ed.). New York: St. Martin's Press.

UPI stylebook: The authoritative handbook for writers, editors & news directors (3rd ed.). (1992). Lincolnwood, IL: National Textbook.

UPI stylebook: Print and broadcast (3rd ed.). (1992). Washington, DC: United Press International.

West's Law Finder: A Legal Research Manual. (1959–). St. Paul, MN: West.

Willis, E. (1993). *Writing scripts for television, radio, and film* (3rd ed.). Fort Worth, TX: Harcourt Brace Jovanovich.

Wren, C. G., & Wren, J. R. (1986). *The legal research manual: A game plan for legal research and analysis* (2nd ed.). Madison, WI: A-R Editions.

Exercises

1. In your Political Communication course, you have been studying the rhetoric of President Bill Clinton. To find verbatim texts of important speeches by national newsmakers, you

consult *Vital Speeches of the Day*. Use the annual index (printed in November) to locate his Inaugural Address (called "American Renewal") delivered between October 15, 1992, and October 1, 1993. When was this speech delivered?

2. For your term paper in Mass Media Management, you will be using an article written in 1985 that cites statistical data, giving the Federal Communications Commission as its source. To see whether the FCC has updated these data, you use the *American Statistics Index*. In the 1994 index volume, you find a reference under this agency to a publication that includes data on "TV station channel allocation." It sounds like this might be what you are looking for.

   a.   What is the accession number for this item?

   b.   Find the abstract for this publication. What is its title?

3. In your seminar on Issues in the Press, you are going to be giving a presentation on newspaper publishing. Although you have compiled a rather comprehensive bibliography on the topic, you find that you need additional facts and figures on circulation trends. You turn to the *Statistical Abstract of the United States* (1994 edition) and find that an entire section of the volume is devoted to Communications.

   a.   Find a table in this section giving data on the number and circulation of daily and Sunday newspapers by states. What is the newspaper circulation per capita for the state of Hawaii?

   b.   How does this figure compare with that given for the District of Columbia?

   c.   What is the number of this table?

   d.   These data are useful, but you would like to find a more comprehensive source. What is the title of the publication given as the source of these data?

4. You are studying the early development of radio in your Media History class. You come across a reference to an early radio station in Madison, Wisconsin, but the reference fails to mention the call letters of the station and when the station began. You consult the index of the 1994 *Broadcasting & Cable Yearbook* and find a listing for a directory of U.S. and Canadian radio stations. Turning to this section, you discover that Madison has several radio stations.

   a.   What are the call letters of the oldest radio station in Madison?

b. In what year did that station go on the air?

c. To whom is the station licensed?

5. You are interning as a communication training specialist in a large company and have been asked to help develop an in-service human relations training program. You've been given the task of identifying commercially available audiovisual materials that might be of use in this program. To identify existing videotapes and to determine their availability, you turn to *The Video Source Book*. Looking in the subject index under the heading "Personnel Management," you find a video with the title *Managing Diversity*. Find the full description of this video.

a. Is this video's level suitable for your audience?

b. Can the video be rented/leased?

c. What is the purchase price?

6. Identify projects or assignments that would require use of the sources listed in this chapter. Which ones would you keep near your desk? Why?

7. Meet in the library reference area and examine a selection of these sources. What interesting new things did you learn? How might you use these sources as a communication professional?

PART THREE

Communication
Research
Processes

Now that we've identified the basic search strategies and sources important for communication research, we will discuss the two processes next encountered by researchers: research and writing. Through the literature review, we determine questions that still need answers and formulate research strategies to uncover those answers. When conducting primary research, we seek to answer those questions. In writing, we determine the best way to present the information found during the literature search and, perhaps, the research investigation.

In Chapter 9, we focus on systematic procedures for conducting a research study. Our purpose in this chapter is to overview the major procedures used in communication research. We also provide several useful sources that you can consult when planning your own research project.

Writing is just as systematic as searching and researching in that specific and rigorous conventions must be followed. In Chapter 10, we focus on basic writing principles, formatting styles, and copyediting. In Chapter 11, we discuss basic writing projects: abstracts, literature reviews, critical essays, research prospectuses, and research reports.

In Chapter 12, we invite you inside the research process to see the decisions and choices that researchers make. We take you through the conceptualization and execution of an actual study. You can find an abridged version of the original report of this study in Appendix B.

Part Three, then, identifies important processes in researching and writing about communication topics. We hope this section will whet your appetite for doing communication research.

Chapter 9

Designing the Communication Research Project

Sometimes a literature review's summary and critical evaluation of past research is an end product of the research effort. In many instances, though, the literature review is only a beginning. We often need to go further to investigate new questions or problems we've uncovered. We'll need to conduct original research to answer the questions not already answered by past studies.

All researchers realize that many facets of communication are not fully understood. Because there are many questions that have yet to be answered adequately, the literature on a specific research topic is seldom complete. When this is the case, researchers must conduct their own investigations to answer the questions. In this chapter, we overview research methods that can be used to bridge these gaps in our knowledge.

Our goal here is only to introduce you to the conduct of research. This will help you understand much of the literature you encounter and design your own research project. In either case, when reading research or doing research, it is important that you consult additional books about research methods, measurement, and analysis. We identify many useful sources at the end of this chapter.

The Research Process

Research is an objective, systematic, empirical, and cumulative process by which we seek to solve theoretical and applied problems. Such problems are obstacles to our knowledge and understanding of communication. Research is *objective* because we try to be impartial when seeking the best solutions to the research problem. It is *systematic* because we move through a series of planned stages when conducting research. It is *empirical* because we look beyond ourselves to observe and to gather evidence. And, research is *cumulative* because it builds upon past knowledge. Research does not stand isolated from what others have learned before.

If a question has already been answered in the literature, there is little need to duplicate the effort. However, many questions are unanswered and duplication or replication of research is warranted if (a) there is reason to suspect the validity of the earlier studies, (b) another view would add to the diversity of knowledge about the problem, or (c) new information might augment or alter previous findings in light of a changing communication environment. For example, the growth of cable television and VCRs in people's homes might change earlier findings about how television is used in family settings.

Descriptive and Explanatory Research

Researchers observe, describe, and often explain the relationships between variables or events. Research can be descriptive or explanatory; our research question guides the choice of method. **Descriptive research** seeks to identify or describe events or conditions. We would conduct descriptive research if we were asking, "What is the present or past state of events?" **Explanatory research** looks for underlying causes and explanations of events. We would conduct explanatory research if we were asking, "Why have these events happened in the manner that they did?"

Let's consider our example of media-related training programs for executives. If our research question is "How have these training programs changed during the past 3 decades?" our focus is descriptive. We would want to describe how the training programs have evolved over the years. If we ask, "How effective is the information contained in these instructional methods?" our focus is explanatory. We would want to evaluate the content of past training programs on the basis of how we define "effective," that is, our criteria to evaluate effectiveness (for example, the ability to field questions or credibility of response). Here, we would arrive at an informed judgment about *why* an instructional training method produces positive or negative, or expected or unexpected, results.

Research Stages

The process of conducting original research consists of several stages:

1. Posing and developing a problem in need of a solution
2. Reviewing past research and writings about that problem or subject
3. Identifying worthy questions unanswered by previous investigators
4. Devising the best method to seek answers to these questions
5. Gathering the necessary information to answer the research questions
6. Analyzing that information
7. Presenting the results of the inquiry
8. Considering the meaning and implications of these results for furthering knowledge of the subject or theory

Problem and Literature

We need to define and to describe our research problem precisely. Once we select and define the problem that we need to solve, we must go to the appropriate literature to see if others have already addressed similar issues. The literature will help clarify the current state of knowledge about our topic. It will also help us identify precise research questions about the problem that we need to answer. For example, suppose our problem concerns the role of nonverbal communication in the classroom. By reading other researchers' published works, we will be able to learn what they have discovered before us. This will help us focus on the precise questions we need to answer.

Research Question

We might narrow our focus to, "How does nonverbal immediacy affect learning in the classroom?" Sometimes, if there's no theory or prior research to guide the study, the research question will suggest an inductive approach to the problem. Observation typically is used to understand the phenomenon well enough to develop a theory about the role of, in our example, immediacy and learning.

Or, if the research literature suggests, we might want to test a *hypothesis*, that is, an expected positive relationship between nonverbal immediacy and learning. Perhaps the literature suggests that, as we increase nonverbal immediacy in the classroom, learning will increase. A **hypothesis**, then, is an educated guess or prediction about the relationship between two or more variables. One of these variables is the **independent variable**. It is the antecedent, or the presumed cause, in the relationship. The other variable is the **dependent variable**. It is the consequent, or the presumed effect, in the relationship.

For example, if our hypothesis is "Communication training will improve a manager's media interview performance," the training program is our independent variable, and interview performance is our dependent variable. Or you might *predict* (in other words, hypothesize) that "Higher degrees of communication competence will result in better academic performance." Communication competence is our independent variable, and academic performance is our dependent variable. What we are predicting is that academic performance (the consequent) will vary *as a result of* a person's level of communication competence (the antecedent).

Whether we seek to answer a research question or to test a hypothesis, we must be sure that all elements, such as nonverbal immediacy and learning, are clearly defined so that we know precisely what answers we are seeking or what it is that we are testing. There are two types of definitions. A **conceptual definition** refers to terms used to describe a variable. For example, a conceptual definition of communication competence might be "being an effective communicator." A conceptual definition of academic performance might be "exhibiting knowledge in the classroom." An **operational definition**, on the other hand, describes the procedures we follow to observe or to measure the variables. For example, an operational definition of communication competence might be "the score obtained on the Communication Competency Assessment Instrument." An operational definition of academic performance might be "overall grade-point average." It is important that an operational definition matches the conceptual definition of the concept being studied.

Method of Inquiry

How we go about trying to answer the question or to test the hypothesis reflects our method of inquiry. Researchers have a wealth of possible methods available to them. We may, for example, choose to conduct an experiment or a survey, or we may want to use observational methods, or we may want to do a critical analysis. Sometimes the question itself suggests the most compatible approach, but often past research suggests the best possible approach. The previous literature can help us design our research method. Different researchers are also more comfortable working with one of the different **quantitative** (that is, deductive and statistical) or **qualitative** (that is, inductive and interpretive) **research** methods that we discuss in this chapter.

Data Gathering and Anlysis

Once the most appropriate method is selected, we need to gather our data. If we use observational methods, for example, we'll conduct our observations of nonverbal immediacy in selected classrooms in a systematic manner. If we use experimental methods, we'll set up a more controlled environment in which we manipulate the amount of nonverbal immediacy and then measure the amount of learning. After we collect our data, we need to analyze them to determine the answer to our research question. We might, for example, look for common themes in classroom discussions or submit the data to statistical analysis.

Writing and Discussing

After completing our analysis, we need to write up our results and to consider the meaning and implications of our findings. Did our analysis support our hypothesis? What does it mean if nonverbal immediacy does lead to better learning in the classroom? Do other factors also contribute to learning? Could we have improved our study in any manner? What does this suggest for future researchers to consider?

Let us return to our earlier investigation into the use of media-related training programs for company executives. That study may have left several questions unanswered. For example:

1. How long have these training programs been in existence?

2. How widespread are such media-training programs in this country or in other countries today?

3. Are these training programs effective in improving an executive's ability to deal with the media?

4. Do training programs simply maintain the power structure of the organization?

After defining our problem and reading the literature, we will refine and seek to answer our research questions. We can probably find answers to questions 1 and 2 in the literature. The literature should also offer tentative but incomplete answers to questions 3 and 4, as well as disagreements among researchers. We might, therefore, need to design our own study or analysis to answer the question. How we go about answering the question reflects our method of approach to the investigation. We discuss various methods of communication research in the remainder of this chapter.

Approaches to Communication Research

We classify the method of communication research into two broad approaches. First, message- or artifact-oriented research looks at communication messages and attitudes associated with messages. It includes archival/documentary and survey/interview research. Second, people- or behavior-oriented research looks at communication behavior. It includes observational and experimental research. We will now briefly discuss these two approaches. Having this preliminary information, you should consult other books on research methods to determine the best procedures for a particular investigation.

Message- or Artifact-Oriented Research

Message- or **artifact-oriented research** focuses on examining and interpreting messages and related ideas, such as people's attitudes and opinions about messages, issues, or events. There are two principal types of message- and artifact-oriented research: archival/documentary and survey/interview research.

Archival/Documenatry Research
Archival or **documentary research** centers on finding, examining, and interpreting messages that have been communicated. Common forms of archival/documentary research include library/documentary, historical, critical/rhetorical, and legal

research, as well as secondary, conversation, textual, and content analysis. First, we'll briefly describe archival/documentary research forms. Then, we'll explain one often-used form, content analysis, in more detail.

Library/Documentary Research When conducting **library** or **documentary research,** we examine all relevant, published materials on our topic. These include printed materials such as published and collected documents (for example, chapters, articles, papers, speeches) and, perhaps, media materials such as films, audiotapes, and videotapes. In other words, when we do library/documentary research, we use many of the materials described in Chapters 5 to 8. We use general sources, finding tools, periodicals, and information compilations to examine a research problem or to answer a research question.

All original research begins with library/documentary research. That is, before we start a study, we must first find out what others have learned about a subject.

Historical Research **Historical research** entails drawing conclusions and presenting new explanations about past communication events or communicators. Historical researchers work with *primary* documents, records, and artifacts, such as original speeches, letters, and recordings that are found in archives and libraries such as a presidential library. They prefer these original works to *secondary* sources, which provide another person's summary or explanation of the original sources.

Historical researchers also seek to collect testimony from authorities or others who can support or disconfirm the written and media materials. Interviews and oral histories are useful for gathering such testimony.

Historical researchers need to be as thorough as possible, examining all relevant and available records and artifacts. They seek to record accurately what transpired and to clarify relationships among societal institutions and conditions, people, events, and the like.

Historical studies may be biographical, movement or idea, regional, institutional, case history, selected, or editorial in nature (Phifer, 1961). For example, an institutional study might consider the societal forces that influenced the development of a particular news organization during the first half of the 20th century. A biographical study might focus on the career of a government leader, business executive, or other personality. A movement study might examine the women's rights or civil rights movements during a certain period.

Critical/Rhetorical Research   **Critical** or **rhetorical research** interprets and evaluates communication events and their consequences. Examples of critical research in communication might include applying Aristotle's concept of "invention" to political debate, doing a fantasy-theme analysis of organizational behavior, conducting a dramatistic analysis of a political campaign, examining the social and economic reasons for the decline in daily newspapers, and exploring how media help foster hegemony and maintain societal power structures. Rhetorical/critical research relies on thorough historical gathering of facts. It also relies on critical methods of choosing and applying appropriate criteria or standards of judgment to evaluate communication events.

For example, a president's televised news conferences might be evaluated by several criteria such as effective use of the medium, directness of response to reporters' questions, degree of control over the ground rules, rapport with members of the press, and the amount and quality of information disclosed. Which of these criteria would be used, of course, evolves from the research question. For example, a critical research project might evaluate how media affected government policy during the past 25 years.

Marxism and cultural approaches are two major branches of critical theory in mass communication. In Marxist theories, the media are seen as powerful agents to restrain change for either ideological or economic reasons. The media are owned by a capitalist class and are organized to serve the interests of that class. Media messages depend on the underlying economic and ideological interests of the owners of the media. Marxist approaches direct us to examine critically the structure of media ownership, the operation of media market forces, and how ideological media messages intentionally influence culture by presenting distorted views of reality and class relationships. Cultural approaches focus our attention on understanding the meaning and role of popular culture for societal groups. They direct us to consider how mass culture subordinates deviant societal groups to nondeviant groups.

Legal Research   **Legal research** is both historical and critical in nature. It seeks to clarify and to understand how law operates in society. It focuses on the evolution and application of legal doctrine such as First Amendment law and Federal Communications Commission (FCC) policy. Legal research centers on issues and cases in several areas: defamation, privacy, restraint of expression (such as censorship and obscenity), freedom of information and news access, newsperson privilege, free press and fair trial, and media regulation. Legal research often considers the origin and evolution of legal precedent, debate over such doctrine, and the role of societal agencies, groups, and the like in the status of the legal or policy issue. It relies heavily on primary documentation from legal codes, court cases, judicial opinions, and administrative rulings.

Secondary Analysis   The goal of **secondary analysis** is to shed new light on previous data and conclusions. Researchers sometimes work with previously gathered or archived data, and their purpose is to reconsider and to reinterpret those data in light of different ways of thinking. They may want to ask different questions, for example, about variables related to voting behavior, and use the same set of data previously used to answer other questions. They may want to reorder the data. For example, they may collapse continuous data such as ages ranging from 18 to 90 years into discrete categories such as younger, middle-age, and older. They may want to see if there are any trends over time by using several data sets. Or, they may use different statistical procedures. For example, they may use multivariate rather than univariate statistics to reanalyze interrelated dependent variables. Or, they may use different statistical packages to see whether previous results were an artifact of a particular package's statistical program. Secondary analysis researchers seek new answers to new questions using not-so-new data.

Conversation Analysis   **Conversation analysis**, also termed *relational* and *interactional analysis* in the 1960s and 1970s, examines the structure, messages, function, rules, and content of conversations. Its purpose is to discover if and how people accomplish their goals when they interact. Interpersonal and small-group communication researchers primarily use this method.

Some researchers gather their data by surreptitiously eavesdropping on conversations. Others design experimental settings to record talk. Most, however, prefer to record the interaction in the most natural environment possible.

To do their analysis, researchers gather samples of conversation. They transcribe these samples into written text. Using one of the selected coding schemes, they categorize the messages and analyze message content and category structure. They then draw conclusions about the conversants' goals, rules, and impact on the interaction.

There are two well-known types of conversation analysis. Rogers and Farace's Relational Control Coding Scheme is used to analyze the power and effects of talk on interpersonal relationships. Bales' Interaction Process Analysis is used to trace the stages of small-group interaction. More recently, researchers have been interested in the beginnings and endings of conversations and in the rules people develop and use in everyday conversation.

Textual Analysis   Textual analysis, or reception analysis, is derived from literary criticism and focuses on "reading" media content or "text." It is interested in the text–audience relationship. Audience interpretations are compared to the media text to explain how meaning is socially constructed and variable. Researchers suggest that audience members "rework" the content.

Researchers generally use ethnography, including in-depth interviews and participant observation, to gather audience interpretations of discourse. They systematically record and categorize these audience reports of experiences with the selected media content, seeking explanations of how the meaning of such content is socially or culturally constructed. Such analyses have been done with television dramas, news, romance novels, and the like.

Content Analysis   Content analysis looks at the characteristics of communication messages. The purpose is to learn something about the content and those who produced the messages. Our eventual interest might lie with the effects the content might have on receivers. However, we would need to link content analysis with another method such as survey or experimental research to ascertain such effects. Speeches, news reports, and television programs are often subjected to content analysis to learn about underlying attitudes, biases, or repeating themes.

If we were to perform a content analysis on the memos superiors send to subordinates, we might decide to code each sentence according to its topic: directive, helpful suggestion, reprimand, request for information, friendly reminder, compliment, and so on. This would let us determine the actual nature of the nonpersonal communication process between superiors and subordinates. The type of topic could be affecting the communication process without the superiors being aware of this effect. Content analysis can thus provide important information.

The methodology of content analysis is a multistage process. Let's consider another research problem here: sex-role stereotyping on television. Here's the process:

1. We select the titles we want to sample (for example, television comedy programs).

2. We select the dates to sample (for example, comedy programs aired on prime-time television in 1993). We can form two **composite weeks** that represent the entire year by randomly selecting two Mondays, Tuesdays, Wednesdays, and so on from throughout the year.

3. We select our units of analysis (for example, the occupations of major characters on the TV shows).

4. We assign these units to predetermined mutually exclusive and exhaustive categories (such as lawyer, physician, teacher, police officer, and so on). By mutually exclusive we mean that all categories differ from one another. By exhaustive we mean that all possible categories are included in our analysis.

5. We then compare whether more men or more women are presented in these different roles. We also might compare our results to U.S. population statistics to see whether television presents an unfair or unflattering bias against women or men.

We will describe different sampling techniques in the next section when discussing survey research. As you can see, though, content analysis is a very systematic process.

Survey/Interview Research

Survey researchers seek to describe or to explain people's current attitudes, opinions, thoughts, and perhaps, reports of behavior (such as whether they voted) surrounding an issue or event (such as an election). Because survey research is the most widely used method of communication research, we will explain it in more depth. We will also briefly identify other survey or interview forms: polls, ratings, interviews, and focus groups.

Survey Research   In our example research study we asked, "How widespread are media-training programs in this country today?" This question leads us to survey research. We can, for example, sample corporate leaders seeking to answer the question. Survey researchers try to obtain the needed attitudinal information systematically and efficiently (that is, in the shortest period of time and as inexpensively as possible). **Survey research** is an efficient means of gathering data from large numbers of people.

Before conducting a survey, we must first determine what it is we are trying to learn. Surveys can be used to measure attitudes and reported behaviors linked to experimental research. Yet, survey research usually employs correlational designs, not looking for cause-and-effect connections but seeking to describe either the opinions of people or the relationships between two or more variables in hypotheses or research questions. Before we can construct the specific questions, we must determine how best to get this information (data-collection methods) and choose a sample of **respondents** (sampling).

There are four basic data-collection methods: personal interviews, telephone interviews, mail questionnaires, and self-administered surveys. Personal interviews are face-to-face encounters between the interviewer and selected respondents. Telephone interviews also require an interviewer but are conducted over the phone. Mail questionnaires are self-administered; a respondent receives a survey in the mail and is asked to respond and return it. Besides mail questionnaires, respondents complete other self-administered surveys without prompting from interviewers, such as in a classroom or work setting. Each technique has its advantages and disadvantages. Consult one of the sources at the end of this chapter for additional information. They contain detailed descriptions of questionnaire design and methods of getting a high rate of return for completed questionnaires.

There are also standard methods of selecting a valid **sample** of people from a population. Samples are chosen because it is too costly, time-consuming, or unnecessary to conduct a *census* of the entire population. Sometimes, in fact, a sample can be better than a census of the whole population; if chosen randomly and care is taken to achieve a high return rate, a sample can better represent the population than could a census with a poor return rate. We use probability (random) and nonprobability (nonrandom) techniques to select samples.

Probability sampling allows us to generalize from the sample being observed to the entire population from which that sample is chosen. It uses random sampling techniques and assures us that the sample is representative of the population. These techniques include simple random, systematic, stratified, and cluster sampling.

A **simple random sample** ensures that each person has an equal or known chance of being chosen for the sample. We may need a list of names to select a sample randomly and a table of random numbers to identify those who are chosen. This is not a very efficient method, though, when a large population is involved.

In a **systematic sample**, every *n*th person is chosen from a sampling frame or list (for example, every *10*th name is chosen from a student directory). We need a current and complete population list for this technique to be useful.

A **stratified sample** ensures that certain subgroups of the population are well represented. For example, if we want to be certain that our sample of 100 includes men and women in proportion to their distribution in the campus population (let's say the campus population is 55% women and 45% men), we would obtain separate lists of the men and women students and then randomly select 55 women and 45 men for our sample.

We could use a **cluster sample** if we find it impractical or impossible to compile a list of everyone in a population but can obtain lists of subgroups. For example, we can easily get a list of all dormitories on campus and then randomly select a sample of these. Then we would select a simple random or systematic sample of the dorm residents.

All these probability sampling techniques assure us that the sample is representative of the population from which it is selected, so that we can generalize our findings from the sample to the population.

Sometimes a probability sample isn't necessary. For example, we may be doing an exploratory, pilot study or assessing relationships between two variables to test a certain hypothesis. **Nonprobability sampling** does not permit generalization, but it is valuable for studying particular groups of people. Its techniques include purposive, quota, and accidental sampling.

With a **purposive sample**, we select a sample that contains either a wide variety of people (for example, to pretest a questionnaire before distributing it to our actual sample) or known groups of respondents that we may want to compare in the future (for example, conservative student leaders, reticent communicators, and so on).

A **quota sample** requires us to identify people with certain traits or who are members of known demographic groups (such as men and women). If gender and class standing are important to our research study of a college population, for example, we may want to sample 25 members of each undergraduate class—first-year to fourth-year students—for our 100-person sample and have 50 of them be women and 50 be men. Quota sampling does not require random sampling among the different groups as does stratified sampling.

An **accidental sample**, or convenience sample, is based on surveying respondents who happen to be available. Surveys done in college classes or with shoppers in malls (sometimes called mall-intercept studies) are examples of this sampling technique.

Nonprobability sampling may lead to conclusions that differ from those we would have reached by using probability sampling. But nonprobability methods are still useful when investigating many research questions.

The methodology of survey research, then, is a multistage process. For example, imagine we want to learn about student attitudes on one university campus toward parking on campus. Here's what we can do:

1. Identify our **population,** or group of interest (in this instance, 20,000 students on the campus).

2. Select a sample, or subgroup, of the population to ask our questions. (Because the student directory is inclusive and up-to-date, we'll use systematic sampling to select, say, 500 people from that directory. We know that we won't reach everyone and some will not want to participate, but we hope to end up with about 300 completed questionnaires.)

3. Determine the method for collecting the information. (We'll use telephone interviewing because the survey is brief and we are working from a good campus phone directory.) Often the method influences Step 2, or how the sample is selected.

4. Construct the survey questions to provide the needed information. (We'll administer a brief questionnaire with precise questions about attitudes toward parking and other relevant information such as class standing, driving behavior, and so on.)

5. Collect and analyze the information gathered.

Successful surveys depend on good questionnaires. We must consider the topic and the audience when we construct our questionnaire. The manner in which we ask questions is crucial to getting the information we seek. Here are some suggestions for writing questions and constructing questionnaires:

1. Instructions at the beginning of the questionnaire should relay the importance of and the voluntary nature of the survey.

2. Instructions for completing the questions (or skipping certain questions) should be easily understood by respondents and interviewers.

3. Make sure the questions are clear, precise, and easily understood by all those who are answering.

4. Each question must ask for only one piece of information at a time. Avoid double-barreled questions such as "Do you agree

with the proposed new program in public information and do you think that the effect of this program will be good for students?"

5. Respondents must have knowledge about the information we seek. So, we can't ask them whether they favor the proposed program without first making sure they know what the program is.

6. How we ask people to respond to the questions should be clear and consistent. Such options must provide enough room for open-ended (for example, fill-in words or sentences) or closed-ended responses (for example, circle a number or check a box).

7. The questions and possible response options must be easy to read and presented in a logical sequence.

8. We need effective transitions between questions or parts of the questionnaire (for example, "Now that you told us how you feel about the proposed program in public information, please tell us how you feel about the following campus issues . . . .").

9. If we give respondents a choice of possible answers, we need to make sure those answers are exhaustive (that is, include all possible options) and mutually exclusive (that is, the answers do not overlap).

10. The questionnaire must be printed clearly and look professional. It should contain sufficient white space in margins and between questions.

We can use surveys for descriptive or explanatory purposes. As a descriptive technique, we can use survey research to identify current attitudes and opinions about issues or persons such as political candidates. Here, we need probability samples so that we can generalize from the smaller sample to the larger population.

As an explanatory technique, we can use survey research to examine the relationships between variables. We often use non-probability samples when using surveys for explanation because we are interested in conceptual questions of relationships among variables, rather than in descriptive generalization. We can, for example, devise and use measures of nonverbal immediacy and of learning in an explanatory survey and see whether learning actually relates to nonverbal immediacy. Of course, it's best if our sample reflects the population.

When doing survey research, we need to consider, among other decisions, our sampling procedure, method of data collection, and questionnaire construction. Regardless of whether we use surveys for description or explanation, the choices for effective conduct of survey research, as you can see, are many. Be sure to consult some of the sources at the end of this chapter for fuller information about survey research techniques.

Polls and Ratings   We use probability sampling techniques when doing polls and ratings research. Polls fit nicely with our discussion of surveys. **Polls** are a descriptive form of survey research whereby we try to learn about the attitudes or opinions of certain groups. Because these groups are usually large (for example, U.S. voters), we draw smaller, representative samples of the population and question those in the sample about our topic of interest. Typically, this has to do with attitudes about issues of importance or toward politicians. We constantly see results of such polls conducted by media organizations (for example, the *CBS News/New York Times* poll) or polling organizations (for example, the Gallup, Harris, and Roper organizations).

Ratings are measures of reported behaviors of viewers or listeners of television or radio programs. They express the percentage of viewers or listeners who tune to a given program at a certain time. For example, a *rating* of 15 for *60 Minutes* means that 15% of all possible television households watched *60 Minutes* at that time. A *share* of 20 for the same program means that 20% of the television sets actually turned on at that time were tuned to that program. Ratings research is often conducted by the A. C. Nielsen and Arbitron companies, although other organizations and individuals also do ratings research. These organizations use probability sampling procedures and, generally, either electronic data gathering (for example, people meters) or viewer/listener diaries.

Intensive Interviews and Focus Groups   Besides their use in survey research, **interviews** can be more in-depth. Such intensive interviews are used as qualitative techniques (that is, answering "why" and "how come" questions) by which we can gather information for several research methods such as oral histories and case studies. They might explore, for example, techniques of film directors or communicative behaviors of personnel directors in organizations. They can probe communication attitudes and behaviors such as views of television programs or reasons for interacting with others. Interviews allow one-on-one contact between the researcher and the respondent for longer periods of time (for example, 1 or more hours). They are usually structured; that is, an interview schedule of questions and question order is prepared ahead of time. They do, though, allow flexibility to follow up and probe reasons for certain attitudes and responses.

The **focus group** is another qualitative technique widely used in marketing research but also gaining favor in some areas of communication research. Essentially, it is intensive group interviewing to understand consumer attitudes and behavior. Groups usually contain 6 to 12 participants, and researchers generally conduct at least two focus groups on a topic. A moderator or facilitator leads the group through a planned discussion of a topic such as attitudes about an organization, its programs, or policies. Such groups are popular to test advertising product and broadcast programming ideas. They require careful planning and recruiting of participants. Controlled group discussion is the key to successful focus groups so that all present get a chance to be heard.

We have included some sources at the end of this chapter that provide more detail about polls and ratings research and about interviews and focus groups.

People- or Behavior-Oriented Research

People- or **behavior-oriented research** focuses on actions and reactions of people that do not rely on self-reports of behavior. There are two primary types of this research: observational and experimental.

Observational Research

Observational research looks and sees how people act in different situations. Here, we don't rely on the self-reports of those being surveyed or interviewed (although we might want to interview people to check on our observations). Instead, we observe people in their typical or natural social settings and describe the actions (that is, behaviors) or messages of people or media being studied.

Suppose we are interested in studying communication between superiors and subordinates in organizations. We could devise a survey or interview selected people to get answers to our questions. But we might find that our questions are not answered sufficiently or that the response rate is low. The workers may feel that their employers might have access to their answers, or they may not respond in enough detail to offer insight into superior/subordinate communication. Observational techniques might be more effective for gathering this information.

There are at least five forms of observational research: ethnography, participant observation, unobtrusive observation, network analysis, and verbal and nonverbal coding.

Ethnography   **Ethnography** is used to form objective descriptions of social norms and events as they occur. When attending to the physical and social ecology of the communication setting, ethnographers try to explain behavioral regularities in social situations. In our superior/subordinate study, for example, a researcher might try to describe the rules of interaction by observing different participants in the organization. These would include the patterns of behavior and use of communication channels in that organization. The ethnographer might also interview employees or examine documents and artifacts to verify these observations. This observational technique often results in a *case study*.

Public relations campaigns are also suited to this case-study format. Here a problem has already been identified. Looking for behavioral norms and regularities, the researcher would observe and describe what the public relations practitioner did to solve the problem and then describe the consequences of this action. Ethnographies should include testimony from participants and examine available records and materials related to the case. Participant observation is often used in ethnographic research.

Participant Observation   **Participant observation** is used to study social situations or organizations from an insider's perspective. Researchers participate in the social environment they are observing. They systematically record and classify their observations. The end result of the research is an analytic description of the social situation or organization, moving from specific observations to generalizations about the situation or organization.

Participant observers rely on their own observations, on information from group members, and on whatever records and materials are available and pertinent. For example, a participant observer may secure a job in an organization, observe superior/subordinate interactions, talk to colleagues who have worked there more than 2 years, examine memos, overhear conversations, and, perhaps, examine personnel files. From all these observations, the researcher would form conclusions about communication patterns in that organization.

Unobtrusive Observation   **Unobtrusive observation** is used when researchers want to study communication in a natural setting, yet choose not to become participants in the group or organization. They may want to remain objective observers because they may feel their participation would contaminate the research setting they are studying or they may have ethical concerns about becoming a participant. They also feel that if those who they're observing knew they were being observed, they might behave differently

Unobtrusive field observers also examine social situations or organizations in a systematic manner similar to participant observation, without becoming a group or social participant. For example, we might observe the use of persuasive sales tactics, the creative advertising process at an ad agency, gatekeeping in the newsroom, or the social climate of viewing television in public places.

Network Analysis   **Network analysis** is the study of behavioral interactions among larger numbers of people. If, for example, we are interested in communication among all members of an organization, we can ask workers to keep a log of the people with whom they communicate, the length of these conversations, and the channels used (speech, memo, meetings, electronic mail, teleconferencing, fax, and so on). Then we can analyze the data to find out whether key individuals have open channels to those with whom they must communicate or what social or task roles different people fulfill in the organization.

Verbal and Nonverbal Coding   Researchers have devised a variety of schemes to code verbal behavior such as self-disclosure and nonverbal behavior (for example, kinesics and facial expression). Also, others have developed systems to code marital, family, and group interaction. **Verbal and nonverbal coding** schemes seek to identify patterns of behavior found in the interaction.

Experimental Research

Like observational research, **experimental research** focuses on people and behavior. It is also more concerned with manipulating and controlling behavior to view reactions better. Experimental research is also markedly different in that observations are made under *controlled conditions*. Experimental research is causal. It is based on the premise that one event, let's say Z, will follow another event, let's say Y. If other factors are present (such as A, B, or C), then we could not be certain it is Y that produces Z. Thus, experimental researchers must **control** all relevant factors other than the one being studied. Laboratory settings provide the most control.

The researcher designs experiments to test hypotheses about the events. That is, if the researcher is examining the effect of variable Y on variable Z, she or he will have formed a hypothesis about the relationship. Evaluation and physiological research are done with experimental designs.

Let's say we want to answer the question "Is a training program effective in improving executives' abilities to deal with the media?" How can we design an experiment to give us an idea of the program's effectiveness? Experimental research employs several **experimental designs**, or blueprints for the study.

Preexperimental Designs We could design an experiment where the executives are given a training program, which we label X. We will measure an executive's ability to deal with the media through a simple test, which we label O. We will have the test consist of a question-and-answer session where we will rate the executives on various factors (for example, keeping cool when questioned intently, speed of answering after a question is asked, perceived honesty, and so forth). We would use the resulting scores to measure the executives' abilities. This research design can be diagrammed like this:

$$X \qquad O$$

This design is known as a *One-Shot Case-Study Design*. It closely resembles descriptive survey or observational research. It is not, however, a controlled observation because many other variables can enter the situation. For example, we don't know what abilities these executives had before receiving the training program.

If we modify our original design and measure the executives' abilities before and after the training, we would be controlling for prior abilities and have a *One-Group Pretest-Posttest Design*:

$$O \qquad X \qquad O$$

This design allows us to say more about the effectiveness of the training program, X, but there are still other variables that might be present. The executives might have improved their abilities on their own time, or ability might be increased normally each time any executive deals with media questions. Or, the first measure of their abilities might cause the executives to become more receptive to training in this area.

Experimental Designs   What we need, then, is a group of executives who do not receive the training program so that we can be more certain that it is the program that influences the executives' abilities. The design that controls for these factors is known as the *Pretest–Posttest Control-Group Design*:

$$\begin{array}{ccccc} \textbf{R} & \textbf{O} & \textbf{X} & \textbf{O} \\ \textbf{R} & \textbf{O} & & \textbf{O} \end{array}$$

In the diagram, *R* refers to the fact that we randomly assign individuals to one of the two groups so that some with higher and lower initial ability are presumably in each group. We give both groups an ability test but have only one group take the training program. The group that does not receive the training is called the **control group**. We then give the ability test again to both groups. We assume that any natural increase in ability from test 1 to test 2 would (because of random assignment to groups) occur in both groups. If ability improves more in the trained group, we can say that the training program had some effect.

What we still have not controlled, however, is the possibility that the group receiving the training program might be more sensitized and influenced by it as a result of the first ability test. We can see whether the initial ability test was influential in increasing sensitivity by dividing the executives into four groups instead of two. We would then give two of the groups the initial ability test and not give it to the other two groups. This is the *Solomon Four-Group Design*:

$$\begin{array}{ccccc} \textbf{R} & \textbf{O} & \textbf{X} & \textbf{O} \\ \textbf{R} & \textbf{O} & & \textbf{O} \\ \textbf{R} & & \textbf{X} & \textbf{O} \\ \textbf{R} & & & \textbf{O} \end{array}$$

This design can help determine if the first test of ability increased executives' sensitivity to the training program. However, it does make our experimental research unnecessarily complicated. For one thing, it requires twice as many subjects as the other designs. It seems that an adaptation of this design, the *Posttest-Only Control-Group Design* might serve our initial purposes well enough:

$$\begin{array}{ccc} \textbf{R} & \textbf{X} & \textbf{O} \\ \textbf{R} & & \textbf{O} \end{array}$$

In this design, we assign executives randomly to one of two groups. One group receives the training program; the other group does not.

At the end, we measure the abilities of individuals in both groups. Now we have controlled for everything we could think of that would provide alternative explanations of our findings. Although we lack a pretest, we have also avoided the potential complications of sensitizing a group to the test and the unnecessary additional demands of the Solomon Four-Group Design. See Campbell and Stanley (1963), Creswell (1994), and Spector (1981) for more information about experimental designs.

Control groups, which do not receive the experimental treatment that **experimental groups** do, then, are crucial for experimental designs. In these experimental designs, we randomly assign **subjects** (that is, participants in an experiment) to either the experimental group or the control group. Only those in the experimental group receive the experimental treatment (the independent variable) before we observe or measure the behavior (the dependent variable) of subjects in both groups.

In our training and media example, only those subjects assigned to the experimental group would be given communication training. We would measure the behavior or performance in media interviews for members of both the experimental and control groups. This enables us to see whether differences on the dependent measure (performance in media interviews) result from the experimental treatment (communication training) because only one of the two groups received that treatment.

Types of Experimental Research   Experimental research is often subdivided into two main types, laboratory and nonlaboratory. In **laboratory research**, people are taken out of their natural surroundings so that more variables can be controlled (for example, noise, other people present, or the surroundings themselves). Sometimes, however, unrealistic results are achieved when people are moved from their normal social surroundings and when they perceive they are being observed. That is, they may communicate differently in a laboratory setting. In **nonlaboratory** (or **field**) experimental settings (which are similar to those used in participant observation and case-study research), people are studied in their natural settings. The researcher, though, has less control over potentially influential variables.

For example, let's imagine you want to study the effects of violent cartoons on children's interactions with one another. In a laboratory study, you would randomly assign children to play groups where half the children view violent cartoons and the other half view nonviolent ones. You would then measure their aggression toward others. However, moving these children into "foreign" surroundings may, in some way, influence their behavior. They may realize they're being watched and curtail their aggression. But if you were to study them in a natural (or nonlaboratory) environment such as a day-care center, other factors might influence their behavior, such as already existing personality conflicts between certain children or the teacher's rules for proper behavior in the day-care center.

Obviously, your decision of where to study communication must take into account the other factors (or **intervening variables**) that could affect the research results. You must make choices about what elements of control can be sacrificed. What we are referring to here are questions of validity.

Measurement of variables must be valid. In general, **validity** refers to measuring what we intend to measure. If an index, test, or scale is used to measure a particular construct, the measure should include items or questions about all aspects of the construct (*content validity*), it should relate to other, similar measures or predict future behavior or attitudes (*criterion-related validity*), and should measure only the construct it purports to measure (*construct validity*).

Measures also must be reliable; **reliability** refers to how dependable, stable, consistent, and repeatable measures are in a study and across several studies. If we use a measure twice and the results are about the same both times, the measure has *test-retest* reliability. If all items in the measure seem to measure the same thing, we say the measure has *internal consistency*. If there are two forms for the same measure (say a test) and people score the same on both, we'd say the forms are *parallel*. And if two or more raters/observers/coders agree on using some sort of scale for their observations, they are said to have *interrater reliability*.

Valid and reliable instruments increase the **internal validity** of a research study. They ensure that no one can derive other possible interpretations of the results. **External validity** refers to how generalizable the results are to people and contexts other than the experimental group and situation.

The various research methods we have described in this chapter are used to seek answers to research questions or to test hypotheses. Original research, then, is another important means of adding to our knowledge about communication. The sources listed at the end of this chapter describe more fully the types of communication research discussed here.

Research Ethics

Now that we've considered how research is conducted, we should consider how researchers meet their ethical obligations to the subjects or participants in their research investigations and to their discipline. **Research ethics** concerns what is right and wrong in the conduct of research inquiries.

Researchers need to be responsible to their discipline, as well as to the participants in their research projects. Researchers must conform to their discipline's professional standards of conduct. It should go without saying that researchers need to be accurate and *honest* when conducting research. By now you can tell that research involves a series of choices about how to address research questions and to conduct such inquiries. Researchers must be careful to remain systematic and objective in the many choices they make when designing measures, selecting and observing participants, analyzing their data, and reporting the results of their studies.

In addition, especially because we involve people in so much of our research, communication researchers must constantly respect the rights of research participants. Researchers adhere to a basic rule: *Do no harm*. If you would not be willing to be a participant in your own research project, you probably shouldn't be doing that project with others. Researchers need to take steps to reduce or to eliminate the risk of physical or psychological discomfort.

Toward this end, universities and many other organizations have Human Subjects Review Boards whose purpose is to balance the needs of the researcher and the rights of the research participants. Researchers who use human subjects need to obtain approval from this Board before conducting their research. Primarily, Human Subjects Review Boards consider whether proposed research projects are of sufficient benefit to offset any potential costs or discomforts to the participants.

Researchers also consider several other ethical concerns. First, subjects or respondents should be voluntary participants in any research project. They should provide their *informed consent*, and should not be coerced to participate. We should engage participants in research with their knowledge and consent. This, of course, is difficult for observational and field research in which observations may take place in crowded public places. This task is easier for survey and laboratory researchers to accomplish.

Second, researchers often withhold the true nature of the research project from the participants because knowing the purpose of the project may influence how participants act and answer questions. Sometimes, *deception* is even a necessary part of an experimental research project. Researchers, though, are obliged to inform participants about the goals and nature of the project at the project's conclusion. This is typically referred to as *debriefing*.

Third, researchers need to protect the *privacy* of their subjects or respondents by promising them anonymity or confidentiality. Anonymity means that participants take part in the research project without the researcher's knowledge of their identity (for example, no names are written on questionnaires). There are times when researchers need to be able to identify their participants, especially when they need to do follow-up questionnaires or interviews with the same people. Confidentiality means that researchers will protect and not reveal the names of participants.

We've just touched upon several important ethical concerns: honesty, harm, informed consent, deception, and privacy. In general, research participants must be treated fairly and shown courtesy and respect. Researchers must address these issues when they plan and conduct communication investigations.

Summary

Research is an objective and systematic process to solve theoretical and applied problems. It can be descriptive or explanatory. It seeks to answer research questions not already answered by past research or to test hypotheses, which specify relationships among independent and dependent variables. The research process moves through several stages from developing a research problem to discussing the implications of the findings of a study. How we seek to answer questions reflects our method of inquiry.

One communication research approach is message- or artifact-oriented research, which includes archival/documentary and survey/interview research. Forms of archival/documentary research are library/documentary, historical, critical/rhetorical, and legal research and textual, secondary, conversation, and content analysis. Survey researchers primarily seek to describe or to explain attitudes. Decisions about sampling procedure, method of data collection, and questionnaire construction are crucial when doing survey research. Other survey or interview forms include polls, ratings, interviews, and focus groups.

Another communication research approach is people- or behavior-oriented research, which includes observational and experimental research. Forms of observational research are ethnography, participant observation, unobtrusive observation, network analysis, and verbal and nonverbal coding. Experimental research is conducted under controlled conditions and employs several designs. It can be done in the laboratory and in the field.

However research is done, measurement of variables must be valid and reliable. Researchers must also address several ethical issues when planning and conducting their studies.

Selected Sources

Comprehensive Texts

Anderson, J. A. (1987). *Communication research: Issues and methods.* New York: McGraw-Hill.

Babbie, E. (1995). *The practice of social research* (7th ed.). Belmont, CA: Wadsworth.

Barzun, J., & Graff, H. F. (1992). *The modern researcher* (5th ed.). Fort Worth, TX: Harcourt Brace Jovanovich.

Bowers, J. W., & Courtright, J. A. (1984). *Communication research methods.* Glenview, IL: Scott, Foresman.

Clark, R. A. (1991). *Studying interpersonal communication: The research experience.* Newbury Park, CA: Sage.

Frey, L. R., Botan, C. H., Friedman, P. G., & Kreps, G.L. (1991). *Investigating communication: An introduction to research methods.* Englewood Cliffs, NJ: Prentice Hall.

Gudykunst, W. B., & Kim, Y. Y. (Eds.). (1984). *Methods for intercultural communication research.* Beverly Hills, CA: Sage.

Judd, C. M., Smith, E. R., & Kidder, L. H. (1991). *Research methods in social relations* (6th ed.). Fort Worth, TX: Harcourt Brace Jovanovich.

Katzer, J., Cook, K. H., & Crouch, W. W. (1991). *Evaluating information: A guide for users of social science research* (3rd ed.). New York: McGraw-Hill.

Kerlinger, F. N. (1986). *Foundations of behavioral research* (3rd ed.). New York: Holt, Rinehart & Winston.

Nachmias, C., & Nachmias, D. (1992). *Research methods in the social sciences* (4th ed.). New York: St. Martin's Press.

Reinard, J. C. (1994). *Introduction to communication research.* Dubuque, IA: Brown & Benchmark.

Smith, M. J. (1988). *Contemporary communication research methods: Introductory perspectives.* Belmont, CA: Wadsworth.

Stacks, D. W., & Hocking, J. E. (1992). *Essentials of communication research.* New York: HarperCollins.

Watt, J. H., & van den Berg, S. A. (1995). *Research methods for communication science.* Boston: Allyn & Bacon.

_____

_____

_____

_____

_____

_____

_____

_____

Content Analysis

Holsti, O. R. (1969). *Content analysis for the social sciences and humanities.* Reading, MA: Addison-Wesley.
Krippendorff, K. (1980). *Content analysis: An introduction to its methodology.* Beverly Hills, CA: Sage.
Weber, R. P. (1990). *Basic content analysis* (2nd ed). Newbury Park, CA: Sage.

_____

_____

_____

_____

_____

_____

Design and Measurement

Blalock, H. M., Jr. (1982). *Conceptualization and measurement in the social sciences.* Beverly Hills, CA: Sage.
Camilli, G., & Shepard, L. A. (1994). *Methods for identifying biased test items.* Thousand Oaks, CA: Sage.
Campbell, D. T., & Stanley, J. C. (1963). *Experimental and quasi-experimental designs for research.* Chicago: Rand McNally.
Carmines, E. G., & Zeller, R. A. (1979). *Reliability and validity assessment.* Beverly Hills, CA: Sage.

Cochran, W. G., & Cox, G. M. (1992). *Experimental designs* (2nd ed.). New York: Wiley.

Creswell, J. W. (1994). *Research design: Qualitative & quantitative approaches*. Thousand Oaks, CA: Sage.

Educational and Psychological Measurement. (1941–). Thousand Oaks, CA: Sage.

Emmert, P., & Barker, L. L. (Eds.). (1989). *Measurement of communication behavior*. New York: Longman.

Hopkins, K. D., Stanley, J. C., & Hopkins, B. R. (1990). *Educational and psychological measurement and evaluation* (7th ed.). Englewood Cliffs, NJ: Prentice Hall.

Huck, S. W., & Sandler, H. M. (1979). *Rival hypotheses: Alternative interpretations of data based conclusions*. New York: Harper & Row.

Miller, D. C. (1991). *Handbook of research design and social measurement* (5th ed.). Newbury Park, CA: Sage.

Spector, P. E. (1981). *Research designs*. Beverly Hills, CA: Sage.

Tardy, C. H. (1988). *A handbook for the study of human communication: Methods and instruments for observing, measuring, and assessing communication processes*. Norwood, NJ: Ablex.

Traub, R. E. (1994). *Reliability for the social sciences: Theory and application*. Thousand Oaks, CA: Sage.

Media Research

Adams, R. C. (1989). *Social survey methods for mass media research*. Hillsdale, NJ: Erlbaum.

Berger, A. A. (1991). *Media research techniques*. Newbury Park, CA: Sage.

Beville, H. M., Jr. (1988). *Audience ratings: Radio, television, cable* (rev. ed.). Hillsdale, NJ: Erlbaum.

Dominick, J. R., & Fletcher, J. E. (Eds.). (1985). *Broadcasting research methods*. Boston: Allyn and Bacon.

Fletcher, A. D., & Bowers, T. A. (1991). *Fundamentals of advertising research* (4th ed.). Belmont, CA: Wadsworth.

Fletcher, J. E. (Ed.). (1981). *Handbook of radio and TV broadcasting: Research procedures in audience, program and revenues.* New York: Van Nostrand Reinhold.

Hartshorn, G. G. (1991). *Audience research sourcebook.* Washington, DC: National Association of Broadcasters.

Hsia, H. J. (1988). *Mass communications research methods: A step-by-step approach.* Hillsdale, NJ: Erlbaum.

Lang, A. (Ed.). (1994). *Measuring psychological responses to media.* Hillsdale, NJ: Erlbaum.

Sharp, N. W. (Ed.). (1988). *Communications research: The challenge of the information age.* Syracuse, NY: Syracuse University Press.

Singletary, M. W. (1993). *Mass communication research: Contemporary methods and applications.* New York: Longman.

Startt, J. D., & Sloan, W. D. (1989). *Historical methods in mass communication.* Hillsdale, NJ: Erlbaum.

Stempel, G. H., & Westley, B. H. (Eds.). (1989). *Research methods in mass communication* (2nd ed.). Englewood Cliffs, NJ: Prentice Hall.

Webster, J. G., & Lichty, L. W. (1991). *Ratings analysis: Theory and practice.* Hillsdale, NJ: Erlbaum.

Williams, F., Rice, R. E., & Rogers, E. M. (1988). *Research methods and the new media.* New York: Free Press.

Wimmer, R. D., & Dominick, J. R. (1994). *Mass media research: An introduction* (4th ed.). Belmont, CA: Wadsworth.

_____

_____

_____

_____

_____

_____

_____

Qualitative and Applied Research

Applied Social Research Methods. (1984–). Thousand Oaks, CA: Sage. (A series of over 35 monographs)

Berg, B. L. (1995). *Qualitative research methods for the social sciences* (2nd ed.). Boston: Allyn & Bacon.

Carter, K., & Spitzack, C. (1989). *Doing research on women's communication: Perspectives on theory and method.* Norwood, NJ: Ablex.

Denzin, N. K., & Lincoln, Y. S. (Eds.). (1994). *Handbook of qualitative research*. Thousand Oaks, CA: Sage.

Herndon, S. L., & Kreps, G. L. (1993). *Qualitative research: Application in organizational communication*. Cresskill, NJ: Hampton Press.

Krueger, R. A. (1994). *Focus groups: A practical guide for applied research* (2nd ed.). Thousand Oaks, CA: Sage.

Lindlof, T. R. (1995). *Qualitative communication research methods*. Thousand Oaks, CA: Sage.

Lofland, J. (1995). *Analyzing social settings: A guide to qualitative observation and analysis* (3rd ed.). Belmont, CA: Wadsworth.

Marshall, C., & Rossman, G. B. (1994). *Designing qualitative research* (2nd ed.). Thousand Oaks, CA: Sage.

Merton, R. K., Lowenthal, M. F., & Kendall, P. L. (1990). *The focused interview: A manual of problems and procedures* (2nd ed.). New York: Free Press.

Miles, M. B., & Huberman, A. M. (1994). *Qualitative data analysis: An expanded sourcebook* (2nd ed.). Thousand Oaks, CA: Sage.

Morgan, G. (Ed.). (1983). *Beyond method: Strategies for social research*. Beverly Hills, CA: Sage.

Murphy, J. W., & Pilotta, J. J. (Eds.). (1983). *Qualitative methodology, theory and application: A guide for the social practitioner*. Dubuque, IA: Kendall Hunt.

Narula, U., & Pearce, W. B. (Eds.). (1990). *Cultures, politics, and research programs: An international assessment of practical problems in field research*. Hillsdale, NJ: Erlbaum.

O'Hair, D., & Kreps, G. L. (1990). *Applied communication theory and research*. Hillsdale, NJ: Erlbaum.

Qualitative Research Methods. (1986–). Thousand Oaks, CA: Sage. (A series of over 35 monographs)

Shaffir, W. B., & Stebbins, R. A. (Eds.). (1991). *Experiencing fieldwork: An inside view of qualitative research*. Newbury Park, CA: Sage.

Spradley, J. P. (1979). *The ethnographic interview*. New York: Holt, Rinehart & Winston.

Stake, R. E. (1995). *The art of case study research: Perspectives on practice*. Thousand Oaks, CA: Sage.

Stewart, D. W., & Shamdasani, P. N. (Eds.). (1990). *Focus groups: Theory and practice*. Newbury Park, CA: Sage.

Strauss, A., & Corbin, J. (1990). *Basics of qualitative research: Grounded theory procedures and techniques*. Thousand Oaks, CA: Sage.

Webb, E. J., Campbell, D. T., Schwartz, R. D., Sechrest, L., & Grove, J. B. (1981). *Nonreactive measures in the social sciences* (2nd ed.). Boston: Houghton Mifflin.

Weitzman, E. A., & Miles, M. B. (1995). *Computer programs for qualitative data analysis*. Thousand Oaks, CA: Sage.

Wolcott, H. (1990). *Writing up qualitative research*. Thousand Oaks, CA: Sage.

Rhetorical and Media Criticism

Brock, B. L., Scott, R. L., & Chesebro, J. W. (1989). *Methods of rhetorical criticism: A twentieth-century perspective* (3rd ed., rev.). Detroit: Wayne State University Press.

Foss, S. K. (1989). *Rhetorical criticism: Exploration and practice.* Prospect Heights, IL: Waveland Press.

Hart, R. P. (1990). *Modern rhetorical criticism.* Glenview, IL: Scott, Foresman/Little, Brown.

Phifer, G. (1961). The historical approach. In C. W. Dow (Ed.), *An introduction to graduate study in speech and theatre* (pp. 52–80). East Lansing: Michigan State University Press.

Rybacki, K. C., & Rybacki, D. J. (1991). *Communication criticism: Approaches and genres.* Belmont, CA: Wadsworth.

Vande Berg, L. R., & Wenner, L. A. (1991). *Television criticism: Approaches and applications.* New York: Longman.

Statistics

Blalock, H. M., Jr. (1979). *Social statistics* (rev. 2nd ed.). New York: McGraw-Hill.

Bruning, J. L., & Kintz, B. L. (1987). *Computational handbook of statistics* (3rd ed.). Glenview, IL: Scott, Foresman.

Cody, R. P., & Smith, J. K. (1991). *Applied statistics and the SAS programming language* (3rd ed.). Englewood Cliffs, NJ: Prentice Hall.

Cohen, J. (1988). *Statistical power analysis for the behavioral sciences* (2nd ed.). Hillsdale, NJ: Erlbaum.

Cooley, W. W., & Lohnes, P. R. (1985). *Multivariate data analysis*. New York: Wiley.

Diekhoff, G. (1992). *Statistics for the social and behavioral sciences: Univariate, bivariate, multivariate*. Dubuque, IA: Brown.

Flury, B., & Riedwyl, H. (1988). *Multivariate statistics: A practical approach*. New York: Chapman and Hall.

Hair, J. F. (1995). *Multivariate data analysis: With readings* (4th ed.). New York: Macmillan.

Harris, R. J. (1985). *A primer of multivariate statistics* (2nd ed.). Orlando, FL: Academic Press.

Healey, J. F. (1993). *Statistics, a tool for social research* (3rd ed.). Belmont, CA: Wadsworth.

Jendrek, M. P. (1985). *Through the maze: Statistics with computer applications*. Belmont, CA: Wadsworth.

Kraemer, H. C., & Thiemann, S. (1987). *How many subjects? Statistical power analysis in research*. Newbury Park, CA: Sage.

Levin, J., & Fox, J. A. (1993). *Elementary statistics in social research* (6th ed.). New York: HarperCollins.

Mantzopoulos, V. L. (1995). *Statistics for the social sciences*. Englewood Cliffs, NJ: Prentice Hall.

Monge, P. R., & Cappella, J. M. (Eds.). (1980). *Multivariate techniques in human communication research*. New York: Academic Press.

Ott, L., Larson, R. F., & Mendenhall, W. (1987). *Statistics: A tool for the social sciences* (4th ed.). Boston: PWS-Kent.

Quantitative Applications in the Social Sciences. (1976–). Thousand Oaks, CA: Sage. (A series of over 100 monographs on statistics and research methodology)

Sirkin, R. M. (1995). *Statistics for the social sciences*. Thousand Oaks, CA: Sage.

Stevens, J. (1992). *Applied multivariate statistics for the social sciences* (2nd ed.). Hillsdale, NJ: Erlbaum.

Tatsuoka, M. M. (1988). *Multivariate analysis: Techniques for educational and psychological research* (2nd ed.). New York: Macmillan.

Walsh, A. (1990). *Statistics for the social sciences: With computer applications*. New York: Harper & Row.

Williams, F. (1992). *Reasoning with statistics* (4th ed.). Fort Worth, TX: Harcourt Brace Jovanovich.

_____

_____

_____

_____

_____

_____

_____

_____

Survey Research

Babbie, E. R. (1990). *Survey research methods* (2nd ed.). Belmont, CA: Wadsworth.

Backstrom, C. H., & Hursh-Cesar, G. D. (1981). *Survey research* (2nd ed.). New York: Wiley.

Converse, J. M., & Presser, S. (1986). *Survey questions: Handcrafting the standardized questionnaire.* Beverly Hills, CA: Sage.

Fink, A., & Kosecoff, J. B. (1985). *How to conduct surveys: A step-by-step guide.* Beverly Hills, CA: Sage.

Fowler, F. J., Jr. (1993). *Survey research methods* (2nd ed.). Thousand Oaks, CA: Sage.

Frey, J. H. (1989). *Survey research by telephone* (2nd ed.). Newbury Park, CA: Sage.

Kalton, G. (1983). *Introduction to survey sampling.* Beverly Hills, CA: Sage.

Lavrakas, P. J. (1993). *Telephone survey methods: Sampling, selection, and supervision* (2nd ed.). Thousand Oaks, CA: Sage.

Wilhoit, G. C., & Weaver, D. H. (1990). *Newsroom guide to polls and surveys.* Bloomington: Indiana University Press.

_____

_____

_____

_____

_____

_____

_____

Exercises

1. Choose a research topic and identify one historical research question and one critical research question that are as yet unanswered by previous research.

2. Identify a research question for that topic that can be answered by content analysis. Describe the procedure you would use to conduct that content analysis.

3. How could you use participant observation to answer such a question on this topic? How would you function in this environment and what artifacts would you need to examine?

4. What research question relating to this topic could be answered by survey research? Explain the strengths and limitations of survey research to examine that question. Which observational technique would best lend itself to this project? Explain why.

5. Describe a possible experiment that could be conducted to provide more information on your topic. Develop two specific research questions about this topic and present an appropriate experimental design for each.

Chapter 10

Writing Research Papers

Writing is a most important part of any research endeavor. Without clear writing, readers cannot understand the writer's research ideas and findings. In this book, it is impossible for us to provide a comprehensive overview of how to write well. Many books written specifically for that purpose contain comprehensive treatments of effective writing. In this chapter, we present basic elements of good writing style, writing and bibliographic formats, and copyediting and proofreading techniques. In general, writers must use a clear, lucid style, adhere to the rules of grammar and spelling, and present the report in an accepted format.

Basic Elements of Good Writing

Clear writing is smooth and consistent. That is, it has no shifts in topic or person, and maintains consistent verb tense. A shift in topic or thought means that the writer begins writing about a particular subject and ends the paragraph or section with a different theme or idea. Writers must read through their drafts to avoid this. Shift in verb tense means that sentences vacillate between the past, present, and future tenses.

Tense and Agreement

Most literature reviews and research reports should use a standard formula for verb tense. The *Publication Manual of the American Psychological Association* (APA), for example, advocates using the past tense (Miller [1983] showed . . .) or the present perfect tense (Miller [1983] has shown . . .) when reviewing the literature. Writers should also use the past tense to describe the procedures of an already conducted study and to describe the results of a completed study. Thus, writers should use the past tense for any research finding, idea, or opinion that has already been published.

When they express their own conclusions or ideas about those results, writers should shift to the present tense to show the reader the difference between the two. The present tense is used to *discuss* the meaning and implications of the results of the study and to present conclusions. Writers should use the future tense for presenting future research directions and in the method section of the research prospectus. Using this standard format helps ensure clear and consistent verb tense and smooth reading.

One problem writers face by adopting the APA rules is that they sometimes put everything into the past tense. But, as the following sentences show, the writer uses past tense in the first sentence to show that the study was conducted in the past. In the second sentence, however, the writer uses the present tense to discuss these results:

■ Brown (1990) found that students who like their instructors asked more questions. Her results suggest that students learn more when teachers use immediacy behaviors in the classroom.

A shift in person means that there are inconsistencies in person and number (that is, between the noun and the singular or plural pronoun). One common mistake is to begin a sentence with a singular noun and shift to a plural pronoun, as in the following sentence:

■ A person who has high communication satisfaction finds that they like conversing with other people.

The "they" in this example is incorrect because "person" is a singular noun. Writers often shift pronouns to the plural to avoid mistakes with noun–pronoun agreement or to avoid using the awkward "he/she" pronoun. They must remember to shift the subject also:

■ People who have high communication satisfaction find that they like conversing with other people.

Actually, a more concise way of writing this sentence is to omit the words "find that they."

Voice

Students often confuse "past tense" with "passive voice." Writers should use the active, not the passive, voice in their writing whenever possible. When using the active voice, writers present the subject of the sentence first and avoid the use of prepositions. It makes writing more interesting and readable. Consider the following two sentences. The first is in the active voice and the second in the passive.

- Livingstone (1989) found that *Coronation Street* viewers actively created clear understanding of the program's characters.
- In a study by Livingstone (1989), it was found that people had a clear understanding of the characters in *Coronation Street*.

Transitions

If you present your ideas in an orderly progression, you will achieve continuity and smoothness. You should identify relationships between ideas and use transitions to maintain the progression of ideas. Transitions often help provide a time link (*then, next, after, while, since*); a cause-effect link (*therefore, so, thus, as a result*); an addition link (*besides, in addition, moreover, furthermore, similarly*); or a contrast link (*however, but, conversely, nevertheless, although, whereas*) (American Psychological Association, 1994, p. 24).

Grammar

Of course, writers should follow standard rules of grammar throughout. Most scholars routinely consult a basic writing or grammar guide or handbook; keep one handy for your writing projects! Day (1994) provided "The Ten Commandments of Good Writing" that aptly illustrate grammatical problems:

1. Each pronoun should agree with their antecedent.
2. Just between you and I, case is important.
3. A preposition is a poor word to end a sentence with. . . .
4. Verbs has to agree with their subject.

5. Don't use no double negatives.

6. Remember to never split an infinitive.

7. Avoid cliches like the plague.

8. Join clauses good, like a conjunction should.

9. Do not use hyperbole; not one writer in a million can use it effectively.

10. About sentence fragments. (p. 160)

Paragraph Structure

Good writing also means writing strong paragraphs with clear thesis statements and complete sentences. A strong paragraph is one that focuses on only one idea. It begins with a thesis (a brief condensation or overview of the paragraph) and uses explanation, elaboration, and supporting material to develop the thesis. Each sentence supports and develops the main idea. Often the paragraph ends with a transition to the next main idea.

Paragraphs can be too long or too short. Lengthy paragraphs (for example, a page long) often have two or more main ideas. They should be split into single-idea paragraphs. On the other hand, one or two sentence paragraphs lack adequate development of the thesis or main idea.

Quoting and Paraphrasing

Plagiarism means using an author's words or ideas without giving credit. Credit for ideas usually is in the form of citing the author and year of publication in the text and reference list. Credit for actual words goes beyond this to giving the page number in the text and using quotation marks around the quoted material.

Babbie (1995) devised a system to help students see the difference between acceptable and unacceptable **citations**, and we've adapted it here. First, here is a paragraph from Rubin and McHugh's (1987) article on parasocial interaction:

> As Horton and Wohl (1956) hypothesized, parasocial interaction is similar to the establishment of social relationship with others. In this investigation, parasocial interaction was related strongly to social and task attraction towards the media personality, and to importance of relationship development with the personality. This supports previous contentions that media relationships can be seen as functional alternatives to interper-

sonal relationships (Rosengren & Windahl, 1972; Rubin & Rubin, 1985). Interpersonal and mediated relationships appear to follow a similar process of development. (p. 288)

Second, here are three acceptable citation methods:

Quotation	As Rubin and McHugh (1987) concluded, "interpersonal and mediated relationships appear to follow a similar process of development" (p. 288).
Paraphrase	Rubin and McHugh (1987) argued that interpersonal and media relationships follow a similar developmental pattern.
Idea	The way in which people develop relationships with others is very much like the way they develop relationships with television characters (Rubin & McHugh, 1987).

Note that all three methods give credit to the source. When we use a string of actual words, we must surround them with quotation marks and give the page number. Names of variables or constructs that authors use in their text need not be "quoted" because they are likely terms that others would use. The key here is *a string of words*.

Third, here are three unacceptable citations; we would term them "plagiarism."

Direct quotation, no citation	Interpersonal and mediated relationships appear to follow a similar process of development.
Edited quotation, presented as one's own	Media relationships can be seen as functional alternatives to interpersonal relationships and follow a similar process of development.
Paraphrased, but ideas presented as one's own	Media and interpersonal relationships follow similar developmental processes.

It is unethical to use another person's words or ideas and present them as your own. Universities and other organizations have specific rules about plagiarism that they expect scholars to follow.

Verb Choice
Often, when introducing quoted material or paraphrasing authors, you find you need a verb to tell the reader what the authors said,

found, and so on. Many verbs are appropriate for scholarly reports, but choosing which one to use depends on the context of the paraphrasing or quotation. For example, the following sentence shows an active way of referring to a particular study (because the authors are listed as the subject instead of as a prepositional phrase):

■ Bell and Daly (1984) _____ four components of affinity seeking.

Now, which verb to use? Here are some commonly found in journal articles. Each has a specific meaning. Which one would be appropriate here?

argued	extended	proposed
assumed	explained	questioned
believed	found	reasoned
concluded	identified	replied
contended	investigated	reported
declared	maintained	showed
defined	noted	suggested
described	observed	thought
developed	presented	viewed

Many of these verbs would fit our sentence, depending on what meaning we want to convey. For example, we could use *argued* to show that there may have been some controversy in the past about the number of components, and Bell and Daly's opinion is that there are four. We could use *presented* to introduce the four components. Or we could use *identified* to suggest Bell and Daly were among the first to see the four-part system; they may also have *described* and *found* them, but *identified* used in the thesis sentence helps us structure a paragraph about what the components of affinity seeking are and how the authors discovered them. Which verb to use depends on the paragraph's purpose.

Style

Writing style has many important elements. The following guidelines should help you improve your writing style.

Tips For Effective Writing

1. Research papers are typically written in a formal style, generally in the third person. Some scholarly journals, however,

have relaxed this guideline and do allow first-person writing. Avoid slang terms and colloquialisms.

2. Avoid an overly descriptive writing style—as in, "The subjects cowered nervously at the thought of spilling their souls to a stranger." That style may be appropriate for a creative writing assignment. It is not appropriate for a scholarly research project.

3. Use the active voice: "Johnson (1992) studied the effects of media viewing on adolescents." Avoid the passive voice: "The effects of media viewing on adolescents were studied by Johnson (1985)." Although you'll often encounter the passive voice in many published research articles, readers find the style tiresome. The tendency to use the third person sometimes encourages passive writing.

4. Avoid jargon in place of common terminology and be precise. You may be familiar with the terms, but your readers may not be. Kessler and McDonald (1984) provide a good example of scientific jargon: "Despite rigid re-examination of all experimental variables, this protocol continued to produce data at variance with our subsequently proven hypothesis" (p. 122). All the authors needed to say was that the "experiment didn't work."

5. Language should be gender neutral. Avoid using sexist language, sexist style, and language that makes the referent ambiguous—for example, *his* (when you intend *his* or *her)* and *men* (when you are referring to people). Also avoid language that stereotypes people—for example, the physician saw *his* patient, the *female* psychiatrist, or the police*man*. In many instances, you can avoid sexist language by using plural forms and being sensitive to stereotypes.

6. Be economical in expression. Say only what needs to be said. Wordiness does not improve comprehension. Yet, be sure to say enough so the reader can understand the point.

7. Make the conclusions you draw and the contradictions you find in the literature clear in your report. Don't simply assume that readers know the subject because you do. It is often wiser to assume that the reader knows little about your topic.

8. Be sure that the pronouns you use (*its, this, that, these, those)* have clear references to their antecedents. Also, use pronouns to focus nouns—for example, this *test,* that *concept,* these *subjects,* those *results.*

9. Use short rather than elongated sentences. Avoid run-on expressions that will lose the reader's attention and comprehension.

10. Move from section to section without abruptness. Use transition sentences to help shift your reader's attention from one section to another. Provide appropriate headings and logical organization.

11. Use correct punctuation to support your meaning.

12. Use proper grammar and spelling. Never submit a manuscript or paper that you haven't checked for spelling and typographical errors. *Proofread your work!*

13. Use consistent tense, topic, and person.

14. *Never plagiarize.* When you use sources closely in your writing, give credit to the original author. It is *never* acceptable to copy anything directly from another's materials without using quotation marks and citing the original source. As we have noted, even paraphrasing requires appropriate citation to that person's work.

15. Do not quote from an abstract. Either summarize the original source (not the abstract) in your own words or quote the original author.

16. Pay attention to the structure and form of published articles. These articles are usually effective examples of how literature reviews can be written.

Writing Formats

There are several different accepted writing and bibliographic formats. You may have become familiar with one style in high school and a different style in college. Commonly used formats in the humanities and social sciences are those of the Modern Language Association (MLA) and the University of Chicago (which is abstracted in Turabian):

Gibaldi, J. (1995). *MLA handbook for writers of research papers* (4th ed.). New York: Modern Language Association of America.

Turabian, K. L. (1987). *A manual for writers of term papers, theses, and dissertations* (5th ed.). Chicago: University of Chicago Press.

University of Chicago Press. (1993). *The Chicago manual of style* (14th ed.). Chicago: Author.

As of early 1995, only one main communication journal (*Text and Performance Quarterly*) requires the **MLA style** and only one (*Journalism & Mass Communication Quarterly*) requires the

Chicago style. All others allow or require submission of articles using the style of the American Psychological Association (APA). Most communication journals have adopted **APA style**:

> American Psychological Association. (1994). *Publication manual of the American Psychological Association* (4th ed.). Washington, DC: Author.

Because almost all of our journals accept or require manuscripts in this style, we have used APA style throughout this book. We hope that, as you read the various chapters, you become familiar and adept with this style. We give an overview of the basics of APA style in Appendix A. This is not meant as a substitute for the APA *Publication Manual*, which presents much more information than we could here. In our overview, we summarize some of the technical aspects of APA style that you will find helpful in constructing literature reviews and research reports.

You should note that MLA style has become similar to APA style in recent years. For instance, in-text footnotes, prevalent in MLA and Turabian (an easy-to-follow guide to the *Chicago Manual of Style*), are now sometimes replaced by endnotes or endnote numbers (enclosed in parentheses), which refer to numbered "Works Cited" listed in the bibliography at the end of the manuscript. The MLA and Chicago (Turabian) footnote styles, however, are similar. For example, if we wanted to refer a reader to page 55 of this textbook or to page 260 of an article on symbolic convergence theory, the MLA footnotes and the Turabian endnotes would look like this (remember, the APA style does not use footnotes for references):

MLA   [1]Rebecca B. Rubin, Alan M. Rubin, and Linda J. Piele, *Communication Research: Strategies and Sources*, 4th ed. (Belmont: Wadsworth, 1996) 55.

[2]Ernest G. Bormann, John F. Cragan, and Donald C. Shields, "In Defense of Symbolic Convergence Theory: A Look at the Theory and Its Criticisms after Two Decades," *Communication Theory* 4 (1994): 260.

Chicago   [1]Rebecca B. Rubin, Alan M. Rubin, and Linda J. Piele, *Communication Research: Strategies and Sources*, 4th ed. (Belmont, Calif.: Wadsworth, 1996), 55.

[2]Ernest G. Bormann, John F. Cragan, and Donald C. Shields, "In Defense of Symbolic Convergence

Theory: A Look at the Theory and Its Criticisms after Two Decades," *Communication Theory* 4 (November 1994): 260.

As mentioned, both MLA and Turabian use a "Works Cited" section for the bibliography, whereas the APA-style bibliography is simply called "References." To show how the three **bibliography styles** differ, we present here one book and one article in each of the three styles:

MLA   Rubin, Rebecca B., Alan M. Rubin, and Linda J. Piele. *Communication Research: Strategies and Sources.* 4th ed. Belmont: Wadsworth, 1996.

Bormann, Ernest G., Cragan, J. F., and Donald C. Shields. "In Defense of Symbolic Convergence Theory: A Look at the Theory and Its Criticisms after Two Decades." *Communication Theory* 4 (1994): 259–294.

Chicago   Rubin, Rebecca B., Alan M. Rubin, and Linda J. Piele. *Communication Research: Strategies and Sources.* 4th ed. Belmont: Wadsworth, 1996.

Bormann, Ernest G., Cragan, John F., and Donald C. Shields. "In Defense of Symbolic Convergence Theory: A Look at the Theory and Its Criticisms after Two Decades." *Communication Theory* 4 (November 1994): 259–294.

APA   Rubin, R. B., Rubin, A. M., & Piele, L. J. (1996). *Communication research: Strategies and sources* (4th ed.). Belmont, CA: Wadsworth.

Bormann, E. G., Cragan, J. F., & Shields, D. C. (1994) In defense of symbolic convergence theory: A look at the theory and its criticisms after two decades. *Communication Theory, 4,* 259–294.

Consult the manuals for more details on these styles.

A standard style for presenting your report or review is essential. (The APA and MLA manuals are helpful because they contain rules for writing.) The other important element is a suitable and consistent physical appearance. Anything that attracts negative attention—such as misspellings, typographical errors, tense shifts, nonparallel headings—will diminish the paper's effect. In short, your ideas may be lost in a maze of stylistic miscues.

Proofreading

Proofread all work before submission. Careless errors only diminish the impact of the work in the eyes of the reader (for example, an employer, a professor, thesis committee, editor). When readers trip over careless word choices or blatant errors, they often lose sight of the important points made in the manuscript and, instead, start looking for additional errors. When this happens, readers miss your important thoughts and ideas. Use the following checklist to proofread your writing.

Proofreading Checklist

1. Are all words spelled correctly? (Remember that word processing spelling checkers cannot tell the usage difference between correctly spelled homonyms.)

2. Is the writing grammatically correct? Do subjects and verbs agree, is the form parallel, is the writing voice active, and is the past verb tense used when appropriate?

3. Are there any punctuation errors? Are all quotation marks outside the punctuation (except for semicolons and colons)? Question and exclamation marks go inside quotation marks only if they're part of the original quote.

4. Is one writing format used consistently throughout? Choose APA or MLA style and stick with it religiously.

5. Are any paragraphs overly long? If so, look for how many main thesis sentences appear in the paragraph and divide it accordingly.

6. Do all sentences flow together? If not, check the thesis sentence to be sure that all sentences are supporting or illustrating it.

7. Do all words have precise meanings? Is there any slang or casual language? Work on using short, clear, standard words rather than slang or technical jargon.

8. Are all quotations in proper form? Is proper credit given to other authors for all ideas and quoted material?

Proofreading Symbols

Many researchers write at the computer or word processing terminal. They can read and correct errors as they view their writing on the monitor. However, it is a good idea to print or type a copy to edit, before printing or typing the final version. Students and instructors find standard proofreading and copyediting symbols useful when proofreading and copyediting manuscripts. We've identified some of the main ones here:

Awk	Awkward
Cap	Use a capital letter
CF	Comma fault
Gr	Error in grammar
Ital	Italics (underlining)
Mng	Meaning not clear
Org	Faulty organization
Par	Paragraph problem (development, length, continuity)
//	Parallel form problem
Pn	Punctuation problem
Pron	Error in pronoun form
Sp	Spelling error
T	Error in use of tense
Trans	Needs better transition
Wdy	Wordy
WW	Wrong word

Many other symbols are also used by journal and book editors when they edit manuscripts for publication. These are also useful for editing your own work before preparing the final copy to submit.

ℰ	Delete character marked
∩	Transpose
∧	Insert
◡	Close up, no space
#	Insert a space
≡	Capitalize
lc	Use lowercase
℗	Start paragraph
no ℗	No paragraph
ital	Italicize or underline

Most instructors use similar symbols or develop their own proofreading and copyediting systems. It's a good idea to ask if you don't understand them. Some journal editors and book publishers send their systems to authors during the proofreading stage. This involves authors in the process so they can be sure that what appears in print is what and how they want it to appear.

Submitting Manuscripts

Occasionally instructors will suggest that you submit your papers or research studies to journals for publication consideration or to professional associations for possible presentation at a meeting. This means that you must pay special attention both to the writing style and to the guidelines for contributors that each journal or association publishes. Not only must the paper be flawless in writing, typing, and word choice, but it must also be appropriate for the particular journal or association to which it will be submitted.

We offer the following suggestions about what to avoid when submitting manuscripts. These are the sorts of things that guarantee failure:

1. *Inadequate Rationale.* The purpose of the study is not clear. A topic is not important to study just because we are interested in it or just because others have studied it before. We need to explain a rationale or guiding force for the study and to support the importance of the investigation. Authors have this burden of proof. Authors have an obligation to present clearly (a) the purpose for the study and (b) a solid rationale for the significance or importance of the study.

2. *Uninteresting Questions.* Authors must ask good questions. We must show that we are familiar with what others have written about our problem in the literature before. We need to present these questions in a compelling manner and build upon the work that has been done before.

3. *Sloppy Methods or Procedure.* Whether the method is quantitative or qualitative in nature, sloppiness is not tolerated. Using questionable scales and measures, coders who cannot agree on their observations, and biased raters, will result in measurement that is not valid or reliable. These can be "fatal flaws" in that the procedure does not allow us to address the research problem adequately.

4. *Inappropriate Sample.* The sample must be chosen with the study's purpose in mind. Convenience samples instead of probability samples need to be justified. The sample must sufficiently represent the population being studied. The size of the sample must be adequate. The number and kind of artifacts or primary documents examined must be appropriate for qualitative and historical research.

5. *Inadequate Analyses.* If we've asked good questions, established the significance of the study, and used sound methods, then we also need to analyze our observations appropriately. If all else is right, computing or reporting the wrong statistics or conclusions, or not providing a complete analysis, will not end the manuscript's future. Reviewers might suggest a different path for analysis. Following the suggestions of reviewers that make sense and revising and resubmitting the work, can put the manuscript back on track.

6. *Lack of Contribution.* Overall, does the manuscript make an important contribution to our knowledge? Reviewers must see the significance of the study and how its publication is essential to furthering our understanding of the topic or problem. Often this comes out in the theory-development and discussion sections of the manuscript.

7. *Inappropriate Journal or Association Division.* Occasionally, the manuscript is simply sent to the wrong place. Highly quantitative studies should not be submitted to *Quarterly Journal of Speech* or *Critical Studies in Mass Communication.* Oral interpretation studies should not be sent to the *Journal of Broadcasting & Electronic Media.* And, generally, mass-communication papers should not be sent to the Organizational division of either SCA or ICA. Discussing the paper with professors, perusing the journals, and reading contributor submission guidelines in the journals can help place the manuscript in the right place.

For additional information on submitting manuscripts for publication, see:

Knapp, M. L., & Daly, J. A. (1993). *A guide to publishing in scholarly communication journals* (2nd ed.). Austin, TX: International Communication Association.

Summary

Writers need to use a clear and lucid style, adhere to rules of grammar, spell properly, and present their reports in an appropriate format. The APA *Publication Manual* standardizes format by setting down rules for writing, bibliography form, and editorial style. It is often used by communication researchers when they are preparing research papers. There is no excuse for sloppy work that is not proofread and carefully edited. Any submitted work must conform to the basic standards of grammar, punctuation, spelling, and format or style. Failure to conform to these standards results in lower credibility and more negative evaluation.

References

American Psychological Association. (1994). *Publication manual of the American Psychological Association* (4th ed.). Washington, DC: Author.

Babbie, E. (1995). *The practice of social research* (7th ed.). Belmont, CA: Wadsworth.

Brooks, B. S., & Pinson, J. L. (1989). *Working with words: A concise guide for media editors and writers.* New York: St. Martin's Press.

Campbell, W. G., Ballow, S. V., & Slade, C. (1990). *Form and style: Theses, reports, term papers* (8th ed.). Boston: Houghton Mifflin.

Day, R. A. (1994). *How to write & publish a scientific paper* (4th ed.). Phoenix: Oryx Press.

Gibaldi, J. (1995). *MLA handbook for writers of research papers* (4th ed.). New York: Modern Language Association of America.

Harvard Law Review Association. (1991). *The bluebook: A uniform system of citation* (15th ed.). Cambridge, MA: Author.

Kessler, L., & McDonald, D. (1984). *When words collide: A journalist's guide to grammar and style.* Belmont, CA: Wadsworth.

Knapp, M. L., & Daly, J. A. (1993). *A guide to publishing in scholarly communication journals* (2nd ed.). Austin, TX: International Communication Association.

Owens, P. (1990). *Dr. Peter Owens' research paper writer* [Computer disk]. Cambridge, MA: Tom Snyder Productions.

Strunk, W., Jr., & White, E. B. (1979). *The elements of style* (3rd ed.). New York: Macmillan.

Turabian, K. L. (1987). *A manual for writers of term papers, theses, and dissertations* (5th ed.). Chicago: University of Chicago Press.

University of Chicago Press. (1993). *The Chicago manual of style* (14th ed.). Chicago: Author.

Exercises

1. Check a paper you have written for effective writing style. Use the "Tips for Effective Writing" and "The Ten Commandments of Good Writing" as guidelines for this examination.

2. Select one recent single-authored book in communication, one multi-authored book, one essay in an edited book, and one single-authored and one multi-authored article in scholarly communication journals. Construct the citations for each of these five sources using correct APA style (see Appendix A).

3. Choose two or three verbs (from page 246) for the following sentences. Compare and contrast the different meanings for those selected.

    a. Smith (1990) _____ verbal qualifiers as terms that connote a great degree of uncertainty.

    b. Smith (1990) _____ a method of measuring verbal qualifiers in speech.

    c. Smith (1990) _____ that women who use more verbal qualifiers are more likely to be perceived as weak.

    d. When Jones (1992) criticized Smith's (1990) new method of measuring verbal qualifiers, Smith _____ that the validity and reliability data were within the bounds of acceptability.

    e. Although Smith (1990) _____ that the method was acceptable, more current research (Jones, 1992; Miller, 1994; Williams, 1993) _____ that Smith's claim was premature.

    f. Smith (1990) _____ that future research should compare perceptions of both men and women as a result of qualifier use.

4. Another finding from the Rubin and McHugh (1987, p. 287) article discussed in this chapter follows. Write a paraphrased summary of this finding in one sentence.

    The fifth hypothesis predicted a positive significant relationship between perceived relationship development importance and parasocial interaction. The correlation between these two variables was significant ($r = .52$, $p < .001$), supporting the fifth hypothesis.

5. Rewrite the following passive sentences in the active voice. Remember to use past tense when necessary.

   a. It was found by Graham (1986) that humor is used by people to get others to like them.

   b. When questionnaires were completed, subjects were allowed to leave the laboratory.

   c. Demographic characteristics of East Liverpool residents have been consistently found by researchers (Barbato, 1987; Offutt, 1990; Perse, 1986) to be representative of the general population.

   d. The scale was submitted to factor analysis to discover how many dimensions were contained in it.

6. Use proofreading and copyediting symbols to edit the following passage. Compare your editing with that of others and with that of your instructor.

We find that the notion of controlalso is very important when we think about and hypothesize about communication bheavior. Rubin (1986) argued that: "we need to consider whether locus of control, alone or in combination with other factors, produces variations in motives for and consequences of using personal and mediated information channels." (p. 135) Locus of control affects behavior (Rotter, 1954). "Internals" feel tehy control events in their lives, "externals" viewing life outcomes as dependent on luck, chance or powerful others. pointing to the reaserch of Williams, Phillips and Lum (1985) and Schoenbach and Hackforth (1987), Levy (1987) asked whether consumers use VCRs for control.

Chapter 11

Preparing Research Projects

Communication students become involved in many different types of research projects during their careers. Many of these are theoretical and involve researching topics for the sake of increasing their own or others' knowledge. Other projects are applied and are geared to solving a problem or answering a question. Often professional organizations have their own format and style for writing and presenting reports. Here we focus on the basic elements of preparing this information. These basics are also used by communication professionals.

We focus this chapter on five main academic projects students commonly undertake: abstracts, literature reviews, critical papers, research prospectuses, and original research reports. For each project, we define what it is, identify different types that exist, explain the format for preparing it, and highlight the steps involved in completing the project.

Abstracts

An **abstract** is an abbreviated version or a condensation of a written work. Writers seem to agree that there are three main types of abstracts, identifiable by their internal purpose.

Indicative abstracts are used for screening, so readers can see if a document is pertinent. They give a description of the scope of the study, the main sections, and other relevant information found in the document. They are short paragraphs (usually 100 to 150 words), giving the purpose and results of the research. They guide the reader rather than informing. Abstracts that precede some journal articles or are in the journal's table of contents are often indicative, to give the reader a flavor for the piece, although many journals prefer shorter versions of informative abstracts.

Informative abstracts are used for information, so readers can identify the main findings and data in a document without having to reread the article. They are more detailed in nature, usually 150 to 400 words, and include information on the purpose and scope, methods, results, and conclusions. They should not contain references to previous literature or to unreported results. This type of abstract allows readers to identify the basic research concepts and findings and to determine whether the study is relevant to their interests. This is the type of abstract to use when preparing bibliography cards. *Communication Abstracts, Psychological Abstracts,* and *Dissertation Abstracts,* for example, publish informative abstracts.

Critical abstracts provide, in addition to main findings and information, a judgment or comment on the study's validity, reliability, or completeness. If a critical abstract becomes too critical, the abstract turns into a review. Often critical abstracts are 400 to 500 words long.

Format

Abstracts, especially of empirical research articles, typically have four sections. The first is an orientation to the general nature of the study and what the research was about (for example, hypotheses and research questions). The second section details the methods, procedures, sample, and other specific information about how the study was done. The third section contains the results of the study. Those unfamiliar with statistics may have a difficult time understanding the elaborate statistical procedures used in many scholarly journal articles. It is important, though, that these results be read and noted, particularly as they relate to the hypotheses or research questions of the study. The last section of the abstract is typically the shortest. It condenses the author's discussion of the results, the relationship of the results to previous research findings, and proposed directions for further research.

Steps

Cleveland and Cleveland (1990) and Collison (1971) have outlined the main steps involved in writing an abstract.

1. Ideally, read the article two or three times before writing the abstract.

2. Identify the main sections of the document and highlight, mark, or note important passages.

3. Write a draft of the narrative. Use complete sentences and your own words. Include the following:

   a. Objectives and scope—Why was the study done and what does it include?

   b. Methodology—What procedures, subjects, instruments, and data analyses were used/performed? How was the study done?

   c. Results—What was found?

   d. Conclusions—What do we now know and what implications does this have?

   e. Additional information—What interesting information doesn't fit into the above categories? What findings are incidental?

4. Edit and rewrite the draft.

   a. Check for brevity, reduce redundancy, and avoid repetition whenever possible.

   b. Use your own words.

   c. Clarify the lead sentence, or thesis. It contains vital information about the purpose of the study and should be clear, concise, and thorough.

5. Prepare and type the final abstract.

   a. Record the reference, accurately and completely, at the top of the abstract.

   b. Give your name at the bottom.

Keep in mind that informative and critical abstracts will be more detailed than indicative abstracts.

Literature Reviews

You may be asked to find specific information in the communication literature, to review the research on a specific topic, and to write a literature review about that research. A **literature review** has two main purposes: to summarize research and to evaluate it. Pure summary is akin to objective and descriptive journalism, whereas evaluation contributes original ideas to our understanding and results in scholarship. Evaluation speaks to the validity of the research findings.

A literature review is a crucial part of the research process. First, it enables us to understand the current status of knowledge about a topic. Second, before you can conduct original research, you must know what scholarship already exists on the topic and evaluate the findings so that you can formulate new research questions to guide your study. As you begin to read original reports of communication scholarship, you will see that researchers explain to the reader how the literature was examined before the research question was formed. The literature review, then, acts as a guide for developing questions not yet answered by the published research literature.

There are two basic types of literature reviews: exemplary and exhaustive. An **exemplary,** or representative, **literature review** is similar to a preface in a research study. In the exemplary review, the writer assumes that the reader knows about the subject and so presents only key references to reacquaint the reader with representative works that relate to the research study.

Key references are those that have directly influenced the study being proposed or conducted. They will be cited and described as they relate to the topic, and they will provide the reader with a starting point for further information. However, the reader is to understand that other, perhaps more general, articles and books exist that may also be related to the subject. Missing key references is a sign of poor scholarship. Most scholarly journal articles begin with exemplary literature reviews; consult journal articles for examples of this type of literature review.

An **exhaustive literature review** is comprehensive. The writer attempts to find all the information pertinent to a topic (usually scholarly journal articles, book chapters, and books) and to summarize and evaluate the major findings. This type of review is typical of review essays in scholarly handbooks or yearbooks, theses and dissertations, and research papers required for communication classes. In an exhaustive review, the writer assumes that the reader has less knowledge of the area than is assumed with an exemplary review. The writer's goal is to emphasize pertinent findings, to review relevant methodological issues, to summarize major conclusions, and to evaluate the status of research on the topic. The reader of this type of review will assume that the writer has examined all the research and theory in the area and that most works on the topic will be referenced in the review.

Format

You are probably quite familiar with writing term papers. The goal of a term paper is usually to summarize information from secondary sources and to make a statement about a particular topic. That is why instructors emphasize the need for creating a thesis statement and supporting it throughout the paper. Literature reviews are similar in this respect. A review of pertinent literature should also be cohesive (in other words, not choppy). In each section of the literature review, the reader should see how the research helps clarify a specific aspect of the problem. The writer of such a review, consequently, must know exactly what that problem is before beginning the writing process.

The thesis statement is a way of clearly stating a position on the subject that you plan to support. It is not a personal opinion or belief. You must demonstrate the proposition with evidence from the research literature. Most often, an understanding of the problem emerges from the literature search process and discussions with the instructor or others. Then, by organizing, integrating, and evaluating the published materials, you consider how adequately the research has clarified the problem. In short, you develop the thesis statement and support various arguments by summarizing and synthesizing those pertinent writings found during the literature search.

Introduction
This first part of a literature review orients the reader to the subject and indicates what is to follow. It is sometimes better to write the introduction after you have completed the paper because you may change your outline slightly during the writing process.

General Statement of the Problem
This second section describes the topic and explains its significance. Answer these questions: What do we mean by the topic? Why is it interesting? How is this topic a significant one in the communication field? Are there controversies that need to be resolved? Is this research area of special interest to a particular group of people?

You can establish the significance of the topic by arguing that this research fills a gap in the literature (in other words, no one else has adequately summarized this essential material), that it provides the possibility for fruitful exploration in the future, and that it relates to a problem that needs to be solved to make communication theory and practice more meaningful. By the end of this second section, then, the problem should be clearly defined and clarified for the reader.

Summary

The third section is the meat of the literature review. Here you summarize previous research, theory, and writings to inform the reader of the state of current knowledge in this area. You also should identify relationships, gaps, contradictions, and inconsistencies in the literature reviewed. There are several organizational strategies that can be used for this summary.

- *Topical order.* Here you present the main topics or issues, one-by-one, and emphasize the relationship of the issues to the main problem. For example, a topical order for a literature review on approaches to group leadership would include the trait approach, the situational approach, and the functional approach. Obviously, without transitions, the topics would appear as a sequence of minipapers and would not seem connected. Thus, you must keep the reader aware of the direction of this organizational scheme and the connections among the topics.

- *Chronological order.* This form of organization is most useful in historical research papers. It doesn't make much sense to describe, chronologically, research studies of group communication if you are emphasizing the need for more research on group cohesion. However, if you are arguing that group research has proceeded from an early emphasis on individual variables to a current emphasis on process variables, chronological order would be consistent with the problem being discussed. Again, this is why it is important that you know the problem before you begin to summarize the literature. The pattern of organization depends on knowing what the end of the paper will look like.

- *Problem-cause-solution order.* Another way to organize this section is to move from the problem to a solution. Several schemes exist for this purpose. The problem–cause–solution order is most typical of this format. You begin by fully describing the problem (for example, we don't know what the influence of friends is on decisions to purchase magazine subscriptions). Then you identify and discuss the cause of the problem (for example, the impact of opinion leaders on newspaper reading has been examined, but the influence of friends on magazine subscriptions has not been investigated). Finally, you propose a solution—what type of research is needed to fill this gap in our knowledge?

- *General-to-specific order.* Here you would examine broad-based research first, then focus on specific studies that relate to the topic. For example, you may first look at writings that have addressed general issues about media effects, then review studies that have looked specifically at the influence of television viewing on children's aggressive behavior.

- *Known-to-unknown order.* Here you examine current literature about the problem, and then identify, at the end, what is still not known.

- *Comparison-and-contrast order.* Here you show how studies are similar to and different from each other.

- *Specific-to-general order.* Here you attempt to make some general sense out of specific studies so that conclusions can be drawn. For instance, you could describe three studies that have tried to measure interpersonal communication competence and then draw some conclusions about how competence should be defined or measured.

Critical Evaluation

A literature review typically ends with a critical evaluation of the literature. This section of the review carefully examines the research done to date by (a) critiquing the conduct and validity of the research on the topic and (b) proposing research questions that are still unanswered in the literature. Through this critical evaluation, the review becomes a piece of scholarship. It creates knowledge by adding new information to the already existing literature about the topic. Through the questions asked, it also sets forth an agenda for researchers to follow. By learning about research methodology, students can understand and evaluate the communication literature and add to the body of knowledge through their own scholarship.

Steps

1. Choose and narrow the topic. How narrow the topic becomes depends on the purpose, scope, and type of project (see Chapter 2).

2. Formulate a working general statement of the problem. According to Hubbuch (1992), it should begin with "What are the basic trends and developments in _____?"

3. Search the literature, employing either a general-to-specific or specific-to-general search strategy (see Chapter 2).

4. Once all sources have been abstracted, examine the bibliography cards for themes, topics, issues, patterns, and developments.

5. Write a thesis that summarizes these trends.

6. Refine your statement of the problem.

7. Choose an organizational strategy for the review and create an outline for the summary section.

8. Write each part of the summary section by focusing on the trends, themes, or ideas, citing studies you've read as illustrations or examples. Use the literature to develop your thesis for each section. Do not merely give abstracts of your studies; show how the studies are connected and how they relate to the themes. Critique, where possible, the validity of the research.

9. Form conclusions about each main section and conclusions about the topic in general.

10. Identify gaps in the literature and propose questions for further study.

11. Write the introduction to the paper, orienting the reader to the subject, what will follow, and the significance of the topic. Make sure you define all terms in need of clarification.

12. Refine the summary section. Write transitions between the sections by pointing out common elements or referring to the thesis and mini-thesis statements.

13. Put the review aside for a few days and prepare the reference list, citing only those sources that actually appear in the review.

14. Reread the review, refine the grammar, and rewrite for clarity. Sometimes reading it aloud will help uncover mistakes.

15. Check it carefully for spelling, typographical, and punctuation errors. Make necessary corrections.

16. Examine the review one last time with an APA manual (or whatever manual you are following) in hand to be sure all stylistic conventions are followed. Make necessary corrections.

17. Print or type the final version of the literature review. Proofread it.

Critical Papers

As we just explained, a critical evaluation is often considered a part of any literature review. Sometimes, however, your goal may be to conduct an exemplary literature review, rather than an exhaustive one, and draw conclusions about the subject based on pertinent evidence. This, then, is a critical paper. **Critical papers** may range from a few pages to monograph length; their size depends on how narrowly defined the topic is and how much pertinent literature exists on it. Article-length critical papers can be found in journals such as *Critical Studies in Mass Communication* and *Quarterly Journal of Speech*.

A key feature of a critical paper is the strong thesis statement. You test the thesis by gathering facts and other evidence and analyzing these materials for authenticity, validity, and relevance. You may change the thesis as you proceed because you want to let the facts guide the paper rather than select only those facts that support a predetermined opinion.

No set format exists for critical papers. The topic, data, and author's perspective determine the format and structure.

Steps

1. Choose and narrow the topic. Consult with people who have written critical papers to adjust the topic to the size appropriate for your specific purpose or goal.

2. Search the literature for relevant data—facts, transcripts, opinions, recordings, research reports, and so on.

3. Develop a working thesis statement.

4. Test the thesis with the data already collected. Adjust as necessary.

5. Search for additional data. Adjust the thesis as the data so suggest.

6. Check for appropriate grammar and sentence structure.

7. Critically evaluate the clarity of the paper's ideas.

8. Check for spelling, typographical, punctuation, and stylistic errors. Make necessary corrections.

9. Print or type the final version of the critical paper. Proofread it.

Research Prospectuses

Some assignments (such as a senior thesis, master's thesis, doctoral dissertation, or independent study project) will require you to move beyond a summary and critical evaluation of the literature to suggest the next step or steps that should be taken to solve the problem. At this point, statements of hypotheses or research questions should clearly and logically emanate from the literature review. Proposed research methods to answer these questions (see Chapter 9) must also be consistent with those used and critically discussed earlier in the paper. These are the basic elements of a research **prospectus.**

Typically, the type of research project proposed will influence which type of literature review one writes. Some institutions, for example, require that the literature review be exhaustive for thesis and dissertation prospectuses, whereas others require only exemplary reviews. An independent study project prospectus may include only several paragraphs or a couple of pages of literature review. So, the purpose of the project and the guidelines of the institution influence the extent of the prospectus. Be sure to ask before proceeding.

Format

Many formats exist for organizing research prospectuses. Most often the format depends on the project being proposed. Many times the format for people- or behavior-oriented studies differs slightly from that used for artifact- or message-oriented studies. The outline that follows contains basic elements of the prospectus and questions that research prospectuses should answer. Depending on the nature of the proposed project, you may not need to include answers to all these questions. Note that some entries in the outline are more relevant for some forms of research (that is, message or behavior) rather than for others. The main difference among these is in the Method section. Also, you may want to shift the order of some sections to reflect your own project. In any case, this outline will guide you to provide a complete prospectus for an adviser or a committee to examine.

    I. COVER PAGE
        A. Title
        B. Author
        C. Date
        D. Purpose of Submission
   II. ONE-PAGE ABSTRACT
 III. RESEARCH PROBLEM (Introduction, Questions, and Overview)
        A. What is the goal of the research project?
        B. What is the problem, issue, or critical focus to be researched?

C. What are the important terms to be defined?

D. What is the significance of the problem?

   1. Do you want to test a theory?

   2. Do you want to extend a theory?

   3. Do you want to test competing theories?

   4. Do you want to replicate a previous study?

   5. Do you want to correct previous research that was conducted in an inadequate manner?

   6. Do you want to resolve inconsistent results from earlier studies?

   7. Do you want to solve a practical problem?

   8. Do you want to test a method or methodology?

   9. What are the limitations and delimitations of such a study?

IV. REVIEW OF LITERATURE

A. What is the theoretical framework for the investigation?

B. Are there complementary or competing theoretical frameworks?

C. What does previous research reveal about the different aspects of the problem?

D. What research questions and hypotheses have emerged from the literature review?

V. METHOD

A. What will constitute the data for the research?

B. What materials and information are necessary to conduct the research?

   1. How will they be obtained?

   2. What special problems can be anticipated in acquiring needed materials and information?

   3. What are the limitations in the availability and reporting of materials and information?

C. Who will provide the data for the research?

   1. What is the population being studied?

   2. Who will be the subjects or respondents for the research?

      a. What is the sample size?

      b. What are the characteristics of the sample?

   3. Which sampling technique will be used?

D. What questionnaire or instruments will be used?

   1. If previously developed:

      a. How reliable and valid are the instruments?

      b. Why use these instruments rather than others?

   2. If developing an instrument for the research:

        a. Why develop a new instrument?

        b. How will items be developed?

        c. What format will be used for the items?

        d. How will reliability and validity be assessed?

   E. What methods or techniques will be used to collect the data?

      1. What are the variables?

      2. How will the variables be manipulated, controlled, measured, and/or observed?

   F. What procedures will be used to apply the methods or techniques?

      1. What are the limitations of this methodology?

      2. What factors will affect the study's internal and external validity?

      3. How will plausible rival hypotheses be minimized?

      4. What sources of bias will exist? How will they be controlled?

   G. Will any ethical principles be jeopardized? How will subjects be debriefed?

VI. DATA ANALYSIS

   A. How will the data be analyzed?

   B. What criteria will be used to determine whether the hypotheses are supported?

   C. What was discovered (about the goal, data, method, and data analysis) as a result of doing a pilot study (if conducted)?

   D. What statistics will be used, if any?

VII. CONCLUDING INFORMATION

   A. How will the final research report be organized? (Outline)

   B. What sources have you examined thus far that pertain to your study? (Reference List)

   C. What instruments, questions, credentials, or data must be made available? (Appendixes of Materials and Instruments)

   D. What time frame (deadlines) have you established for collecting and analyzing the data and for writing the report? (Timetable/Schedule)

These questions indicate that planning is vital to any research project. You must have a clear plan of action and stick to it throughout the project. Remember, research is systematic, and objective methodological conventions must be followed.

Steps

We will not repeat, here, all the steps involved in conducting a literature review or critical essay, even though they are pertinent, but will focus instead on the main steps in constructing the research prospectus.

1. Determine what it is that you want to study. Discuss the topic with an adviser who is interested in this topic and willing and able to advise your research.

2. Review the literature and develop specific research questions that you want to answer or hypotheses that you want to test.

3. Consult with your adviser on the feasibility of conducting such research. Your adviser may want to see your literature review before this meeting. If you need to have a prospectus committee, now is the time to begin to set it up.

4. Construct the research problem section and orient the literature review to your particular problem area.

5. Determine which procedures or methods will best answer your questions or test your hypotheses. Explain these thoroughly and review other research that has used these procedures/methods.

6. Submit the plan to your adviser and discuss the wisdom of proceeding as planned.

7. Polish (rewrite, edit, proofread) the prospectus and submit it.

Original Research Reports

Original **research reports** are comprehensive summaries of what happened when a research project was carried out. Besides the literature review, they include information on what was planned and what was discovered.

Reports differ slightly depending on the type of research conducted. Archival and documentary research reports emphasize support for arguments and procedures for analyzing the contents of documents. Survey research reports focus on data sampling procedures and statistical analysis of results. Observational research reports detail methods for observing behavior and the findings of the observations. Experimental reports emphasize controlled procedures and statistical analysis of results.

Format

As previously outlined, the research process involves careful planning and execution. A specific convention for reporting research results should also be followed. Although research reports vary depending on the type of research project conducted, some elements are common to all research reports.

In the first section, the *introduction*, you need to develop the problem and its significance and provide background information on the study. You should include the rationale for the study, the purpose of the investigation, and a review of the most pertinent literature. If the report will be submitted to a journal for publication, this review should be exemplary (briefer than that required for a classroom literature review). If the report will be a thesis or dissertation, the review should be exhaustive.

In the second section, you detail the *method* and materials used in the study. Include in this section the sample you studied, the research design, the measures you used, and the specific procedures you followed in conducting the study. In other words, how did you examine, observe, or measure your data? These details should be specific so that another researcher could reproduce or replicate your study.

In the third section, you present your *results*. This might be the shortest section of an experimental research report because you are limited here to just the results of your investigation. It could, however, be the longest section of a report if the study is archival/documentary in nature. You may find tables and figures helpful for relating complicated or summary data here, especially for survey and experimental research.

The last section of the report is the *discussion*. In this section, you should *discuss* (not recapitulate) the results that you found. Point out where expected results were not found. Show how your results agreed or disagreed with previous research. Discuss the theoretical implications and/or the practical applications of your results. Identify the limitations of your study and point to future directions for investigation. It is your job here to make sure that the meaning of the results and the significance of the study are clear.

Steps

We outlined the basic steps in conducting research in Chapter 9. In Chapter 10, we summarized some basic concerns of reviewers when they read a submitted manuscript. You should keep these concerns in mind both as you prepare to conduct a research study and as you write the research report about that project. Earlier, in the literature review and prospectus sections of this chapter, we detailed the steps for writing research reports. Here we'll take you through the steps that follow a completed prospectus.

1. Conduct the research study.

2. Analyze the data and summarize the results.

3. Review the findings in relation to what you expected to find and in relation to what has been found before. Generate important ideas that need further explanation or elaboration in the discussion section.

4. Write the discussion section, pulling together the main themes or issues that are important and the new findings from your study. Also include ideas for new research projects that emerged from your findings.

5. Check the research report for coherence and clarity.

6. Submit the report to your professor or committee, for convention presentation, or for publication.

The last step can be very involved. Students submit projects to their instructors, and researchers often consider submitting literature reviews and research reports to professional associations for convention presentation and for publication in scholarly journals. Each year the professional associations publish a "Call for Papers" for the next year's convention. Contact the organization for further information (see Chapter 1).

The choice of where to submit a completed research report to be considered for publication largely depends on the nature of the work. To find the right place for your manuscript, scan *Current Contents* (see Chapter 7) and examine the contents of recent issues of a variety of journals. Look at the prefaces and the "Instructions to Authors" in the journals to see which one is most likely to consider your paper for publication.

Two other publications offer detailed descriptions of communication journals and may help you decide where to submit your articles:

Dyer, C. S., & Heim, S. (Comps.). (1995). *The Iowa guide: Scholarly journals in mass communication and related fields* (6th ed.). Iowa City: Iowa Center for Communication Study.

Knapp, M. L., & Daly, J. A. (1993). *A guide to publishing in scholarly communication journals* (2nd ed.). Austin, TX: International Communication Association.

It is, of course, important to consider the prestige of publishing in a quality journal, but you also must consider where the article will have the most impact for the audience you have in mind. A small-scale study or a study focused on a state or regional issue might be more appropriate in a state or regional journal, whereas a study having national implications would be better placed in a national journal. Discussions with colleagues and professors can help you decide on the best market for your paper.

Each journal details its policies and procedures for submitting manuscripts for consideration. These guidelines explain the journal's review policy, the appropriate manuscript style (such as APA or MLA), and the number of copies to send. Most journals do not ask you to send the original typed copy and do not return copies if the manuscript is not accepted for publication. So be sure to make a copy for yourself or keep the original before you send the paper out for review. Address inquiries about specific journal policies and procedures to the editor whose name is listed on the inside cover or first pages of each journal. Because editors change every 3 or so years, be sure to consult the most recent issue of the journal.

Typically, you would send three or four copies of a manuscript to the editor of the selected journal. It is important that the paper be written in the style acceptable to that journal. You will often have to provide an abstract with your manuscript. Examine the journal to decide whether to send an indicative or an informative abstract.

The editor will decide whether the manuscript is of sufficient quality and within the purview of the journal. If it is not, you will receive a letter saying so. If it is, the editor will send you an acknowledgment of receipt and send the manuscript, usually with author identity removed, to two or three reviewers chosen for their expertise about the paper's content or methodology. These reviewers will send their recommendations to the editor. After receiving all recommendations, the editor will evaluate the manuscript and the reviews and send you a letter. The letter will advise you whether the editor has accepted the paper for publication. He or she will usually include copies of the reviews. The review process typically takes about 3 months (sometimes longer).

To be publishable, a study has to investigate significant research questions in a rigorous and methodologically sound manner. It should extend knowledge in one's field. Most seminar papers and many convention papers do not meet these criteria.

The editor's decision letter may accept or reject the paper or ask you to resubmit a revision after you have incorporated the editor's and reviewers' suggestions. Don't be disheartened by a less than enthusiastic review. A vast majority of manuscripts (often up to 85% or 90% in the best journals) are either rejected or in need of revision. If you're asked for a revision, follow the specific editor and reviewer suggestions, and rewrite. The process may be time-consuming and demanding, but often the results are rewarding. If a paper is rejected and you feel the manuscript really does have merit, use the editor and reviewer comments to revise the paper and submit it to a different journal. Most journal editors will tell you that they want to see only your best work, and reviewer comments help you make the manuscript better.

Summary

Abstracts are condensations of research reports. They indicate what can be found in a document or what the major findings are; sometimes critical comments are added. Taking notes by abstracting articles on bibliography cards saves researchers time and energy.

Literature reviews, the bases of most research projects, have standard patterns of organization: an introduction to the subject, a general statement of the problem, a summary of previous research to inform the reader of the state of current knowledge, and a critical review of the literature. An exemplary or representative literature review is similar to the introductory section of a research study. In an exhaustive literature review, the writer attempts to summarize all major investigations on a topic. Both types of reviews require the writer to select and narrow a topic and to search the relevant literature for appropriate sources.

Critical papers include a literature review, but concentrate on developing new understandings or conclusions about the literature. The thesis of such papers is supported by the literature and information reviewed.

A literature review is also part of a research prospectus. After identifying the problem, thoroughly reviewing the pertinent literature, and posing the research questions at hand, the prospectus writer describes the method, sample, and procedures for the study. Included with the prospectus is a reference list of sources, appendixes of the instruments (that is, the questionnaire, scales, or coding system) used in the study, and a timetable for the investigation.

A research report must also be systematically organized. The first section is an introduction that provides background information, the rationale, and the purpose of the investigation, as well as a review of the pertinent literature. The second section contains the method and procedures used in the study. The third section describes the results or findings. In the final section, the author discusses the meaning and significance of these findings.

When you submit research reports to be considered for convention presentation or for publication, they must follow the association's or the journal's guidelines. Journals follow systematic procedures for reviewing manuscripts. Manuscripts must address important questions, advance knowledge, be methodologically and stylistically appropriate, and include abstracts to help readers quickly identify the purpose, findings, and relevance of the research. The following sources can help guide you through these writing projects.

References

American Psychological Association. (1994). *Publication manual of the American Psychological Association* (4th ed.). Washington, DC: Author.

Barzun, J., & Graff, H. F. (1992). *The modern researcher* (5th ed.). Fort Worth, TX: Harcourt Brace Jovanovich.

Becker, H. S. (1986). *Writing for social scientists: How to start and finish your thesis, book, or article.* Chicago: University of Chicago Press.

Bowers, J. W., & Courtright, J. A. (1984). *Communication research methods.* Glenview, IL: Scott, Foresman.

Cleveland, D. B., & Cleveland, A. D. (1990). *Introduction to indexing and abstracting* (2nd ed.). Littleton, CO: Libraries Unlimited.

Collison, R. L. (1971). *Abstracts and abstracting services.* Santa Barbara, CA: ABC-Clio Press.

Day, R. A. (1994). *How to write & publish a scientific paper* (4th ed.). Phoenix: Oryx Press.

Dyer, C. S., & Heim, S. (Comps.). (1995). *The Iowa guide: Scholarly journals in mass communication and related fields* (6th ed.). Iowa City: Iowa Center for Communication Study.

Glatthorn, A. A. (1984). *Writing the dissertation: A manual for doctoral students.* Philadelphia: University of Pennsylvania, Graduate School of Education.

Henson, K. T. (1995). *The art of writing for publication.* Boston: Allyn & Bacon.

Hubbuch, S. M. (1992). *Writing research papers across the curriculum* (3rd ed.). Fort Worth, TX: Harcourt Brace Jovanovich.

Knapp, M. L., & Daly, J. A. (1993). *A guide to publishing in scholarly communication journals* (2nd ed.). Austin, TX: International Communication Association.

Locke, L. F., Spirduso, W. W., & Silverman, S. J. (1993). *Proposals that work: A guide for planning dissertations and grant proposals* (3rd ed.). Newbury Park, CA: Sage.

Madsen, D. (1992). *Successful dissertations and theses: A guide to graduate student research from proposal to completion* (2nd ed.). San Francisco: Jossey-Bass.

Roth, A. J. (1995). *The research paper: Process, form, and content* (7th ed.). Belmont, CA: Wadsworth.

Tucker, R. K., Weaver, R. L., & Berryman-Fink, C. (1981). *Research in speech communication.* Englewood Cliffs, NJ: Prentice Hall.

Exercises

1. Choose a scholarly journal article and write informative, indicative, and critical abstracts of it. After writing these, compare them with one about that same article in *Communication Abstracts.*

2. Prepare an outline of a research prospectus for a topic of interest.

3. Examine a thesis or dissertation and an article that has been written and published based on that work. Look at the scope of the literature covered and depth of coverage. When comparing the two, identify what was omitted, condensed, changed, or added.

4. Compare the publication submission guidelines for three or four different journals. What do they have in common? What elements differ?

Chapter 12

Conducting a
Research Study

Now that you're well versed in the strategies and sources for searching and researching communication topics, we thought you might like a behind-the-scenes look at the research process. The best way for us to provide this inside look is to explain how we conducted one research study. We'll talk about how we conceptualized the study, chose the procedures, and analyzed the data. The actual research report can be found in:

> Rubin, A. M., & Rubin, R. B. (1989). Social and psychological antecedents of VCR use. In M. R. Levy (Ed.), *The VCR age* (pp. 92–111). Newbury Park, CA: Sage.

We have included an abbreviated version of the research report in Appendix B.

Conceptualization

In a study we did about 15 years ago, we began to understand how confinement in a hospital affected the television viewing habits of patients (A. Rubin & Rubin, 1981). Before entering the hospital, younger and older people had different reasons for watching television. Once within the confines of the hospital room, however, their reasons became very much alike—both younger and older patients watched television for companionship and to fill time. This may seem like common sense (actually, much research supports common sense), but it led us to wonder whether confinement was the *only* factor that diminished chronological age differences.

After reading through much of the social gerontology literature, we concluded that other important elements also affect aging and communication. We decided we should examine age, not as the number of years a person has lived, but as a constellation of factors that define a person's position in life. These *life-position* elements were physical health, mobility, social activity, interpersonal interaction, life satisfaction, and economic security. We named this *contextual age* and created a scale to measure the various aspects of this construct (A. Rubin & Rubin, 1982a).

We received a small grant from the ABC television network and began to look at how life position affected the way people used television. We published a few reports of research studies in which we used these contextual-age measures to examine viewing patterns of older and younger people (A. Rubin & Rubin, 1982a, 1982b; R. Rubin & Rubin, 1982). One theoretical perspective helped guide our research: uses and gratifications.

Uses-and-gratifications theory is based on several basic principles. It assumes (a) a person's behavior is motivated or goal-directed; (b) people (for example, media audiences) actively seek communication sources (for example, television or friends) to satisfy their needs or wants; (c) people select from among different communication sources when trying to satisfy their needs; (d) people are influenced by social and psychological factors (such as age, education, personality, and life position) when they communicate; and (e) people can identify their own reasons for communicating.

At about the same time, we began to look carefully at how interpersonal and mass communication might interface within uses and gratifications and other theoretical perspectives. We developed an agenda for research (A. Rubin & Rubin, 1985). All the while, we saw contextual age as an important antecedent to communication because the literature we read and our own research suggested that life position strongly influences how we communicate. We generated several research questions in that article and focused on the links among personal and mediated communication theory and research.

Our research then took separate paths to try to answer some of the questions posed in the research agenda. Among other topics, we looked at how lonely people have a sense of interpersonal interaction (called parasocial interaction) with television newscasters (A. Rubin, Perse, & Powell, 1985), how involved soap opera viewers are when they watch (A. Rubin & Perse, 1987), and why people use videocassette recorders (VCRs) (A. Rubin & Bantz, 1987).

The VCR was an expanding home communication technology, and the popular and scholarly literature began to emphasize the need to understand why people use VCRs. (We found much of this literature by using computerized searching techniques that we will update later in this chapter.) We found eight major reasons why people use their VCRs: for library storage, time shifting, socializing, critical viewing, and occupying children, and to watch music videos, exercise tapes, and rented movies. As you can see, some of these reasons are closely entwined with interpersonal communication.

Other lines of our research looked at parasocial relationships with television characters (Perse & Rubin, 1989; R. Rubin & McHugh, 1987) and why people talk interpersonally with others (R. Rubin, Perse, & Barbato, 1988). In this last study, we created a scale to measure the motives people have for conversing with others. This interpersonal motives scale was modeled after uses-and-gratifications scales that looked at why people use media such as television. We found several primary interpersonal motives: communicating for pleasure, affection, inclusion, control, relaxation, and escape.

At the conceptual level, based on uses-and-gratifications theory, we expected a link between using media (here, the VCR) and communicating interpersonally. We felt it was time to look at this part of the theory. We wanted to study this problem: What are the relationships between motives for using the media and motives for communicating interpersonally with others? This is the general problem statement that guided our research.

Computer Search

We were aware of the uses-and-gratifications literature in communication because we had worked closely with it over the years. We were not, though, up to date on the VCR literature that had appeared in print since the earlier VCR study had been completed. So we decided to update our knowledge of this area through a limited (in terms of years) computer search.

We first searched *ABI/Inform* to find articles focusing on business aspects of VCRs. We used such key terms (derived from the database's glossary) as *videocassette* AND-ed to *recorder* AND *home use*, but NOT *instruction* (because we didn't want articles dealing only with using VCRs to teach classes). We asked for articles published from 1986 (a similar computer search for the earlier VCR article covered the period through 1985) to 1988 (when we did the study). This resulted in 10 hits. The articles came from sources we may not have found on our own: *Marketing News*, *Incentive Marketing*, *Marketing & Media Decisions*, *Marketing*, *Advertising Age*, *IEEE Spectrum*, *Discount Merchandiser*, *Journal of Advertising Research*, and *Consumer Electronics*. These articles gave more of a "trade" than a theoretical perspective on VCR use.

We also used *PsycINFO* to update our search of *Psychological Abstracts*. We used *videotape recorders* as our key term and excluded education-related articles by NOT-ing the key terms *educational television*, *teaching*, and *videotape instruction*. This resulted in three hits for the 1986 to 1988 period, including articles from the *British Journal of Occupational Therapy*; *Behavior Research Methods, Instruments, & Computers*; and *Journal of Fluency Disorders*. These were interesting but not highly useful sources.

We then searched *ERIC*. Here our key terms were *videotape cassettes* AND *videotape recorders* NOT *educational television*, *television curriculum*, or *teaching*. There were 10 hits for the 2-year period. These included articles from *Clearing House*, *Computing Teacher*, *Communication Quarterly*, and *Library Hi Tech* and six convention papers (from the *Research in Education* section).

We also updated our earlier search of *Sociological Abstracts* using such key terms as *videotape* AND *cassette* AND *recorder*. There were no hits for 1986 to 1988. We then used the library's CD-ROM of *Dissertation Abstracts* to see what dissertations may have looked at VCRs during this time. We located three and printed their citations and abstracts at the terminal.

Model

We used the abstracts found in the computer database searches to determine which articles might be relevant for our study. Besides the earlier literature we had read about personal and mediated communication, life position, and VCRs, we also read these newly found articles. Based on this review of the pertinent literature and our earlier research, we created a model to represent the relationships among the variables we expected to influence how VCRs are used (Figure 16).

In our model we expected that (a) locus of control and demographic characteristics such as age and gender would influence a person's life position, (b) life position would affect reasons people communicate with others, (c) these interpersonal motives would influence why people use VCRs, and (d) these VCR motives would affect how often someone uses his or her VCR. This conceptual model guided our investigation.

Thus, by now we had identified our research problem and searched the relevant literature. We had developed a model and were focused on the following research question: What are the social and psychological antecedents of VCR use? Now we were ready to plan the method of our study to answer this research question.

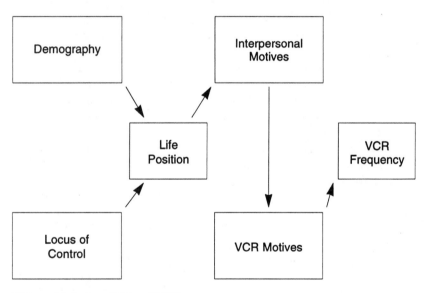

Figure 16. Antecedents of VCR use.

Questionnaire

We decided to use survey research to answer the research question. Recall that survey research is an efficient means of gathering information from large groups of people. We felt that a self-administered questionnaire was the most appropriate survey technique. Uses-and-gratifications research typically uses questionnaires for data gathering. Remember that one assumption of uses and gratifications is that people can report their reasons for communicating. Also, we felt that they can best provide information on their own life position, sense of control in their lives, and demographic information. These variables have been measured with survey questionnaires in the past. The study also was correlational in nature, making survey research an appropriate choice.

So we aimed to conduct a survey that included several scales to measure the variables in our model. First, we had to devise demographic questions to tap social elements that are known to influence communication behavior. Respondents anonymously filled in their *age* and the number of people who lived in their home or apartment (*household size*). They circled responses to indicate their *gender* (male or female), their highest level of completed *education* (elementary school, some high school, high school graduate, some college, college graduate, or advanced degree), and their current *employment* status outside the home (full-time, part-time, or unemployed).

As is the convention in survey research, we placed these demographic questions on the last page of the questionnaire. This is done so that important information would have already been gathered if someone feels these questions are too personal and chooses not to respond to them.

Second, we needed a measure of personality. During our literature search and past research, one personality variable often seemed to influence communication: *locus of control.* This construct refers to how much people feel in command of their lives. Externally controlled people feel that others or luck determines how events in their lives turn out. Those who are internally controlled feel that their own actions influence their destinies.

One scale, developed in 1966, to measure this construct had become a standard in the psychology literature, but our literature search suggested that another scale might be more precise. We turned to the *Social Sciences Citation Index* to see how many others had used Levenson's (1974) scale since its development. We found impressive data supporting the scale's validity and reliability. Valid scales measure what they intend to measure, and reliable scales are dependable and used consistently by respondents. So we chose to go with the more recent scale and cited some supporting research in the paper.

Third, we needed measures of life position, interpersonal motives, and VCR motives. In our own research, we had already developed such measures. Based on some of our previous research mentioned earlier in this chapter, we were able to use slightly shortened, but still valid and reliable, versions of the scales so that the questionnaire would not become too long. Lengthy questionnaires are tedious and troublesome. Respondents can become fatigued when trying to answer all the questions. Respondents also are volunteers who have limits on their available time.

We adapted the life-position scales from our contextual-age measures of physical health, mobility, interaction, life satisfaction, and economic security (A. Rubin & Rubin, 1982a; R. Rubin & Rubin, 1982). So we asked respondents how much they agreed with questions about their physical health (for example, "I usually feel in top-notch physical condition"), mobility (for example, "I have to rely on other people to take me places"), life satisfaction (for example, "I find a great deal of happiness in my life"), and so on.

And we adapted the communication-motives scales from our interpersonal-motives research (R. Rubin et al., 1988) and VCR-motives research (A. Rubin & Bantz, 1987). So we asked respondents how much certain statements were like their own reasons for talking with other people (for example, "to get something I don't have" and "because I need someone to talk to or be with") or for using a VCR at home (for example, "because I want to entertain people who come over" and "because it gives you more choice over what to watch"). In Figure 17 we've included examples of a few of the VCR motivation items from the original questionnaire.

Fourth, we needed a measure of how often people use their VCRs. For years, media researchers have struggled with the problem of how to measure media exposure. For example, merely asking people one question—how many hours they usually watch television—may result in a socially desirable underestimation. Because VCRs are not used in the same manner every day, we needed two different questions. One question asked respondents to fill in the number of days each week they use a VCR. The other question asked them to fill in the number of hours they use a VCR on those days. We created an index of *VCR frequency* by multiplying the number of days by the number of hours.

We constructed the questionnaire so that it began with a brief introduction to the study. Each section included basic instructions about completing the questions. We systematically arranged the sections to prevent earlier questions from biasing answers to later questions. We presented the sections in the following order: interpersonal motives, interspersed contextual-age and locus-of-control items, VCR frequency, VCR motives, and demographics. We prepared the pages so that instructions for answering questions were clear, tran-

HERE ARE SEVERAL REASONS OTHER PEOPLE HAVE GIVEN FOR WHY THEY USE A VCR AT HOME. FOR EACH REASON, PLEASE CIRCLE THE NUMBER TO INDICATE HOW MUCH EACH REASON IS LIKE YOUR OWN REASONS FOR USING A VCR AT HOME.

If the reason is **exactly** like your own reason, circle a **5**.

If the reason is **a lot** like your own reason, circle a **4**.

If the reason is **somewhat** like your own reason, circle a **3**.

If the reason is **not much** like your own reason, circle a **2**.

If the reason is **not at all** like your own reason, circle a **1**.

I Use a VCR at Home Because	Exactly	A Lot	Some-what	Not Much	Not at All
1. I like to have movies or programs that can be viewed many times.....	5	4	3	2	1
2. It is convenient to rent tapes.	5	4	3	2	1
3. I like to have tapes available for members of the family.	5	4	3	2	1
4. I like the freedom to set my own schedule.	5	4	3	2	1
5. I want to entertain others at parties...	5	4	3	2	1
6. I want to re-watch a program and review it critically.	5	4	3	2	1
7. I like to have the ability to view programs any time.	5	4	3	2	1

Figure 17. VCR study questionnaire.

sitions between sections were smooth, questions were not crammed together, there was plenty of white space, and the questionnaire could be professionally reproduced in 8 ½ -inch by 11-inch booklets.

Procedure

The multivariate statistics that we used to analyze the collected information required a sample size of about 300 respondents. However, we know that some surveys are lost, others are not usable (for example, incomplete or unreadable), and some people surveyed would not even use VCRs. So we had almost 500 questionnaires printed and distributed about 450 of these, hoping to end up with 300 usable surveys.

We were concerned about how to get responses from a sufficiently broad sample. We did not have the funds to hire a survey research team to conduct door-to-door interviews or a marketing firm to conduct telephone interviews. Yet we wanted to survey a wide range of people of varied backgrounds and interests.

We decided to use purposive, quota-sampling procedures (see page 219) and to have the students in our upper-division communication research classes serve as research assistants. We trained these assistants in data-collection techniques and in the ethics of conducting surveys (for example, the voluntary and anonymous nature of questionnaire completion). We gave the assistants specific instructions about when and how to collect the data. They were told to choose a wide variety of people to represent the general population and to solicit one man and one woman of various educational backgrounds from each of four age groups: 18 to 34 years, 35 to 49, 50 to 64, and 65 years and older.

The demographic questions in the survey allowed us to check the breadth of the sample. For example, the average age of our sample was 43 years. The descriptive statistics about the sample are reported in the method section of the research report.

Our assistants collected these data during spring break in 1988. Some students took the surveys home or on vacation to other states, but most (85%) respondents were from Ohio. We received 428 completed questionnaires; 299 respondents owned or used a VCR. These 299 VCR users became the sample for our study.

Once our assistants returned the surveys to us, we had to "clean" all questionnaires. This means we went through each questionnaire to (a) place numeric codes on certain questions that needed them, (b) declare "missing" for the data analysis any questions that were not answered, (c) write answers clearly in the margins for any questions where the handwriting was not sufficiently legible to prevent errors when entering the data into the computer, and (d) make sure, in general, the survey was usable.

When the questionnaires were clean, we entered the data into a file on the university's mainframe computer. We then prepared the data for statistical analysis. Before proceeding with the analysis, though, we first checked 10% of the data to see whether any typing errors had occurred in data entry. Finding only a single error (in the 3,200 numbers we checked), we felt reassured that our data were ready for analysis.

Analysis

The analysis for the study was systematic and straightforward but complex. As is true for any quantitative study, our conceptual model and the level of measurement of our variables dictated the nature of our statistical tests. We used a standard statistical software package, SPSS, for our analyses (SPSS, 1988).

We first ran a *frequency analysis* on each measure. This gave us summary statistics (such as means and standard deviations) of all our variables. It also allowed us to find possible errors in our data. For example, we used 5-point scales to measure locus of control, life position, and communication motives. In other words, a question would ask whether the respondent "strongly agreed" (coded 5), "agreed" (4), "agreed some and disagreed some" (3), "disagreed" (2), or "strongly disagreed" (1) with the item. The frequency analysis could not tell us if a 3 was entered on the computer for a response when a 4 should have been entered. However, it could tell us if a 0 or 6 was entered by mistake (remember, the responses had to range from 1 to 5). Fortunately, all our data complied with expectations.

We included several variables for each component of the model. For example, *locus of control* included internal control, powerful-others external control, and chance external control. *Life position* consisted of physical health, interaction, mobility, life satisfaction, and economic security. And *interpersonal motives* included relaxation, pleasure, control, inclusion, affection, and escape.

In addition, a survey often includes several questions for each variable to measure different aspects of that variable and to ensure the reliability of the measure. We followed this practice. So, for example, we asked three questions to measure internal locus of control, another three questions to measure life satisfaction, another three questions to measure the inclusion interpersonal motive, and so on. We added the numeric responses to all three questions together to create the scales to measure each of the variables. As suggested by past research, we did this for the locus-of-control, life-position, and interpersonal-motive variables.

Because past research was not as clear about VCR motives, we could not simply add up the answers to the different questions. Instead, we used a statistical procedure known as *factor analysis*, which determines the different dimensions of motivation that might exist. In this way, we could identify five primary motives for using the VCR: library storage, social interaction, freedom of choice, learning, and time shifting.

After creating our scales for each variable in this manner, we were ready to try answering our research question. We employed several other statistical procedures in the analysis. These included partial correlation, multiple regression, and canonical correlation.

Epilogue

So what did we find? Well, we did identify specific social and psychological antecedents of the different motives for using VCRs and for how often a VCR is used. For example, we found that we could predict social-interaction reasons for using a VCR from specific interpersonal motives—seeking companionship and affection and putting off doing something else—and from restricted mobility but a tendency to interact with others.

We went on to discuss the implications of our results. We observed that "the VCR is a convenient and economical mechanism for communication storage and retrieval" (A. Rubin & Rubin, 1989, p. 106). And we pointed to how our findings support the principles of uses and gratifications and how our reasons for communicating with others help predict how and why we use VCRs.

Having read this book, you are now ready to read the results for yourself. They are found in Appendix B. We have great faith in your ability to understand the literature and basics of research methodology.

We have tried to infuse you with our love for discovery, and hope you'll extend your own literature reviews and research papers into do-able research projects. If you fear venturing out on your own the first time (the second time will be a breeze!), ask a fellow student or professor to work with you on the research project. By conducting research, you'll gain even more insight into the strategies and sources of communication research than we can provide here. We wish you the best!

References

Levenson, H. (1974). Activism and powerful others: Distinctions within the concept of internal-external control. *Journal of Personality Assessment, 38*, 377–383.

Perse, E. M., & Rubin, R. B. (1989). Attribution in social and parasocial relationships. *Communication Research, 16*, 59–77.

Rotter, J. B. (1966). Generalized expectancies for internal versus external control of reinforcement. *Psychological Monographs, 80*(1), 1–28.

Rubin, A. M., & Bantz, C. R. (1987). Utility of videocassette recorders. *American Behavioral Scientist, 30*, 471–485.

Rubin, A. M., & Perse, E. M. (1987). Audience activity and soap opera involvement: A uses and effects investigation. *Human Communication Research, 14*, 246–268.

Rubin, A. M., Perse, E. M., & Powell, R. A. (1985). Loneliness, parasocial interaction, and local television news viewing. *Human Communication Research, 12,* 155–180.

Rubin, A. M., & Rubin, R. B. (1981). Age, context and television use. *Journal of Broadcasting, 25,* 1–13.

Rubin, A. M., & Rubin, R. B. (1982a). Contextual age and television use. *Human Communication Research, 8,* 228–244.

Rubin, A. M., & Rubin, R. B. (1982b). Older persons' TV viewing patterns and motivations. *Communication Research, 9,* 287–313.

Rubin, A. M., & Rubin, R. B. (1985). Interface of personal and mediated communication: A research agenda. *Critical Studies in Mass Communication, 2,* 36–53.

Rubin, A. M., & Rubin, R. B. (1989). Social and psychological antecedents of VCR use. In M. R. Levy (Ed.), *The VCR age* (pp. 92–111). Newbury Park, CA: Sage.

Rubin, R. B., & McHugh, M. P. (1987). Development of parasocial interaction relationships. *Journal of Broadcasting & Electronic Media, 31,* 279–292.

Rubin, R. B., Perse, E. M., & Barbato, C. A. (1988). Conceptualization and measurement of interpersonal motives. *Human Communication Research, 14,* 602–628.

Rubin, R. B., & Rubin, A. M. (1982). Contextual age and television use: Reexamining a life-position indicator. *Communication Yearbook, 6,* 583–604.

SPSS, Inc. (1988). *SPSS-X user's guide* (3rd ed.). Chicago: Author.

Appendix A

APA Style Basics

The *Publication Manual of the American Psychological Association* (1994) contains seven main sections: content and organization of a manuscript, expression of ideas, APA editorial style, manuscript preparation and sample paper, manuscript acceptance and production, journals program of the American Psychological Association, and bibliography. Here we are going to highlight some of the basic principles of the APA style that are most important to consider when writing literature reviews, prospectuses, and research papers. First, we will explain the basic bibliographic format used for references; then we will present some basic elements of the editorial style for the text of the paper. Because there have been recent changes to the APA system (in 1994), we will place in **boldface** those aspects that have been changed.

Bibliographic Format

A bibliography is a list of sources compiled on a specific topic. It is not just the end product of communication research—it is a necessary component of any project. Bibliographies sometimes include citations for sources in addition to those sources actually cited in a paper. However, the *reference list* attached to research reports, literature reviews, review articles, term papers, and the like includes *only* those works that were consulted (that is, actually read) during research and that are cited in the paper. No extraneous sources should be included. The purpose of a reference list is not to show all the works you've found but to give necessary information so that readers can identify and retrieve those sources that were actually used. In APA style, the reference list is given the heading *References*.

The APA *Publication Manual* suggests that reference lists be double-spaced when typed. However, to save paper, your instructor may allow you to single-space the entries and double-space between them. As you may have noticed by now, the second and succeeding lines of each citation are indented three spaces **when they are typeset**. This allows a reader to distinguish more easily between the entries when looking for a specific source. **When you type the references, however, type each entry like a miniparagraph, with the first line indented 5 to 7 spaces, using the tab key.**

As an experienced researcher, you will find that the more you consistently use any style, the easier it is to organize your findings for the final product, be it a research paper, seminar paper, speech, editorial, newspaper article, debate, or report.

Books

Learning the APA style for books is not difficult. For a single-authored book (see Example 1), the first element in the citation is the author's last name, followed by a comma, and then the author's initial(s). Next, place in parentheses, followed by a period, the year the book was published. Then give the title of the book. Capitalize only the first letter of the first word (except for proper nouns), and underline the entire title. End the title with a period. The final elements in the citation include the city (and state postal abbreviations for smaller cities) where the book was published, followed by a colon and the name of the publisher. End the citation with a period. Note that **only single spaces are used to separate each element in all citations**. For example:

■ Example 1: Single-Authored Book

Perloff, R. M. (1995). The dynamics of persuasion. Hillsdale, NJ: Erlbaum.

Underlined words are typeset in *italics*. Thus, every time you see italics in our text (or others), read it as underlining in typed manuscripts. If only a specific part of a source such as a chapter is used, this is indicated in the text citation itself. For example: (Perloff, 1993, chap. 3). Typeset, the preceding citation would appear like this:

> Perloff, R. M. (1995). *The dynamics of persuasion.* Hillsdale, NJ: Erlbaum.

If a book has been reissued since its first edition, that should be indicated in the citation:

■ **Example 2: Reissued Book**

> Newcomb, H. (Ed.). (1995). <u>Television: The critical view</u> (5th ed.). New York: Oxford University Press.

Note the abbreviations used. The lowercase "ed." is an abbreviation of *edition*. When this term is capitalized, it is an abbreviation of *Editor*.

If the book has two authors, use a comma and an ampersand between the names (see Example 3). If the reference is an essay in an edited book, the essay's title is not underlined, but the book's title is (see Example 4). Inclusive pages of the essay in an edited book should be indicated in the reference. Doctoral dissertations (Example 5), films (Example 6), and television programs (Example 7) are stylistically similar.

■ **Example 3: Dual-Authored Book**

> Baran, S. J., & Davis, D. K. (1995). <u>Mass communication theory: Foundations, ferment and future</u>. Belmont, CA: Wadsworth.

Note the use of the ampersand before the name of the last author in a series of authors. Also use the ampersand in the text of the paper, but only when the names appear as a citation in parentheses; for example, (Baran & Davis, 1995). We could have eliminated the state in this reference if it were a one-of-a-kind city (such as Chicago or Boston, see Example 2). Had this been an edited book, "(Eds.)." would have been inserted between the last editor's name and the year of publication.

■ **Example 4: Essay in an Edited Book**

> Bryant, J. (1989). Messages features and entertainment effects. In J. J. Bradac (Ed.), <u>Message effects in communication science</u> (pp. 231–262). Newbury Park, CA: Sage.

As you can see, the page numbers of the essay are included in parentheses following the book's title. If an edited book has two editors, use an ampersand between the two names; if there are three or more editors, separate all names with commas and use an ampersand before the last name.

■ Example 5: Doctoral Dissertation

Rodgers, R. V. P. (1991). An analysis of rhetorical strategies in the recruitment literature directed to prospective black student populations at The Pennsylvania State University (Doctoral dissertation, The Pennsylvania State University, 1991). <u>Dissertation Abstracts International, 52,</u> 4147A.

If you read the dissertation on microfilm, you would also include the University Microfilms number in parentheses at the end of the entry. When an unpublished doctoral dissertation does not appear in *Dissertation Abstracts International*, underline the title. Follow the title with the words "Unpublished doctoral dissertation," a comma, the name of the university where it was completed, another comma, the city where the university is located, and the country if the city is not well known. The year when the dissertation was completed sometimes is 1 year earlier than when the abstract appears in *Dissertation Abstracts International*. If that is the case, both dates are slashed (for example, 1991/1992) when the dissertation is cited in the text. Also note that the first letters in "The Pennsylvania State University" are capitalized because it is a proper noun.

Nonprint Media

The style for nonprint media is explained in the APA *Publication Manual* (pp. 216–222). The producer is the first author (see Example 6); sometimes the director is listed as second author. Example 7 also shows the producer as the first author for a series in the first citation, and a writer as the author for an episode in that series for the second citation.

■ Example 6: Film

Lehman, E. (Producer), & Nichols, M. (Director). (1966). <u>Who's afraid of Virginia Woolf?</u> [Film]. Burbank, CA: Warner Brothers.

■ Example 7: Telecast (Series and Episode)

Lasiewicz, C. (Producer). (1995). <u>48 hours</u> [Telecast]. New York:CBS.

Kandra, G. (1995). Stopping the clock (E. Shapiro, Director). In C. Lasiewicz (Producer), <u>48 hours</u>. New York: CBS.

The APA *Publication Manual* provides other examples for broadcast programs and other electronic media. As in any referencing style, it is most important to be accurate, complete, and consistent.

Government Publications

The style used for government publications is not fully explained in the APA *Publication Manual*. If the report is available from the National Technical Information Service (NTIS) or from the U.S. Government Printing Office (GPO), use the style shown in Example 8. If the report is not available from these agencies, do not include it in the bibliography but treat it as a footnote along with other not widely or easily accessible material.

Technical reports of nongovernmental organizations that are available to the public are treated like books (see Example 9).

■ Example 8: Government Document

U.S. Senate, Special Committee on Aging. (1980). <u>How old is "old"?</u> <u>The effects of aging on learning and working</u> (DHHS Publication No. NIH 78-1446). Washington, DC: U.S. Government Printing Office.

■ Example 9: Technical Report

Balkema, J. B. (Ed.). (1972). <u>A general bibliography on aging.</u> Washington, DC: National Council on the Aging.

Note that in Example 8 the primary government body is identified as the document's author, followed by the subsidiary agency (in this case a committee). The reference also includes the issuing department's report number. This report is issued by the National Institute of Health (NIH) of the Department of Health and Human Services (DHHS). It can be purchased by the public from the U.S. Government Printing Office. Example 9 is very much like a single-authored book reference (Example 1) except that the author is an editor (Ed.) of the work and the publisher of the report is an agency.

The APA *Publication Manual* (pp. 201–215) presents biblio-graphic formats for books and nonprint materials not discussed here. Consult the *Publication Manual* for assistance when the pre-ceding examples do not fully apply.

Periodicals

The format for periodicals is slightly different from that used for books. Capitalize the first letter of each word (except prepositions and articles) in the name of the periodical. (Capitalize only the first letter of the first word of the article's title.) Underline the name of the periodical, not the title of the article, and the volume number of the journal in which the article appears. The page numbers of the article come after the periodical's volume num-ber. The standard format for a journal article with one author is shown in Example 10 and that for a coauthored article is given in Example 11.

■ Example 10: Single-Authored Article

Garramone, G. M. (1985). Effects of negative political advertising: The roles of sponsor and rebuttal. <u>Journal of Broadcasting & Electronic Media, 29,</u> 149–159.

■ Example 11: Dual-Authored Article

Suzuki, S., & Rancer, A. S. (1994). Argumentativeness and verbal aggressiveness: Testing for conceptual and measurement equivalence across cultures. <u>Communication Monographs, 61,</u> 256–279.

If each issue of a particular journal starts with a page 1, include the issue number in parentheses after the volume number to make locating the article easier (see Example 12).

■ Example 12: Issues Beginning With Page 1

Turow, J. (1994). Hidden conflicts and journalistic norms: The case of self-coverage. <u>Journal of Communication, 44</u>(2), 12–31.

In Example 12, the number 2 in parentheses indicates that the arti-cle appears in Volume 44's second issue.

■ **Example 13: Book Review**

> Benjamin, L. (1982). [Review of <u>Telecommunications, mass media, and democracy: The battle for the control of U.S. broadcasting, 1928–1935</u>]. <u>Journal of Broadcasting & Electronic Media, 38,</u> 241–242.

Similar to a journal article title, if the review had its own title, the title would follow the date. The information in the brackets indicates the title of the book being reviewed.

Articles appearing in general-interest or trade periodicals and magazines, such as *Advertising Age* or *Time*, are identified by date **and by volume number**. If the article begins in one place and is continued elsewhere, give all page numbers, but use a comma to separate the page numbers. Similar to journal articles, **do not use "Vol." before a volume number or "p." before a page number.**

■ **Example 14: Magazine Article**

> Bell, N., & Amdur, M. (1994, January 24). NBC Super Channel looks to make mark in Europe. <u>Broadcasting & Cable, 124</u>(4), 112.

When the author is unknown, begin the citation with the name of the article and alphabetize it according to the first significant word in the title (not *a, an, the,* and so on). Bibliographic format for newspaper articles is similar to that of general-interest periodicals, but omits the volume number and uses "p." or "pp." before the page numbers. Consult the APA *Publication Manual* (pp. 194–201) for other examples of periodical citations.

Unpublished Papers, Reports, Personal Communications, and Speeches

Professional convention papers or other reports are often available though the ERIC Document Reproduction Service. Example 15 shows how these are referenced. However, not all convention papers are submitted to or accepted by ERIC. When unpublished papers and reports are available for use in a research project, they are cited as in Examples 16 and 17.

■ **Example 15: ERIC Report/Paper**

> Feeser, T., & Thompson, T. L. (1990). <u>A test of a method of increasing patient question asking in physician-patient interactions</u>. Paper presented at the annual meeting of the Speech Communication

Association, Chicago. (ERIC Document Reproduction Service No. ED 325 887)

■ Example 16: Unpublished Convention Paper

Thomas, S., & Gitlin, T. (1993, May). <u>Who says there's a dominant ideology and what happens if that concept is falsified?</u> Paper presented at the annual meeting of the International Communication Association, Washington, DC.

■ Example 17: Unpublished Convention Poster Session

Sharkey, W. F., & Kim, M-S. (1994, November). <u>The effect of embarrassability on perceived importance of conversational constraints</u>. Poster session presented at the meeting of the Speech Communication Association, New Orleans, LA.

Do not list oral interviews, personal conversations, memos, letters, and unpublished speeches with the references because the text is not permanently stored for others to examine. They are, however, referenced in the text. Be sure to include the name, type of communication, and date. An example is: (R. Jacobs, personal communication, March 27, 1995).

Legal References

The field of law has its own conventions for citing work in legal periodicals. In most legal periodicals, citations of court cases, statutes, and such are placed in footnotes. In the APA style, legal references are placed in the reference list along with the other references.

In the text of a manuscript, cite the legal materials in the same way as other references. Begin with the first few words of the reference list entry. Then give the date. This information will help the reader identify the citation in the References. Underline the names of court cases, but not statutes. The APA *Publication Manual* (pp. 223–234) offers examples of typical citations of legal materials, but refers the user to *The Bluebook: A Uniform System of Citation* for more information.

Citing Sources in the Paper

You have probably seen APA style used in many sources you've already examined. It is easily recognizable. First, books or other publications are generally not cited in footnotes or notes. There are usually only a few, if any, notes in an article. When the work of an author is referred to in the text of the paper, it is cited by using the author's last name and year the source was published. For example:

Scott (1992) identified . . .

Several researchers (Anthony, 1990; Gregory & Smith, 1985; Polk et al., 1980) reported . . .

Douglass (1986) concluded: "The research findings clearly indicate support for the hypotheses" (p. 55).

These sources are then fully listed at the end of the article or chapter. This eliminates the need for most footnotes in the text.

As the preceding examples suggest, there are rules governing where in the sentence the citation occurs. As the first example shows, if an author's (or authors') name is used in the sentence, the year of publication directly follows the name. If an author (or authors) has two or more works published in the same year that are cited in the reference list, the works are alphabetized in the list by the first significant word in the title of the article or book. The first receives an *a* after the year, the second a *b*, and so on. The *a* and *b* are also used in the text reference so the reader can find the exact source being referenced. See Chapter 12 for an example of this.

In the second example, several specific researchers are being identified, so their names (alphabetically arranged by first author) and years are enclosed in parentheses and works are separated by semicolons. When a source has two authors, always give both names (joined by an ampersand). When there are three to five authors, list all names the first time the reference is mentioned in the text—for example, (Polk, Erickson, Adams, & Johnson, 1980)—and abbreviate, as in the second example, for the next and subsequent mentions (Polk et al., 1980). Whenever a source has six or more authors, always use this abbreviated convention (et al.) in the text, even the first time the reference is mentioned.

The third example shows how sources of quotations are cited. Note the page number of the quotation is given at the end of the sentence before the period. Had the author's name not been integrated into the sentence as it was here, it would be placed, along with the year, with the page number, as follows:

"The research findings clearly indicate support for the hypotheses" (Douglass, 1986, p. 55).

Manuscript Style

Typing

Using standard 8 $\frac{1}{2}$ -inch by 11-inch paper, **create margins of at least 1 inch** on the top, bottom, and sides. This allows a maximum 6 $\frac{1}{2}$ -inch typed line (65 characters in pica [10 pitch] and 78 characters in elite [12 pitch]). Do *not* justify the right margin or hyphenate words, even if your software program wants to do it automatically for you. *Double-space everything.* Just set your typewriter or computer software on "2" and everything should conform to APA style. Put no more than 27 lines of text on a page. Check with your instructor, adviser, or graduate school for possible alterations to these standard typing instructions.

Format

APA style suggests a standard system of setting up and ordering the pages of a manuscript. See pp. 7–21 and the sample paper on pp. 258–272 of the APA *Publication Manual.*

Title Page

Papers begin with a title page. Type a "page header" (the first few words of the title) in the upper right-hand corner, with the page number several spaces to its right. Page headers should be consistent on every page of the manuscript. Then, starting flush left across the top of the page (but below the page header), type "Running head: " and insert a shortened title in the space. This would be the abbreviated title appearing at the top of published pages (50 characters or less, all in capital letters). Then, about centered in the middle of the page are the paper's complete title (in uppercase and lowercase letters), below which are the author's name and institutional affiliation. Double-space between lines of the title, as well as between title, author, and affiliation.

Abstract

On the next page (page 2), comes the abstract. In one double-spaced paragraph, concisely summarize what the paper or study is about: the problem, method, findings, and conclusions. Do not indent the first line of the abstract as you would normally indent paragraphs. The abstract should be 100 to 120 words for empirical papers and 75 to 100 words for review or conceptual papers.

Text

The text begins on the next page (page 3). Most research reports are broken into sections, and headings help the reader see where the different sections begin and end. Headings and subheadings also help readers see the flow of the text and orient them to the thesis of each area.

Most journal articles have two or three levels of headings; longer manuscripts might use more than three levels. The headings should be precise and clearly worded and their format standardized throughout the paper. The form of the heading depends on how many levels you need throughout the paper. For example, if you need three levels of headings beyond the title, center the first level and type in both uppercase and lowercase letters. Position the second level flush left and type in both uppercase and lowercase letters and underline. Indent (as you would a normal paragraph) and underline the third level heading; type the heading in lowercase letters (with the first letter of the first word capitalized) and end the heading with a period. The paragraph begins one space after that period. This format is follows.

First-Level Heading

<u>Second-Level Heading</u>

 <u>Third-level heading.</u> Begin text of paragraph . . .

Because the entire manuscript is double-spaced when typed, the text is double-spaced before and after the first- and second-level headings (extra space is not used above and below headings). Pages 92–93 of the APA *Publication Manual* contain examples of headings when more than or fewer than three levels are needed.

References

These begin on a new page following the end of the text of the manuscript. Center the word "References" at the top of the page and begin typing them, after a normal double space. Check with others to see if there might be a different style operating at your university.

Appendix

If you have appendixes, they come next. Center "Appendix A" at the top of the first appendix and center the title in uppercase and lowercase under it. Remember to double-space before the title.

Notes

Author notes and content foototes follow any appendixes. Content foototes are used sparingly in APA style. They are occasionally used to add important information to the points made in the text. Use footnotes only when the flow of the discussion would be broken by incorporating this information directly into the text.

Center the word "Footnotes" on the top of the page and then sequentially number and enter each note, using a 5 to 7 space paragraph indentation for the first line of each; place the footnote number slightly above and to the left of the first word of each note. In the text, number all notes consecutively and type the numbers (called superscripts) slightly above the end of the line of text (following any punctuation marks except a dash).

Tables, Figure Captions, and Figures

Place tables, figure captions, and figures at the end of the manuscript. Tables and figures require a very specific format. Quantitative tables contain exact values of data (usually statistics) in columns and rows. Qualitative tables contain words instead of numbers. Figures are charts, graphs, pictures, or drawings that extend and clarify the content of the paper.

APA style suggests you use tables and figures sparingly. If you have only a few statistics to report, incorporate them into the text of the paper. For a large number of statistics, use a quantitative table and do not duplicate the numbers in the text. Tables need descriptive headings and clear labels for the variables in the columns and rows. Headings for both tables and figures should clearly identify the content. Table 1 is an example of how to present a table. Again, the APA

Table 1
Percentage of Employed U.S. College Students

WORK HOURS PER WEEK	REGION			
	SOUTHEAST	NORTHEAST	MIDWEST	WEST[a]
0	25	20	21	22
1–10	35	39	40	37
11–20	19	20	30	30
21–30	10	12	6	9
31–40	8	8	3	2
Over 40	3	1	0	0

Note. These are fictitious data created just for this book.
[a] Includes Alaska and Hawaii.

Publication Manual provides more specific information on how to format tables (pp. 120–141) and present figures (pp. 141–162).

References

American Psychological Association. (1994). *Publication manual of the American Psychological Association* (4th ed.). Washington, DC: Author.

Harvard Law Review Association. (1991). *The bluebook: A uniform system of citation* (15th ed.). Cambridge, MA: Author.

Appendix B

Social and Psychological Antecedents of VCR Use[1]

The videocassette recorder (VCR) has become a socially significant communication technology as it moved into the home in the 1980s. VCRs provide expanded content and context options over traditional media. They accentuate choice, involvement, and control, and highlight the active and interactive nature of personal and mediated communication. Research about the nature and impact of VCRs, however, is limited even though over 60% of all U.S. households now have VCRs.

We take a uses and gratifications (U&G) approach to studying VCRs. U&G is based on the tenet that social and psychological factors influence people's motives to communicate, choices of communication alternatives, behavior, and communication effects. An underlying U&G assumption is that people choose to communicate purposely to satisfy felt needs; this behavior produces gratifications. . . .

U&G is especially appropriate for studying VCRs, which invite active audience participation by allowing greater control over viewing choices than traditional media. . . . Our goal is to explain social and psychological antecedents of VCR use, and to consider the interplay of personal and mediated communication. We test a model by which we expect VCR motives to complement interpersonal communication motives, which are influenced by life position, which is affected by personality and demographic factors.

Motives for Using VCRs

Harvey and Rothe (1985–1986) identified six basic reasons to use VCRs: to zap commercials, to time shift, to establish an environment for children, to increase viewing choices, to increase noncommercial viewing by building a library of programs, and to fast view by zipping through programs. Time shifting and increasing viewing choices were the most important uses. . . .

Rubin and Bantz (1987, 1988) . . . found eight interrelated motives for using VCRs [and] . . . proposed that VCR use is active behavior that complements and extends other modes of communication. VCR use is a functional alternative to interpersonal communication. They argued that we need to examine VCR use in relation to interpersonal communication and to examine the social and psychological antecedents of VCR use, including how an individual's life position and sense of life control affect VCR use. . . .

Personal and Mediated Communication

Although U&G typically has been used in mass communication, we have proposed its relevance for interpersonal communication (A. Rubin & Rubin, 1985). Interpersonal channels are need-gratification alternatives, which may be coequal to mediated channels. For example, one can gratify companionship needs by conversing with a friend or by listening to talk radio. Social and psychological antecedents affect both interpersonal and media motives. . . .

The social nature of VCR use requires consideration of interpersonal and social interaction. Schoenbach and Hackforth (1987) found that West German video households have more leisure-time activities, and that nonusers of VCRs are not more physically active than VCR users. In a study of interpersonal communication and media consumption in Saudi Arabia, Al-Attibi (1986) found that interpersonal communication fulfills adolescents' affective, entertainment, and escape needs, whereas the media gratified information needs. . . .

Life Position and Communication

Life position affects both personal and mediated communication. We have conceptualized life position as "contextual age," a constellation of social, psychological, economic, health, and communication indicators of age (A. Rubin & Rubin, 1982). We developed contextual age as an alternative to chronological age because the latter improperly assumes homogeneity along such life-position dimensions as life satisfaction, mobility, and interaction (A. Rubin & Rubin, 1986). . . .

Life position affects how people use media (A. Rubin & Rubin, 1982; R. Rubin & Rubin, 1982). For example . . . those low in life satisfaction and economic security tend to watch television for companionship and escape. Wenner (1976) found that . . . socially mobile elderly, for example, use television to avoid social contact with others, but socially isolated elderly use television content to facilitate interaction with others. . . .

Locus of Control

The notion of "control" also is important when addressing communication behavior. . . . Locus of control affects behavior (Rotter, 1954). "Internals" feel they control events in their lives, whereas "externals" view life outcomes as dependent on luck, chance, or powerful others. Pointing to the research of Williams, Phillips, and Lum (1985) and Schoenbach and Hackforth (1987), Levy (1987) asked whether consumers use VCRs for control.

Locus of control commonly refers to a person's mastery of his or her environment and life. Locus of control is consistent with U&G's active audience concept. Active audience members seek to gratify their needs and control their actions. According to Brenders (1987), "internals should be motivated to seek out, exert greater effort in, and derive greater satisfaction from situations allowing personal control" (p. 96). . . .

Demographic Characteristics

Demography affects life position and communication behavior. For example, we have found . . . age to relate positively to economic security and life satisfaction but negatively to health and mobility

(A. Rubin & Rubin, 1986). Demography also affects VCR use. When examining the social context of VCR viewing in Great Britain, Gunter and Levy (1987) found male/female differences and that most VCR playback is done alone. A. Rubin and Bantz (1987) identified age and gender differences in why VCRs were used. And, Dobrow (1987) linked VCR use with education, income, and ethnic background. . . .

Model of VCR Use

In this study, then, we employed a U&G orientation to examine antecedents of VCR use. . . . The model outlines an expected sequence to the social and psychological antecedents of VCR use: demography and locus of control influence a person's social and psychological well-being or life position, life position affects motives for interpersonal communication, interpersonal motives lead to VCR motives, and VCR motives affect the frequency of VCR use.

Method

Sample and Procedures

Similar to past survey-research studies (e.g., A. Rubin & Bantz, 1987; R. Rubin, Perse, & Barbato, 1988), we included a wide range of people in the sample by using purposive quota sampling. Students enrolled in two undergraduate communication research classes at Kent State University were given specific age and gender sampling quotas. We trained these assistants in data collection and research ethics, and instructed them to solicit one male and one female of various educational backgrounds from each of four age groups to represent the general population: 18–34, 35–49, 50–64, and 65 years and over. Questionnaires were anonymous and individually self-administered. . . . A total of 428 completed questionnaires were returned; 299 of these respondents (69.9%) owned or used a VCR at home. The latter group constituted the sample for this study.

Respondents in the VCR sample ranged in age from 18 to 75 (M = 42.99, SD = 15.39); 52.8% were male (0 = male, 1 = female),

67.6% were presently married, and 79.4% were employed outside the home. . . .

Measurement

Locus of control. We measured locus of control (LOC) with Levenson's (1974) scale. . . . Respondents reported their agreement with 12 statements (1 = strongly disagree, 5 = strongly agree). Four summed and averaged items represented each of three LOC dimensions: *Powerful Others Control* (M = 2.43, SD = .69, alpha = .70), *Internal Control* (M = 3.69, SD = .57, alpha = .64), and *Chance Control* (M = 2.46, SD = .66, alpha = .66). . . .

Contextual age. Contextual age (CA) reflects life position rather than just chronological age (A. Rubin & Rubin, 1986). Respondents stated their agreement with 18 statements (1 = strongly disagree, 5 = strongly agree). Three summed and averaged items were used for each of four CA dimensions: *Physical Health* (M = 3.66, SD = .77, alpha = .62), *Mobility* (M = 4.11, SD = .85, alpha = .65), *Life Satisfaction* (M = 3.66, SD = .71, alpha = .72), and *Economic Security* (M = 3.10, SD = .92, alpha = .81). To improve reliability, we combined the six interpersonal interaction and social activity items into a fifth CA dimension of *Interaction* (M = 3.31, SD = .63, alpha = .62). . . .

Interpersonal communication motives. We used the Interpersonal Communication Motives scale to measure interpersonal (IP) motives (R. Rubin et al., 1988). Respondents reported how much each of 18 statements was like their own reasons for talking to people (1 = not at all, 5 = exactly). Three summed and averaged items were used for each of six IP motives: *Relaxation* (M = 3.02, SD = .85, alpha = .75), *Pleasure* (M = 3.48, SD = .87, alpha = .80), *Control* (M = 2.47, SD = .88, alpha = .69), *Inclusion* (M = 2.99, SD = .97, alpha = .77), *Affection* (M = 3.75, SD = .76, alpha = .74), and *Escape* (M = 2.25, SD = .87, alpha = .66). . . .

VCR motives. We adapted earlier measures of . . . VCR use (A. Rubin & Bantz, 1987) to assess motives for using a VCR. Respondents stated how much each of 22 reasons for using a VCR at home was like their own reasons (1 = not at all, 5 = exactly). Given the exploratory level of this analysis compared with the previous established scales, responses were subjected to principal components factor analysis with iterations and oblique rotation (SPSS, 1988). The factor solution explained 63.9% of the total variance. . . . There were five factors [*Library Storage, Social Interaction, Freedom of Choice, Learning,* and *Time Shifting*] . . . Freedom of choice and time shifting were the two most salient VCR motives.

VCR frequency.   We asked respondents to estimate . . . how many days each week they usually use a VCR at home, and, on those days they use a VCR, how many hours each day they usually use the VCR to watch or record programs or tapes. . . . Daily VCR use averaged 2.51 hours ($SD = 1.64$) on an average 2.29 days ($SD = 1.77$) each week. We multiplied the days per week and hours per day of VCR use to create an index of weekly VCR Frequency ($M = 6.63$ hours, $SD = 8.49$).

Results

Correlates of VCR Motives and Frequency

We first looked at the partial correlates of VCR motives and frequency. Several conclusions are evident from the data. . . . First, VCR motives were interrelated. The strongest associations were between using the VCR for: library storage and both time shifting and social interaction, and freedom of choice and time shifting. Second, VCR motives correlated more with interpersonal motives than with other antecedents. . . . Third, VCR frequency of use was linked more to motives for using VCRs than to other variables. VCR frequency correlates were: library storage, freedom of choice, time shifting, and social interaction VCR motives; less education; LOC external, powerful others, and chance control; and IP control.

Predictors of VCR Motives and Frequency

Next, we asked which antecedent variables best explained VCR motives. We regressed each VCR motive on blocks of antecedent variables, which were entered into the equation based on the conceptual model: (a) demography, (b) locus of control, (c) contextual age, and (d) interpersonal motives. . . . To locate predictors of VCR frequency, we also regressed frequency on the same blocks of antecedent variables with the addition of VCR motives on a fifth step. . . . Five of the six equations were significant. . . .

Significant final predictors of the library storage VCR motive were: communicating interpersonally for control, larger household size, and male gender. The measures explained 11.7% of the library storage variance. . . .

Significant final predictors of the social interaction VCR motive were: communicating interpersonally for inclusion, escape, and affection, CA interaction, CA immobility, and younger age. The measures explained 31.1% of the social interaction variance. . . .

At the conclusion of the analysis, the only significant predictor of the freedom of choice VCR motive was LOC internal control. The measures explained 12.6% of the freedom of choice variance. . . .

Although communicating interpersonally for control predicted the learning VCR motive, the regression equation was not significant. The predictors explained only 8.3% of the learning variance. . . .

Significant final predictors of the time shifting VCR motive were: communicating interpersonally for control, CA life dissatisfaction, and younger age. The measures explained 12.8% of the time shifting variance. . . .

Significant final predictors of VCR frequency were: VCR library storage and freedom of choice motivation, LOC external control, and less education. The measures explained 21.1% of the VCR frequency variance.

Multivariate Relationships: VCR Use and Antecedents

In the last stage of the analysis, we used canonical correlation to assess the multivariate relationships among the set of antecedents to VCR use and the set of VCR motives and frequency. We included only those antecedents that were significant contributors in the regressions. . . . The analysis identified two significant roots.

The first canonical root (R_c = .58, lambda = .47, p < .001) explained 33.1% of the common variance between the variates. . . . Across the sets, younger, interactive, but less mobile persons, who communicated with others for reasons of inclusion, escape, and affection, used VCRs primarily for social interaction, and to store tapes, for convenient choice, and to time shift.

The second canonical root (R_c = .39, lambda = .70, p < .001) explained 14.9% of the common variance between the variates. . . . Across the sets, less educated and externally controlled persons, who were less satisfied with their lives, were more frequent users of VCRs primarily to shift time rather than for convenient choice.

Discussion

The VCR is an evolutionary technology that is more than an appendage to television. VCRs allow us to use traditional channels of communication, such as television and interpersonal interaction, in different ways. . . .

Our results reinforce previous U&G notions. First, communication motives are interrelated. . . . The VCR is a convenient and economical mechanism for communication storage and retrieval. Convenience, choice-making ability, time restructuring, and social utility are central to VCR use. Such components reinforce earlier contentions that "VCR use is indeed active behavior" (A. Rubin & Bantz, 1988, p. 191).

Second, motives to communicate interpersonally predict motives for using a VCR. Communicating interpersonally for reasons of inclusion, affection, and escape, predicted social interaction motives for using the VCR. . . . VCR use links interpersonal and mass communication (A. Rubin & Bantz, 1987); and VCR use increases time spent with family and friends (Harvey & Rothe, 1985–1986; Roe, 1987). . . .

In addition, communicating interpersonally to achieve control (i.e., getting others to do something) predicted several VCR motives: time shifting, library storage, and learning. This supports Schutz's (1966) notion that control is an interpersonal communication need, yet further suggests that those who seek to achieve control can do so in both personal and mediated contexts. . . .

Third, there are social and psychological antecedents to communication motivation, which explain VCR use. External locus of control and less education predicted frequency of VCR use. Perhaps the externally controlled use VCRs as a way to increase feelings of control in their lives. . . . Internal locus of control was the best predictor of the VCR freedom of choice motivation, which was a personal control factor emphasizing choice over what to watch, freedom to set one's own schedule, and multiple viewing options. . . .

We found support, then, for U&G assumptions that there are social and psychological antecedents to communication motives and behavior, which must be examined and understood. In this study, social demography, psychological predispositions, and life position contribute to our understanding of VCR motives and behavior.

There are several directions for future research. Beyond motives, we need to consider . . . what is being taped or replayed by VCR users and . . . to examine the consequences of VCR use for social interaction and interpersonal relationships. How do VCRs alter family interaction and the home environment? . . . Do VCRs compensate for interpersonal communication deficiencies of the immobile or media dependent? Consequences also extend to societal structures. For example, how do VCRs affect network television programming and . . . the music industry?

References

Al-Attibi, A. A. M. (1986). Interpersonal communication competence and media consumption and needs among young adults in Saudi Arabia (Doctoral dissertation, Ohio State University, 1986). *Dissertation Abstracts International, 47*, 10A.

Brenders, D. A. (1987). Perceived control: Foundations and directions for communication research. *Communication Yearbook, 10*, 86–116.

Dobrow, J. R. (1987). The social and cultural implications of the VCR: How VCR use concentrates and diversifies viewing (Doctoral dissertation, University of Pennsylvania, 1987). *Dissertation Abstracts International, 48*, 03A.

Gunter, B., & Levy, M. R. (1987). Social contexts of video use. *American Behavioral Scientist, 30*, 486–494.

Harvey, M. G., & Rothe, J. T. (1985–1986). Video cassette recorders: Their impact on viewers and advertisers. *Journal of Advertising Research, 25*(6), 19–27.

Levenson, H. (1974). Activism and powerful others: Distinctions within the concept of internal-external control. *Journal of Personality Assessment, 38*, 377–383.

Levy, M. R. (1987). Some problems of VCR research. *American Behavioral Scientist, 30*, 461–470.

Roe, K. (1987). Adolescents' video use. *American Behavioral Scientist, 30*, 522–532.

Rotter, J. B. (1954). *Social learning and clinical psychology*. Englewood Cliffs, NJ: Prentice Hall.

Rubin, A. M., & Bantz, C. R. (1987). Utility of videocassette recorders. *American Behavioral Scientist, 30*, 471–485.

Rubin, A. M., & Bantz, C. R. (1988). Uses and gratifications of videocassette recorders. In J. Salvaggio & J. Bryant (Eds.), *Media use in the information age* (pp. 181–195). Hillsdale, NJ: Erlbaum.

Rubin, A. M., & Rubin, R. B. (1982). Contextual age and television use. *Human Communication Research, 8*, 228–244.

Rubin, A. M., & Rubin, R. B. (1985). Interface of personal and mediated communication: A research agenda. *Critical Studies in Mass Communication, 2*, 36–53.

Rubin, A. M., & Rubin, R. B. (1986). Contextual age as a life-position index. *International Journal of Aging and Human Development, 23,* 27–45.

Rubin, R. B., Perse, E. M., & Barbato, C. A. (1988). Conceptualization and measurement of interpersonal communication motives. *Human Communication Research, 14,* 602–628.

Rubin, R. B., & Rubin, A. M. (1982). Contextual age and television use: Reexamining a life-position indicator. *Communication Yearbook, 6,* 583–604.

Schoenbach, K., & Hackforth, J. (1987). Video in West German households. *American Behavioral Scientist, 30,* 533–543.

Schutz, W. C. (1966). *The interpersonal underworld.* Palo Alto, CA: Science and Behavior Books.

SPSS, Inc. (1988). *SPSS-X user's guide* (3rd ed). Chicago: Author.

Wenner, L. (1976). Functional analysis of TV viewing for older adults. *Journal of Broadcasting, 20,* 77–88.

Williams, F., Phillips, A. F., & Lum, P. (1985). Gratifications associated with new communication technologies. In K. E. Rosengren, L. A. Wenner, & P. Palmgreen (Eds.), *Media gratifications research: Current perspectives* (pp. 241–252). Beverly Hills: Sage.

_____

_____

_____

_____

_____

_____

_____

_____

_____

Note

[1] This chapter is condensed from Rubin, A. M., & Rubin, R. B. (1989). Social and psychological antecedents of VCR use. In M. R. Levy (Ed.), *The VCR age: Home video and mass communication* (pp. 92–111). Newbury Park, CA: Sage. Copyright 1989 by Alan M. Rubin and Rebecca B. Rubin. Reprinted by permission of the authors.

Glossary[1]

Abstract (a) A paragraph-length or longer summary or condensation of an *article*, book, or other work. (b) A *periodical* composed of summaries of scholarly *research reports* and theoretical articles that have been published in *journals* and books. Some abstracts also include summary descriptions of books and dissertations.

Abstracting service (a) An organization that produces *abstracts*. (b) Abstracts supplied to subscribers by an organization.

Accidental sample A *nonprobability sampling* technique in which those people who happen to be available are chosen for the *sample*.

Annotated bibliography A list of writings or other materials that includes short descriptions or evaluations in addition to *citations*.

Annotation A short description of a published work. Critical annotations also evaluate the works described.

Annual A publication that appears once a year.

Annual review An *annual* that provides summaries of scholarly research activities in a particular content area.

Anonymous FTP A network service that allows users to retrieve publicly available documents, stored on remote servers, by using the file transfer protocol (*FTP*) and logging in as "anonymous."

APA format or **APA style** The style recommended by the American Psychological Association for referencing information in scholarly

---

1 *Note.* Terms appearing in *italics* are included in this glossary.

publications and for arranging information in *citations* and *bibliographies*.

Appended bibliography A list of writings or other materials that appears at the end of a book, *article*, or other work.

Archival/documentary research Inquiry that centers on finding, examining, and interpreting messages. Common forms include *library/documentary, historical, critical/rhetorical,* and *legal research,* as well as *textual, secondary, conversation,* and *content analysis*.

Archie A network service that searches *FTP* sites for publicly available files on a given topic.

Archive (a) An organized body of public records or historical documents. (b) An institution that collects, preserves, and provides services related to the use of archival materials.

Article A manuscript published in a *journal,* other *periodical,* or an *encyclopedia*.

Artifact-oriented research See *message- or artifact-oriented research*.

Behavior-oriented research See *people- or behavior-oriented research*.

Bibliographic database A *computerized database* that consists primarily of *citations* to publications and sometimes includes *abstracts*.

Bibliographic style The style used for arranging information in a *citation* or a *bibliography*. Examples: *APA format, MLA format*.

Bibliography A list of writings or other materials, usually compiled on the basis of topic, author, or some other element common to the entries, and systematically arranged. Types of bibliographies include: *annotated, appended, current, general, retrospective,* and *selective topical*.

Bibliography card A note card on which the complete *citation* for a publication is entered by a researcher as a record-keeping and record-finding device. It includes a brief summary of the contents of the publication.

Bimonthly A publication that appears every other month.

Broadcast index A list of programs archived via audiotape or videotape that can be searched by title or subject.

Browser Software that provides an interface to the *World Wide Web*.

Catalog A systematic list of books and/or other materials that records, describes, and indexes the resources of one or more libraries or *collections*. Many library catalogs are available on cards; some are published in book format or on *microfilm* or *microfiche*. Library catalogs are increasingly being placed on storage media that will allow *on-line* access through terminals or micro-computers.

CD-ROM An abbreviation for "compact disk–read-only memory," this term usually refers to a small laser disk that stores electronic data.

Citation A reference note on the source or authority for facts, quotations, and opinions. A complete citation contains sufficient bibliographic information to enable a researcher to locate the item.

Citation index A list of works that have been cited by subsequently published works. The listing is usually by cited author, enabling one to locate later works that have cited that author's *research*.

Client A computer or program that requests a service of another computer or program (called the *server).*

Cluster sample A *probability sampling* technique in which subgroups of a *population* are identified in stages and then the *sample* is drawn randomly from the final subgroup.

Collection A compilation of documents or media of a similar type that are gathered together and published as *periodicals*, books, or in *microform.*

Communications software A software program that enables a computer equipped with a *modem* to communicate with another computer over telephone lines.

Composite week In *content analysis*, when a week is created by randomly selecting one Monday, one Tuesday, one Wednesday, and so on from all possible Mondays, Tuesdays, Wednesdays, and so on for the year.

Computerized database A *database* stored on a magnetic or optical medium so that it can be accessed by computer. Types of computerized databases include *bibliographic, referral,* and *source.*

Comserve An electronic information service for the communication field available through electronic mail.

Conceptual definition Terms used to describe the true meaning of a *variable.*

Content analysis Examination of the structure and content of messages, particularly those in the media.

Control (a) One aim of science (in addition to theory, explanation, understanding, and prediction). (b) To test or verify by means of conducting an experiment in a contained atmosphere.

Control group The group of individuals that does not receive the experimental treatment.

Controlled vocabulary The set of *subject headings* or *descriptors* used by a particular *index, abstracting service, catalog,* or *computerized database* to describe listed works.

Conversation analysis Examination of the structure, messages, function, rules, and content of conversations.

Critical paper A treatise that analyzes and evaluates literature and draws conclusions about the subject.

Critical/rhetorical research Selection and application of appropriate criteria to interpret and to evaluate a communication event and its consequences.

Cumulation The contents of successive volumes of a title incorporated into one volume. The current issues of *periodical indexes*, for example, are usually cumulated into volumes covering a longer time period.

Current bibliography A list of writings or other materials that is updated on a regular basis.

Data Information that is observed or gathered in the conduct of research.

Database A collection of information organized in such a way that specific items can be retrieved.

Database producer An organization that compiles and publishes *computerized databases*.

Dependent variable The consequent or presumed effect in a relationship between two or more *variables*.

Descriptive research An identification and description of events or conditions.

Descriptor A term used in *computerized database* access systems to denote a *subject heading* or *keyword*.

Dictionary A book containing an alphabetically arranged collection of words, together with their meanings, equivalents, derivation, syllabication, and other useful information. *Subject dictionaries*, which define terms in a particular *discipline* or of a highly specialized nature, often include relatively extended *encyclopedia*-type entries.

Directory A systematically arranged list of individuals, institutions, or organizations, giving addresses, activities, publications, and other information.

Discipline A branch of knowledge and the individuals who teach and *research* in it.

Document delivery service A service offered by *database vendors*, allowing users to order publications *on-line* for delivery through the mail.

Documentary research See *archival/documentary research*.

Domain Portion of an *Internet* address that specifies the location of the addressee.

Downloading The practice of transferring *data* from a larger computer to a smaller one.

E-mail Electronic mail or messages that are sent via computer networks.

Encyclopedia A comprehensive compilation of information, usually arranged alphabetically by topic in *articles* or essays and providing overviews that typically include definitions, descriptions, background, and bibliographic references. General encyclopedias attempt to encompass all branches of knowledge, whereas subject encyclopedias limit coverage to a specific *discipline.*

Ethnography *Observational research* used to describe social norms and events as they occur.

Exemplary literature review An examination and description of only those materials that pertain most closely to the topic.

Exhaustive literature review An examination and description of all materials on a topic.

Experimental design A plan or blueprint for the conduct of *experimental research.*

Experimental group The group in an experiment that receives the experimental treatment or manipulation.

Experimental research An investigation of communication events under *controlled* conditions. Usually, the goals are to explain and to predict relationships among *variables.*

Explanatory research Inquiry that looks for underlying causes and explanations of events.

External validity The results of an empirical *research* study that are generalizable to other people, situations, times, and so forth.

Field research See *nonlaboratory research.*

Finding tool Any bibliographic work that can be used to locate sources of information on a topic. Examples include *periodical index, abstracting service, bibliography, catalog, on-line* or *computerized database,* and *directory.*

Focus group Intensive group interviewing used to understand consumer attitudes and behaviors.

Free-text searching A method of searching *computerized databases* in which all words in a document or *citation* can be searched. Free-text searching uses *natural language* rather than a *controlled vocabulary.*

FTP Abbreviation for File Transfer Protocol, the *Internet* tool for moving files from a remote computer to the user's service provider's machine.

Full-Internet connection A direct connection to the *Internet* that permits use of a *World Wide Web browser* with a graphical user interface.

Full-text database A *computerized database* that contains the complete text of publications such as *journals*, newspapers, books, and so forth. Every word of the entire text of these publications can be searched.

General bibliography A list of writings or other materials that includes *citations* of materials on a variety of topics.

Gopher A menu-driven information system that transparently connects users to other *Internet* sites.

Gopher servers Software stored on remote computers that allows users to use *Gopher* to access information at *Internet* sites worldwide.

Gopherspace The universe of *Gopher* sites on the *Internet*.

Government document Any printed matter originating from or printed at the expense or with the authority of an office of a legally organized government. Types include hearings, committee prints, and reports.

Guide to the literature A type of reference that lists and annotates available sources (for example, *directories*, *indexes*, and *journals*) for a specific *discipline* or subject area. Guides sometimes offer descriptions of the literature in a field, recommend effective *search strategies*, and identify organizations that may provide additional information to researchers.

Handbook A compact book of facts, sometimes called a *manual*. Scholarly or subject handbooks organize, summarize, and make readily accessible a body of information about a field of study.

Historical research An examination of past observations to understand the events that occurred.

Hits The records that the computer has found containing the *descriptors* that are used with a *computerized database* search. These are sometimes termed "postings."

Homepage The default document *World Wide Web* users see when connecting for the first time to a particular WWW *server*.

html (Hypertext Markup Language) The language used to write *hypertext* documents for *World Wide Web*.

http (Hypertext Transport Protocol) The program that establishes connections between *hypertext* documents on *World Wide Web*.

Hyperlink A reference within one *hypermedia* document to another document, which, when selected, connects the user to the second document.

Hypermedia *Hypertext* that includes links to other forms of media.

Hypertext A document that includes links to other documents.

Hypothesis An educated guess or prediction about the relationship among two or more *variables*.

Identifiers A type of *controlled vocabulary* used by *ERIC* for subject retrieval.

Image database A *computerized database* that contains graphic images such as photographs, reproductions of art works, and textual material.

Independent variable The antecedent or presumed cause in a relationship between two or more *variables*.

Index A list (usually alphabetical) giving the location of materials, topics, names, and so forth, in a work or group of specified works. Also, a shortened form of *periodical index*.

Interlibrary loan system A cooperative arrangement between libraries and groups of libraries by which one library may borrow material for its patrons from another.

Internal validity Indicates that the results of a study cannot be explained in any other way. That is, little or no fault can be found with the study's sampling method, measuring instruments, and *research* design.

Internet An international network of computer networks used to access computerized databases, communicate with others, and retrieve document files.

Intervening variable A factor other than the *independent variable* that can affect the *dependent variable*.

Interview A qualitative technique used to probe *respondents'* attitudes and behaviors.

IP address An *Internet* address expressed numerically.

Journal A *periodical* containing *research reports* and *review articles* in a specific scholarly field or *discipline*.

Jughead A program installed on many *Gopher servers* that allows the user to search a particular *Gopher* menu for *keywords*.

Keyword A significant word, often drawn from the title of a work, under which entries for references to that work are filed in a *catalog*, *bibliography*, *index*, or *computerized database*.

Laboratory research Investigations conducted in surroundings that are new to the individuals being studied. Usually, laboratory research is conducted to strengthen the *control* of extraneous *variables*.

Legal research Inquiry into how law operates in society.

Library of Congress classification A system of subject classification of materials developed by the Library of Congress for its *collection*. It is widely used by college and university libraries in the United States to arrange and locate materials on shelves. Call numbers are composed of letters and numbers.

Library/documentary research A review of existing documents or written, printed materials such as those found in a library.

LISTSERV An electronic discussion group on a particular topic, which uses a mailing list to distribute messages to all members' electronic mail boxes.

Literature review A summary and synthesis of previous research about a topic. Two types are *exemplary* and *exhaustive*.

Literature search A systematic search for published material on a specific subject.

Logical operators Words such as AND, OR, or NOT, which are used in *database* searching to combine words and concepts.

Magazine A type of *periodical* intended for general reading or for a particular profession.

Manual A compact book of facts. Manuals are similar to *handbooks*, but the term "manual" is used more specifically to denote how-to guides for accomplishing specific tasks.

Media index A finding tool for newspaper materials, films, television videotapes, and reviews of these.

Message- or artifact-oriented research Scientific inquiry that examines messages and attitudes associated with messages. Types include *archival/documentary* and *survey/interview research*.

Microfiche Positive or negative sheet film (usually 4 inches by 6 inches) used for compact storage of information.

Microfilm Positive or negative roll film, loose or in a cartridge, which is used for compact storage of information.

Microform The general term for either *microfiche* or *microfilm*.

MLA format or **MLA style** The style recommended by the Modern Language Association for referencing information in scholarly publications and for arranging information in *citations* or *bibliographies*.

Modem A piece of equipment used with computers to translate digital computer signals into analog telephone signals, making it possible to transmit *data* between computers over telephone lines.

Monograph A book that treats a single subject within a single volume.

Mosaic A *World Wide Web* graphics-based *browser* or *client* program that allows *hyperlinks* to sound, video, and textual resources.

Multimedia database A collection of *data* that includes media such as audio, graphic images, and video.

Natural language A term used in *computerized database* searching to distinguish the vocabulary available for *free-text searching* from *controlled vocabulary* (consisting of *descriptors* listed in a *thesaurus*).

Network analysis The study of behavioral interactions among organizational members.

Newsgroup An electronic discussion group on *Usenet*.

Newspaper index A list of articles, editorials, and reviews that have been published in a newspaper.

Newsreader A program that allows the user to access and participate in *Usenet newsgroups*.

Nonlaboratory research An investigation conducted in naturalistic surroundings. The subjects may or may not be aware that *research* is being done.

Nonprobability sampling The nonrandom selection of members of a *population* for a *sample*.

Numeric database A *computerized database* that consists primarily of numerical or other statistical *data*.

Observational research A *nonlaboratory research* procedure where trained observers describe the behaviors or messages of the people or media being studied. Observational research includes *ethnography, participant observation, unobtrusive observation, network analysis*, and *verbal and nonverbal coding*.

OCLC (Online Computer Library Center) This service is used by many libraries to automate their cataloging and *interlibrary loan* procedures. OCLC terminals located in libraries can be used to consult a *bibliographic database* that includes the holdings of many libraries in the United States.

On-line A term used in on-line *database* searching designating the direct interactive process of retrieving computer *data* while a search is in progress.

On-line catalog A *bibliographic database* consisting of the holdings of a particular library.

On-line search service Service offering access to *on-line databases* using search *protocols* usually specific to the service *vendor*.

Operational definition Procedures followed to observe or to measure a *variable*.

Operator A word or symbol used to create logical sets that can then be used to retrieve terms in various combinations. Boolean operators include AND, OR, and NOT.

Participant observation An observational technique used to study social situations or organizations where researchers participate in the observed environment.

People- or behavior-oriented research Scientific inquiry that examines people's behavior. Types include *observational* and *experimental research*.

Periodical A publication with a distinctive title intended to appear at some specified interval (for example, daily, weekly, monthly, or quarterly). See also *journal* and *magazine*.

Periodical index An *index* to *articles* published in many different *periodicals*, generally issued at regular intervals and cumulated annually. This term is often shortened to *index*.

Permuterm Subject Index A subject *index* consisting of title *keywords* arranged alphabetically.

Plagiarism Using an author's words or ideas without giving credit.

Poll *Survey research* used to describe the attitudes or opinions of a *sample*.

Population People or objects that have some common characteristic. Researchers often draw a *sample* of this group to investigate for the purpose of generalizing to the larger population.

Primary source A document, manuscript, record, recording, or an original published report of *research*. Primary sources are often written about or reworked, resulting in *secondary sources*. Legal primary sources include statutes, court decisions, executive orders, and treaties.

Probability sampling The random selection of members of a *population* for a *sample*. The purpose is to generalize observations from that sample to the population.

Professional/trade magazine See *magazine*.

Prospectus A proposal for a research study in which the author thoroughly reviews the supporting literature, sets up *hypotheses* or research questions, and details the methods that will be followed to answer the questions or test the hypotheses.

Protocol The particular commands and techniques used in *on-line search* systems to create *search statements* to retrieve *citations* and other types of information.

Proximity operators A word or symbol used to specify the closeness of *natural-language* terms in *free-text searching* of *computerized* or *on-line databases*.

Purposive sample A *nonprobability sampling* technique in which the *sample* is selected to represent either a wide variety of *respondents* or respondents who possess a certain trait.

Qualitative research Inductive, interpretive methods of scientific inquiry.

Quantitative research Deductive, statistical methods of scientific inquiry.

Quarterly A publication that appears four times a year.

Quota sample A *nonprobability sampling* technique in which members of a *sample* are chosen because they have a certain trait or demographic characteristic.

Ratings Measures of the size of broadcast audiences.

Reference See *citation.*

Reference librarian A librarian who staffs the reference desk and can assist library patrons in locating suitable materials.

Referral database A *computerized database* that contains references to organizations, people, grants, *research* projects, contracts, and so forth. It sometimes includes summaries or *abstracts.*

Reliability A measure's stability, consistency, and repeatability.

Research Objective, systematic, empirical, and cumulative inquiry into a subject.

Research ethics What is right and wrong in the conduct of *research.* Issues include honesty, harm, deception, informed consent, and privacy.

Research report A summary of an original *research* study typically consisting of four main sections: introduction, method, results, and discussion.

Respondent A participant in *survey research.*

Retrospective bibliography A list of writings or other materials that appears at a particular point in time and is not updated.

Review article A published manuscript that thoroughly examines the literature on a particular topic and presents previously undrawn conclusions about the strength, sufficiency, or consistency of the information.

Rhetorical research See *critical/rhetorical research.*

Sample A subgroup of a *population* that is examined in a *research* study. Two methods of sampling are *probability* and *nonprobability.*

Scholarly journal See *journal.*

Search statement A request for information entered by a user of *computerized databases* that instructs the search system to retrieve a specified *set* of documents.

Search strategy The organized plan by which a person conducts a *literature search.* In *computerized database* searching, it refers to a set of planned search statements that are to be entered into the search system to retrieve the desired records.

Secondary analysis Examination of previously gathered or archived *data.*

Secondary source A work that consists of information compiled from *primary* or original sources. Examples include *annual reviews, dictionaries,* document sourcebooks, *encyclopedias,* and *textbooks.*

Selective topical bibliography A list of writings or other materials that includes only *citations* to those materials judged to be most pertinent or valuable to a particular topic. It is not comprehensive.

Semiannual Published twice each year at 6-month intervals.

Semimonthly Published twice each month.

Series Separate works usually related by subject, author, or format that are assigned a collective series title and issued successively by a publisher.

Server A computer whose software allows it to store *data* and make it available to network users; users employ client software on their own workstations in order to access the *data*.

Set A group of records retrieved from a *computerized database* as the result of a particular *search statement*.

Shareware Software programs that are distributed freely for trial purposes; those who adopt a program are usually expected to pay the developer a fee.

Simple random sample A *probability sampling* technique in which each person has an equal or known chance of being chosen for the *sample*.

Source database A *computerized database* that includes sufficiently complete information to satisfy an information need without the necessity of retrieving additional documents. Types of source databases include *numeric, full-text,* and *image*.

Specialized index Type of *periodical index* in an academic *discipline*.

Statistical source A reference work where census and other governmental or media statistics are reported.

Stratified sample A *probability sampling* technique in which the *sample* is selected from certain subgroups of the *population* to ensure adequate representation.

Subject A participant in *experimental research*.

Subject dictionary A *dictionary* that resembles an *encyclopedia* in that it contains elongated meanings for the terminology of one subject area or discipline.

Subject heading A word or group of words under which publications dealing with a particular subject are listed in a *catalog, periodical index, computerized database, abstracting service,* or *bibliography*. Subject headings are usually arranged in alphabetical order. See also *descriptor*.

Survey research A *research* procedure used to collect information about conditions, events, opinions, people, organizations, and so forth. Survey researchers question members of a *sample* often to describe a *population*.

Systematic sample A *probability sampling* technique in which every *n*th person or event is chosen for the *sample* from a list of persons or events.

Telnet An *Internet* protocol that allows the user to connect to a remote computer.

Terminal emulation A program that allows a user's workstation to adopt the characteristics of a particular type of computer terminal, permitting access to a remote computer.

Textbook An overview and explanation of one or more topics presented in an easy-to-understand manner.

Textual analysis Examination of media content or text in relation to audience interpretation.

Thesaurus (a) A list of *descriptors* or *subject headings* and their related terms that accompanies a particular *computerized* or printed *index, abstracting service,* or *catalog* to indicate the specific indexing terms used in that source. (b) A book of synonyms and antonyms.

Topical bibliography A list of *references* on one specific topic or theme.

Tracing A listing at the bottom of a *catalog* record of an additional heading under which the described work is entered in the catalog.

Trade magazine See *magazine*.

Unobtrusive observation *Nonlaboratory research* where the researcher observes participants without their being aware that they're being observed.

URL (Uniform Resource Locator) A standardized way of representing different documents, media, and network services on *World Wide Web*.

Usenet A worldwide network of electronic discussion groups, or *newsgroups*, that can be accessed on most college and university campuses through a *newsreader* program.

Validity Measuring what one intends to measure.

Variable Something that can assume different values. A concept to which numbers are attached and that changes in value. For example, television viewing can be a variable with values that range from 0 to 24 hours each day; eye color can be a variable (blue = 1, green = 2, brown = 3, hazel = 4, and so forth).

Vendor An organization supplying *on-line databases* to other organizations or individuals. Vendors are essentially retailers of on-line databases.

Verbal and nonverbal coding Application of schemes to describe messages systematically.

Veronica A network service that allows users to search *Gopher* menus worldwide for documents.

World Wide Web A system based on *hypertext* that allows the user to explore and connect to other *Internet* resources.

Yearbook An annual volume describing current developments in a specific field. Information may be given in narrative or statistical form.

Subject Index

A

Abstract and index abbreviations, 164
Abstracting services, 134, 137
Abstracts:
  citing, 59
  defined, 120, 259–260, 315
  format, 230, 300
  selected list, 144
  services, 134, 137, 315
  writing, 34, 35, 230, 261
Accidental sample, 14, 219, 315
American Forensic Association, 14
American Marketing Association, 14
American Newspaper Publishers
  Association, 177
American Psychological Association, 26
Analysis:
  content, 216, 217
  conversation, 216
  interactional, 216
  reception, 216
  relational, 216
  secondary, 215
  textual, 216
Annotated bibliography, 121, 315
Annual, 183, 315
Annual reviews:
  defined, 104–105, 315
  selected list, 113–114
Anonymous FTP, 78, 315
Antecedent, 210
APA format or style, 26, 291–303,
  249–250, 315–316
Appended bibliography, 121, 316
Approaches, communication
  research, 212–229
Arbitron Ratings Company, 177
Archie (Internet finding tool), 78–79
Archival/documentary research,
  212–217, 316
Archive collections, directories, 172–
  173

Archives, 171–173, 316
Article, 316
Artifact-oriented research, 212–223,
  316
Association for Education in
  Journalism and Mass
  Communication (AEJMC), 12
Association of American Publishers,
  177
A. C. Nielsen Company, 177

B

Behavior-oriented research, 223–229,
  316
Bibliographic database, 43–44,
  316
Bibliographic format:
  book, 292–294
  government publication, 295
  introduction, 291
  legal reference, 298
  nonprint media, 294–295
  periodical, 296–297
  styles, differing, 248–250, 316
  unpublished paper, 297–298
Bibliographies:
  selected list, 138–139
  types, 120–122, 316
Bibliography card, 24–26, 316
Biographical study, 213
Bookmarks:
  Gopher, 82–83
  World Wide Web, 86
Books:
  APA style, 292–294
  evaluating, 31–34
  reviews, 129
Boolean logical operators, 49–51, 282
Broadcast Education Association
  (BEA), 12, 13
Broadcast indexes, 133–134, 316

Source Index

A

ABI/INFORM, 43, **61**, 129, 282
Abstracts and Abstracting Services, 276
Abstracts of Popular Culture, 164
Academic Index, 43, **62**
Academy of Management Review, 159
Administrative Science Quarterly, 159
Advances in Content Analysis, 106
Advances in Experimental Social
    Psychology, 113
Advances in Psychological Assessment,
    175, 188
Advances in Semiotics, 114
Advances in the Study of Behavior, 114
Advances in the Study of
    Communication and Affect, 114
Advancing Communication Science, 106
Advertising Age, **154**, 162
Adweek, 162
Almanac of American Politics, The,
    195
Alternative Press Index, **133**, 143, 171
America: History and Life, 164
American Behavioral Scientist, 160
American Cinematographer, 162
American Historical Review, 161
American Journal of Political Science,
    161
American Journal of Psychology, 160
American Journal of Sociology, 160
American Journal of Speech-Language
    Pathology, 158
American Journalism, 157
American Journalism History, 139
American Journalism Review, 162
American Jurisprudence Second, 103,
    112
American Orators before 1900, 112
American Orators of the Twentieth
    Century, 112

American Periodicals Series, 188
American Periodicals, 1741–1900: An
    Index to the Microfilm Collections,
    190
American Political Dictionary, The,
    199
American Political Science Review, 161
American Politics Quarterly, 161
American Sociological Review, 160
American Speech, 158
American Statistics Index (ASI), **62**,
    176–177, 181, 191
America's Watching: Public Attitudes
    toward Television, 192
Analyzing Gender, 108
Analyzing Social Settings, 236
Ancient Greek and Roman
    Rhetoricians: A Bibliographical
    Dictionary, 199
Annual Report of the Federal
    Communications Commission,
    180, 193
Annual Review of Anthropology,
    114
Annual Review of Applied Linguistics,
    114
Annual Review of Information Science
    and Technology, 114
Annual Review of Psychology, 114
Annual Review of Sociology, 114
Annual Review of the Institute for
    Information Studies, 114
AP Broadcast News Handbook, 201
Applied Communication Theory and
    Research, 236
Applied Multivariate Statistics for the
    Social Sciences, 238
Applied Psycholinguistics, 158
Applied Social Research Methods, 235
Applied Statistics and the SAS
    Programming Language, 238

I

K

L

Q

R